T0295864

Rise of the North East

Rise of the North East

The Path to Prosperity, Inclusion and Sustainability

Research and Information System for
Developing Countries (RIS)

Tata Trusts

RIS
Research and Information System
for Developing Countries
विकासशील देशों की अनुसंधान एवं सूचना प्रणाली

TATA TRUSTS

OXFORD
UNIVERSITY PRESS

OXFORD
UNIVERSITY PRESS

Great Clarendon Street, Oxford, OX2 6DP,
United Kingdom

Oxford University Press is a department of the University of Oxford.
It furthers the University's objective of excellence in research, scholarship,
and education by publishing worldwide. Oxford is a registered trade mark of
Oxford University Press in the UK and in certain other countries

Published in the United States of America by Oxford University Press
198 Madison Avenue, New York, NY 10016, United States of America

British Library Cataloguing in Publication Data

Data available

Library of Congress Control Number: 2022947311

ISBN 978-0-19-284934-2

DOI: 10.1093/oso/9780192849342.001.0001

Links to third party websites are provided by Oxford in good faith and
for information only. Oxford disclaims any responsibility for the materials
contained in any third party website referenced in this work.

Contents

Foreword

Dr Rajiv Kumar
Vice Chairman, NITI Aayog

NITI Aayog is steadfastly working towards fulfilling the India's aspiration of a five trillion dollar economy by 2025 and Prime Minister's vision of a New India. In its efforts towards strengthening India's robust framework of cooperative federalism, NITI Forum for North East was constituted in February 2018. NITI Aayog is also the nodal agency for coordinating the implementation of the Sustainable Development Goals (SDGs) in India and has imparted special focus on India's North Eastern Region (NER) towards enhancing their capacities and unleashing their full potential through drivers of economic growth and strengthening their resource base.

The NITI Forum for North East aims at improving rail, road, and air connectivity, tapping the potentials of hydel resources in the region, development of agriculture and allied sectors, and promotion of tourism in the region. The Forum would also endeavour to support industrialization and diversification in the region by focusing on select sectors such as tourism, startups, horticulture, bamboo, and food processing and their contribution to the national economy. This would go a long way in further improving the prospects of the North Eastern States in contributing to the national aspiration of five trillion economy by 2025. National policy initiatives are also currently being guided by key monitoring frameworks being developed by NITI Aayog including the SDG India Index.

This report titled *Rise of the North East: The Path to Prosperity, Inclusion and Sustainability* prepared by RIS and TATA Trusts comprehensively covers major dimensions such as: state initiatives and localization of SDGs; drivers of economic prosperity and sustainable livelihood; climate adaptive agriculture and diversification; nutrition, health, and well-being; education, skill development, and entrepreneurship; communication, connectivity, and infrastructure development; and financing of SDGs. These themes are aligned with the SDG Conclave 2020 which took place during 24–26 February 2020 in Guwahati under the patronage of the NITI Aayog. While the region has enormous potential for economic resurgence, development needs to be inclusive and sustainable.

The region's development has to be informed of its diverse potential and possibilities, regional aspirations, and need for context-specific and localized development models with strong safeguards for its ecology. The role of civil society and private entrepreneurs needs to be promoted for localization of SDGs and in furthering partnerships and collective ownership of development processes. The North Eastern states also need to work together for evolving joint areas of cooperation on SDGs, focusing on sustainable infrastructure and carbon neutral growth models. The region is intimately nested in India's eastern neighbourhood, and the Agenda 2030 offers new opportunities to reinvigorate development cooperation to fulfil the shared aspirations in the region with due leadership from India.

Rajiv Kumar

Preface

Professor Sachin Chaturvedi
Director General, RIS

Before the world plunged into a deep crisis in 2020 with the global spread of the COVID-19 pandemic, RIS had already made substantial efforts at coming up with research-based policy roadmaps for North East India to connect the region with the vision of 'New India'. The following were the two key considerations in this endeavour: the desire to meet the SDG targets for the region and the obligation towards supporting determined national efforts at unleashing the full potential of the North East particularly as the bridge with India's eastern and South East Asian neighbours. With certain setbacks in terms of time and money due to the pandemic, it is all the more necessary to explore all options to consolidate previously ongoing efforts and set the roadmap informed of evidence, details, and causal implications. This report titled *'Rise of the North East: The Path to Prosperity, Inclusion and Sustainability'* published in times of the pandemic is expected to fulfil that requirement to a great extent.

India's strong urge for rapid socio-economic transformations under the paradigm of collective efforts and inclusive development was manifested in the leadership and vision of the Prime Minister. Such a paradigm shift in national aspirations and policymaking guided by stronger faith on inclusivity and sustainability moving away from informalization, embedding low-carbon pathways and minimizing exclusions since 2014, predates adoption of the SDGs in 2015. It has often been stated, therefore, that the SDGs mirror India's development agenda and serve well as a relatable and organic framework towards India's international commitments as a responsible member of the global community.

An exploration of economic potential and development prospects in the North Eastern states of India under this transformative and integrated policy framework informed by SDG aspirations should lead to good governance, optimum utilization of resources, and harnessing local capabilities an idea very strongly embedded in the framework of the Agenda 2030. Along with the rest of the country, this region would have to enhance its contributions both in the social and economic spheres to contribute to the national goal of reaching five trillion economy by 2025. In this direction, this report makes several recommendations on drivers of economic growth and enablers of social sector development.

India's North East comprising eight states have been looked at from the perspectives of India's Act East Policy; development cooperation with the neighbouring countries; promoting trade including border trade; and connectivity, infrastructure, and industrialization. This report sheds light on the aforementioned parameters and deepens the understanding on prospects of localization of the SDGs and state-level efforts with focus on finance, technology, value addition, markets, and skills.

I thank Dr Rajiv Kumar, Hon'ble Vice Chairman, NITI Aayog for guiding and inspiring us in this effort. I am also very grateful to Shri Biplab Kumar Deb, Hon'ble Chief Minister of Tripura with whom I had a chance to discuss this report. I am thankful to Chairman, RIS, Dr Mohan Kumar for his constant encouragement in this endeavour. I am also thankful to Ms Shireen Vakil, Head, Policy and Advocacy, TATA Trusts for the collaboration with RIS towards a long-term partnership in this area.

I wholeheartedly thank all my colleagues at RIS who contributed to the report: Prof S. K. Mohanty, Prof Milindo Chakrabarti, Prof Amitabh Kundu, Dr P. K. Anand, and Mr Krishna Kumar. Last, but not the least, my colleagues Dr Sabyasachi Saha and Dr Priyadarshi Dash from RIS, who planned and coordinated the production of this voluminous report, deserve compliments for their painstaking efforts. I also acknowledge the efforts put in by the RIS Publication team comprising Mr Tish Malhotra, Mr Sanjay Sharma, and Mr Sachin Singhal towards timely compilation of the manuscript. I am sure that the Report would be found useful reference by all stakeholders including policymakers, think tanks, academicians, business and industry circles, civil society, and media.

Sachin Chaturvedi

Executive Summary

COVID- 19 and Development Process in
North- Eastern States

More than 79.7 million people have been affected across the world by the COVID-19 pandemic as of 28 December 2020, causing significant economic, social, and financial losses, particularly in developing economies and underdeveloped countries (WHO Website). By the end of October, NER confirmed cases made up 3.6 per cent of all cases in India. The NER, in contrast to the rest of the nation, was able to reasonably control the virus's rapid spread thanks to quick action from state governments, border guards, and the local public, who backed the immediate closing of 5,000 km of foreign borders in the area. All tourism-related activities were restricted by the state governments in the NER, interstate border crossings were restricted, and all public health care facilities were required to adhere to strict criteria regarding their readiness for COVID-19 cases.

Even though all of India's states are experiencing comparable economic effects, smaller states may be harder hit. For instance, given their size compared to the rest of India, the states in the NER experienced higher severity of economic slowdown. The COVID-19 epidemic in NER had the biggest immediate effect on the various progresses of SDGs. The region was at the forefront of implementing proactive measures and adopting localization for the accomplishment of SDGs before the pandemic outbreak.

In the NER region, the loss of jobs, income, and livelihood was very high. With the closure of economic sectors, unemployment in the states increased, negatively hurting people's livelihoods and reducing the likelihood that the SDGs will be achieved. The efforts taken by Reserve Bank of India by announcing a Regulatory Package on 27 March 2020 to decrease the burden on Indian financial markets and by Central Government especially through Pradhan Mantri Garib Kalyan Anna Yojana, and many other NER state initiatives like COVAAS App, Gyan Brikshya, Dhanwantri, Start- Up Manipur Initiative and Restart Meghalaya Programme etc., contributed to the NER's improved recovery.

State Initiatives and Localization of SDGs

The SDGs mirror India's national development priorities and India's commitment to them may be seen in that light. Implementation of SDGs, within the national policy agenda, has received strong institutional support through the combined efforts of NITI Aayog and the Ministry of Statistics and Programme Implementation, and their integration at the sectoral level is being pursued by line ministries and the State governments in the spirit of cooperative federalism. The monitoring exercise on SDGs has gained momentum through the adoption of the National Indicator Framework and publication of SDG India Index for States.

The NER states have been at the forefront of SDGs' adoption in the country with formulation of Vision and Strategy, assigning nodal departments/units/cells and orchestrating inter-departmental coordination on SDGs in the government. In fact, Assam has been the first state in the country to launch the initial roadmap on SDGs right in the beginning of 2016, coinciding with commencement of the Agenda 2030 implementation phase. This was followed up with creation of SDG-related research unit and nodal agency, mapping of development policies, monitoring framework, and multi-stakeholder partnerships with civil society organizations.

The other states of the NER have also emerged as serious partners on SDG implementation on their own merit and have offered novel approaches on development interventions for people's welfare, prosperity, and environmental sustainability through comprehensive strategy documents that carry aspirations for achieving the SDGs by bringing in integration, resource efficiency, and focus. The new policy articulation has come in the form of re-aligning state-level policies and programmes, localization/district-level interventions, last mile delivery, entrepreneurship development, state indicator frameworks, and multi-stakeholder models. The NITI Forum for North East is a new platform, beyond the Strategy for New India @ 75, which seeks to elevate collaboration and dialogue to the level of executive leadership from the region and the Centre, reach out to experts from the region, and robustly support NER states in their efforts to boost economic activity in the region.

Drivers of Economic Prosperity and Sustainable Livelihood

In keeping with India's aspiration of reaching five trillion dollar economy by 2025, expectations from the NER have multiplied. The Gross State Domestic Product (GSDP) of the Northeastern states constituted 2.7 per cent of India's GDP in 2018. For the NER in particular, there is an urgent need to orient policymaking towards creation of 'drivers' of economic prosperity. The most important growth drivers for the region would comprise of macroeconomic foundations; local production, industrialization, and value addition; and market linkages through trade and competitiveness. In 2018, exports of the region were 0.73 per cent of its GSDP as against 12 per cent for the country as a whole. Financial inclusion continues to be a major issue in context of NER. The credit-deposit ratio has been significantly lower than the all India average.

The growth of industry in the NER was higher as compared to all India level. The double digit industrial growth is evident from Arunachal Pradesh, Assam, Manipur, Mizoram, and Tripura while Meghalaya has recorded a negative growth. The NER has a high concentration of industrial clusters (8 per cent of all India figures; 433 out of 4,103), however, mainly in the handicraft sector (86.1 per cent), followed by handloom (7.5 per cent), and far less in the industrial category (6.5 per cent). In terms of all India figures, the NER shares 10.3 per cent of handicraft clusters in India, 12.8 per cent of handloom clusters, and 1.5 per cent of industrial clusters in the country. Under the handicraft category, there are as many as sixteen sectors existing in the region, and under each sector, there are several clusters that can be identified by distinct product varieties. The sectors that hold potential for NER include textiles, wood products, leather, gems and jewellery, base metal, art and culture, and stone-based products. In handicrafts, substantial number of clusters (144, equivalent to 50 per cent of total handicraft clusters in the region) is engaged in the production of basketry, mat weaving and cane articles.

Export profile of the region in the broad economic activities indicates that agricultural sector shared the largest proportion of the region's trade, followed by mining and manufacturing. Exports from the region in 2018 reported to be $433 million, which was only 0.13 per cent of India's total exports. Broadly, three aspects with regard to trade may be of significance: (a) the scale of trade of the region is very low, (b) the region has production and export base for several products, and (c) these products are thinly spread across the region even as these products can be exported to several destinations driven by existing competitiveness. As per current estimates, the NER has as many as 836 products that can be exported to the rest of the world including Southeast and East Asia, and the region is already exporting to all eight member states of SAARC, eight Association of Southeast Asian Nations (ASEAN) member countries, and to all regions in the rest of the world.

Overall, services sector contributes 30 per cent–70 per cent of GSDP of individual states. However, Gross Domestic Value Added and Gross Fixed Capital Formation are lower than the national average that indicates the constraints with regard to expansion of economic activities in the region as a whole. Further, the NER has by and large failed to industrialize in a significant way despite policy push from Central and State governments. The other level of challenge is that the evidence on industrialization is scattered across several information sources including Annual Survey of Industries, privately available databases such as Prowess, Indian economy statistics of RBI, Cluster Analysis database of RIS, DGCIS of the Department of Commerce, and UN Comtrade, etc. There is very little clarity about the manufacturing sector activities at the regional and sub-regional level (i.e. at the state, district, and further sub-regional level). Of the 370 corporate sector firms operating in the NER, 170 were in the services sector, 160 in manufacturing, and the rest in electricity, gas, and construction sectors. In manufacturing sector, tea, cement, miscellaneous manufactured items have dominant presence, whereas financial services and wholesale trade are important sectors in services. The data for contribution of the tourism sector (often perceived to be potential growth driver for the region) are scattered across various sources, and the fact that tourism creates direct and indirect revenue and employment presents difficulty for objective comparison.

While widespread services sector offers avenues of income generation through IT and ITeS, hospital, tourism, education and repair services, etc., non-manufacturing industrial activities in the industrial sector currently supports economic growth of the region. However, manufacturing *per se* has been suboptimum for NER. The region has comfortable power supply situation compared to the rest of the country, which can pave way for greater industrialization. As per the last census in 2011, the share of NER for people below poverty line was 4.89 per cent, evidently higher than its national population share. In terms of employment, the NER region has low level of workers' participation than several states in rest of India, with high level of rural unemployment. Another area of concern is that of Ease of Doing Business indicators. While the national score has significantly improved, some NER states demonstrated deterioration in ranks as compared to other states of the country.

Climate Adaptive Agriculture and Diversification

Agriculture, agriculture-based products, and plantation crops are of immense significance in the NER. Notably, out of the limited cultivable land available, non-food grain produce components are predominant, whereas paddy is the main food grain crop. The NER is gifted with favourable topography that is highly suitable for pisciculture, animal husbandry, and cultivation of fruits, vegetables, plantations, spices, etc. The region had very high national shares in specific fruits such as kiwi (96.7 per cent), pineapple (47.6 per cent), strawberry (40.3 per cent), and jackfruit (28.5 per cent) in 2015. There are several other important citrus and other fruits originating in the region in substantial quantity (banana, guava, lemon, litchi, orange, and plum). Naturally, such products have high demand in both domestic and international markets. The region has also specialized in number of spices and medicinal plants and has a large share in vegetable production. It is a major producer and consumer of meat and poultry. Prosperity and livelihoods of the region crucially depend on value addition on the wide range of agricultural, dairy, and meat products from the region, and hence the need for strong push for the food processing industry. It is pertinent to note that, even with existing scale of operations, in aggregate, this sector in the NER is perhaps enjoying better competitiveness scores compared to rest of the country in terms of lower input to value addition ratio.

The NE region is more vulnerable to climate change due to its fragile geology, high and skewed rainfall necessitating forward looking climate mitigation and adaptation initiatives. Water stress, floods, and likewise high-monsoon rainfall-caused high soil erosion are hitting the same areas over different periods of a year. Further, seen from the lens of specific sectors, the climate change poses larger threats to diverse livelihood activities like tea/rubber plantations, spices, floriculture and fisheries, etc. A large number of policy and programme responses of the Central and State Governments are under implementation, many of which directly or indirectly strengthen the mitigation and adaptation measures.

Nutrition, Health, and Well-being

Social sector and quality of human life are foundational to any developmental agenda. For the NER, the latest National Family Health Survey-4 (NFHS-4, 2015–16) confirms that the incidence of malnutrition among the children below five years of age and pregnant and lactating women reduced across NE states during the ten-year period since NFHS-3. The NER has lower levels of stunting (in seven of eight states) against national average. Proportion of children challenged with deficiencies of the nature of wasting in all the eight states of NER was lower than the national average. The NER states also have relatively less burden of underweight children compared to rest of India. On anaemia among children, all NE states had lesser proportion, and on anaemia among pregnant women, most states in the region have lower scores than the national average. The challenges for the region include affordability and access to nutritious food, especially among the people in lower deciles of income.

The NER compares well with other regions on health indicators covering life expectancy, infant mortality rate, and maternal mortality rate, and most states have better scores than national average. The State of Assam, given its overwhelming population size in the region, is, however, facing severe shortfall against these indicators. The non-communicable diseases account for close to 60 per cent of all deaths in the NER. Another area of serious concern is that communicable maternal, neo-natal, and nutritional diseases contributed to over 30 per cent of all deaths in NER, while deaths on account of communicable diseases were higher than the national average. The NER also face stiff challenges vis-à-vis national average on diarrheal diseases, stroke, tuberculosis, heart ailments, and cancer. While standard health infrastructure is satisfactory in many cases as compared to national average, remoteness of regions poses significant challenges even for primary healthcare. Government remains the most important player in the region for health services delivery, and private sector faces constraints for a variety of reasons.

Education, Skill Development and Entrepreneurship

The NER has higher literacy than the rest of the country. Clubbed with better proficiency in English this unlocks many opportunities to match the needs of domestic and international markets. Some key issues may need to be addressed to harness the existing potential of the region. It is well known that, due to limited opportunities of skilling and employment, outmigration from the NER to other parts of India is high. Occasional internal disturbance also prompts youth to look for opportunities outside the region. Skilling and education is the enabling environment for upward socio-economic mobility, which is a key to eradicating poverty. However, some NER states needs to address high dropout rates in schools and create more infrastructures for higher education in the region. The focus areas for better outcomes include professional courses for higher employability of youth, provision of basic amenities in schools, and optimal utilization of funds.

The skilling ecosystem in the NE has specific needs to meet the challenges to address the aspirations of its youth to equip them in a holistic manner with the upcoming demands like 4th Industrial Revolution, green buildings, modern logistics, etc., and at the same time upgrade skills at all age levels in the traditional sectors to enhance productivity and competitiveness. A major challenge perceived in the region is that while sector-specific skills are needed in the tourism, travel and hospitality, fashion designing, and in specific areas such as gas, petroleum, etc. sectors, much of the potential remains locked in food processing and plantation-based value addition including value chains of bio-tech parks, agro-food clusters/parks, rubber, bamboo, medicinal plants; IT/ITeS parks, physical and digital infrastructural projects, etc. A number of Central and State Government Skilling initiatives are facilitating youth of the NER to equip themselves, in order to effectively harness the demographic dividend. Another set of emerging opportunities is in establishing own startups supported by schemes such as Atal Innovation Mission, MUDRA, and other innovative funding options, leading to entrepreneurial initiatives. Towards this endeavour, Startup India can facilitate aspiring youth.

Communication, Connectivity, and Infrastructure Development

The NER is often considered distant from the prosperous economic hubs in India. The total road length in the NER was reported to be 498,545 km in 2016–17 with a net addition of 127,815 km in the preceding six years. All the eight states of NER have experienced steady addition to their road network during 2010–17. Seven major railway projects covering 122.91 km (Rs. 21,412.8 crore) were completed during 2014–19 that included modernization of railway network and conversion to broad gauge. The completion of 4.94 km long road-cum-rail Bogibeel Bridge and Bhupen Hazarika Setu over Brahmaputra have been major milestones for the region. The Government of India agencies such as the National Highway Authority of India (NHAI) and the Border Road Organisation (BRO), along with state governments, are transforming their strategies towards economic corridor-oriented approaches beyond narrow dimensions of physical connectivity and are implementing projects to promote regional development in partnership with neighbouring countries. The ongoing mega cross-border connectivity projects covering NER such as the Trilateral Highway and Kaladan Multimodal Transport Transit Project upon completion would be major steps in the direction of economic corridors.

Brahmaputra has historically been a major waterway for trade connecting NER with other parts of India and Bangladesh, hence the current focus on better utilization of NW-2 and revival of cargo traffic. This should be studied in the backdrop of declining cargo and passenger traffic through this mode. Compared to 865.1 thousand tonnes in 2009, the volume of cargo transported through waterways declined to 178.7 thousand tonnes in 2015 for waterways in Assam. Likewise, total number of passengers ferried by water vessels seems to have also gone down in Assam with reduction in the number of powered vessels (both for cargo and passenger traffic) introduced in recent times.

Leaving aside Sikkim, which so far did not have civil aviation services, several other states in the region witnessed considerable improvement in passenger and cargo traffic between 2015 and 2018. New routes under new schemes such as Ude Desh Ka Aam Naagarik (UDAN) (including in helicopters) will boost intra-regional connectivity in NER, even as state capitals remain poorly connected except for some hub and spoke connectivity between Guwahati and other cities in the region. On digital connectivity, it may be noted that with regard to mobile and wireline connectivity between 2010–11 and 2015–16, the NER registered significantly higher growth vis-a-vis all India. However, tele-density remains much below all India levels, even as there is improvement in penetration in terms of broadband as well as internet. The rate at which broadband connectivity has improved in the NER is better than national average, but the number of times internet connectivity has grown during the same period is much less than the national average. The Bharat Net programme under Digital India initiative, which is expected to provide broadband connectivity to 11,252 gram panchayats in the NER, is facing significant implementation gaps across most states excepting one. To overcome existing implementation gaps, on account of unique geographical and climatic challenges including long monsoon, the states in the North East are going to be connected through satellite media aided by GSAT-11.

For all practical purposes, the NER is pivotal to India's Act East Policy and is at the heart of sub-regional initiatives like Bay of Bengal Initiative for Multi-Sectoral Technical and Economic Cooperation (BIMSTEC), Bangladesh, Bhutan, India, Nepal (BBIN), and Bangladesh-China-India-Myanmar (BCIM). The region has the capacity to reach South East Asian countries through trade in goods and services. Prosperity in NER is directly linked to trade, investment, and connectivity with India's extended neighbourhood, a perception also shared by local citizens. New domestic and international air routes between NER and neighbouring countries would revive people-to-people connect and facilitate trade in primary products of shorter self-lives in which the region excel. To that extent, beyond competition in certain products, several products exported by NER matches import demand in ASEAN countries. The region evidently exports to most countries in the ASEAN.

Financing of SDGs

With the introduction of SDGs, global community and individual countries have also multiplied their efforts to mobilize resources from all possible sources (government, private, multilateral financing, as well as local sources) for financing the SDGs. While the financing gaps for the developing regions remain daunting, resource pooling and blending through robust partnerships, capacity building, and accountability have been found to be the most convincing way forward. The NER of India has specific challenges in this regard as the region has sub-optimum level of economic activity, widespread informalization, greater regional diversity, and longstanding internal discord. The government has overwhelming presence in financing development and capacity building in the region.

As has been the practice, in addition to the transfer of central funds to the NER states, 10 per cent of the Annual Plan Budget of fifty-two Ministries of the Union Government is earmarked for NER since 1998–99. It is also known that the capacity of the states in the NER is low in raising tax revenues compared to states outside the NER. Their accounts, however, have higher share of non-tax revenue. The extent of support currently received by the NER states is reflected in the very high share of gross transfers (often above 45 per cent) in the aggregate disbursements reaching them. However, it has been observed that perhaps expenditure on the social and economic services in the NER, particularly on health and education, is not commensurate with higher levels of resource flows. However, a few states have performed better than the national average. Non-development expenditure remains high for the NER states. Many states continue to have disproportionately high fixed expenditure on interest payments, salaries and wages, pensions, and subsidies. The region has benefitted from external financing through multilateral development banks such as Asian Development Bank (ADB) and World Bank (WB) in connectivity, infrastructure, capacity development, and livelihood promotion.

Acknowledgements

We are grateful to Dr Rajiv Kumar, Hon'ble Vice Chairman, NITI Aayog for guiding and inspiring us in this effort. We are thankful to Chairman, RIS, Dr Mohan Kumar for his constant encouragement in this endeavour. Prof Sachin Chaturvedi, Director General, RIS has been the moving spirit behind this report, and his vision and meticulous guidance to the research and editorial teams is gratefully acknowledged. We are also thankful to Ms Shireen Vakil, Head, Policy and Advocacy, TATA Trusts for the collaboration with RIS towards a long-term partnership. We wholeheartedly thank all faculty members at RIS who contributed to the report: Prof S. K. Mohanty, Prof Milindo Chakrabarti, Prof Amitabh Kundu, Prof T. C. James, Dr P. K. Anand, and Mr Krishna Kumar. Dr Sabyasachi Saha and Dr Priyadarshi Dash from RIS who contributed to this report as well as planned, edited, and coordinated the production of this voluminous report, deserve complements for their painstaking efforts. Editorial comments received from Dr P. K. Anand on initial drafts of the chapters are gratefully acknowledged. We also acknowledge the guidance and support received from Mr Rajeev Kher, Ambassador Amar Sinha, Ambassador Bhaskar Balakrishnan, and Mr Augustine Peter of RIS.

During the preparation of the report, we received valuable suggestions and comments in meetings held with various stakeholders and resource persons. Preparatory meetings with partners and State Governments convened by NITI Aayog and North Eastern Council on SDG Conclave 2020 were informative and useful. We thank Shri Ram Muivah, former Secretary, North Eastern Council for his guidance and support. Ms Sanyukta Samaddar, Adviser, NITI Aayog and her team have shared their detailed comments on the draft report, which has enormously benefitted from their insights and observations. We are also grateful to all State Government departments in the North East who extended their support in sharing valuable information which was found extremely useful.

We are grateful to all invited experts, and members of the North East Training, Research and Advocacy Foundation (NETRA) who participated in the workshop at Guwahati on 16 October 2019. We specially acknowledge the insightful interactions with Prof T. G. Sitharam, Director, IIT Guwahati, and initial inputs and comments received from Prof Chandan Mahanta, Dr Shiladitya Chatterjee, Prof E. Bijoykumar Singh, Mr Rudra Mani Dubey, Dr K. Ahmed, Mr Jiban Chandra Phukan, Ms Supriya Khound, Dr Sudarshan Rodriguez, Dr Jayanta Choudhury, Dr Narayan Sahoo, Dr Subhrabaran Das, and Dr Durga Prasad Chhetri.

The Report has benefitted from substantive inputs and comments by eminent scholars and practitioners including Shri V. K. Pipersenia, Dr Ashok Jain, Prof Manmohan Agarwal, Dr Bala Prasad, Dr Yogesh Gokahle, Dr Nitya Nanda, Dr C. S. C. Sekhar, Dr Harsha Chaturvedi, Dr Kanak Haloi, and Mr Pratim Ranjan Bose. Contributions and support received from Dr Nimita Pandey, Dr Namrata Pathak, Dr Sushil Kumar, Ms Prativa Shaw, Mr Ankur Jaiswal, and Ms Neeharika Agnihotri. We also acknowledge the assistance by the RIS interns Ms Sakhsi Nigam and Ms Lavanya Sayal for contributing to the COVID-19 chapter. The support from Dr Manorama Bakshi, Mr Anirudh Menon, and Mr Amar Chanchal of TATA Trusts are duly acknowledged.

Finally, we express our gratitude to the Oxford University Press for coming forward to publish this report. The comments received from anonymous reviewers were extremely insightful and encouraging. Last, but not the least, we thank Mr Dhiraj Pandey, Commissioning Editor of OUP for facilitating the publication of this report.

1

COVID-19 and Development Process in North-Eastern States

Introduction

Gifted with unique natural resources and flora and fauna, the North Eastern Region (NER) comprising eight states—Arunachal Pradesh, Assam, Manipur, Meghalaya, Mizoram, Nagaland, Sikkim, and Tripura, is an important aspirational region of India. Over the years, NER has recorded significant expansion of economic activity, improvement in physical connectivity and digital infrastructure, higher trade and investment with bordering countries such as Bangladesh and Myanmar, better access to education and health, greater tourist attraction, among others. The adoption of Sustainable Development Goals (SDGs) has created ample opportunities for the states in NER to scale up and streamline existing efforts for consolidating development gains, hence striving towards achieving the SDGs. Besides pooling own resources and machinery, the north-eastern states have received strong institutional support from the central government and institutions. Before the outbreak of the corona virus, the states showed positive symptoms which perhaps created hope among the regional governments that the region would make faster progress in SDG indicators. However, the disruption in activity across the region due to long period of lockdown and partial lockdown has made the progress on SDGs uncertain.

As of 28 December 2020, more than 79.7 million people have been affected across the world by this COVID-19 pandemic inflicting heavy economic, social, and financial costs, especially in developing economies and poor countries (WHO Website). The pandemic has caused abrupt disruptions in domestic and regional supply chains and have eroded the incomes of people and business prospects in the economies at large. The

Rise of the North East, RIS, Oxford University Press.© Research and Information System for Developing Countries 2023.
DOI: 10.1093/oso/9780192849342.003.0001

wear and tear of the pandemic for the developing world has become massive as countries continue to operate with shutdown of major economic sectors. Besides domestic distortions, there could be spillover of external shocks from South East Asia and the ASEAN region in terms of incidence of the disease, stringency, and its impact on the NER region. Thus, from the point of view of policymaking, it is crucial to focus on curbing the effect of the pandemic in the short-term and revive the NER economy in the medium-term in terms of trade, investment, and connectivity.

In view of this evolving situation, this chapter briefly covers the attempts to understand the nature of economic impact of the pandemic in the NER and discuss the range of policy measures implemented by the governments and issues related to the consequences of this shock for the development process.

Spread and Severity of COVID-19 in NER

The novel corona virus pandemic has taken a heavy toll on people, economies, and societies across the world. The pandemic that was initially hailed as health crisis has turned out to be a global economic crisis due to its exponential spread and severity worldwide. The magnitude of economic collapse manifested so far, made it the worst crisis the world has faced in the past century. Countries are struggling to cope with the public health and economic challenges still unfolding in many parts of the world. Although the world has faced similar fatal disease outbreaks in the past such as Spanish flu (1918–1919), Asian flu (1956–1958), Hong Kong flu (1968–1969), Sars-CoV-1 (2003–2004), Swine flu (2009–2010), Zika virus (2014–2016), and Ebola virus (2014–2016), the devastating and unpredictable spread of corona virus has made it the worst and unique.

India reported its first COVID-19 case on 30 January 2020 in Kerala. By 3 February, India had three cases (Worldometer, 2020). Within four months, the confirmed cases in India had exponentially increased from 9,385 in March 2020 to 9.84 million in June 2020 (Figure 1.1). By the end of August, India ranked among the worst-hit countries after the United States and Brazil. As of 28 December, India has registered 10.2 million confirmed cases of COVID-19. With rapid surge in cases, India was counted as one of the most-affected country in the world after Brazil,

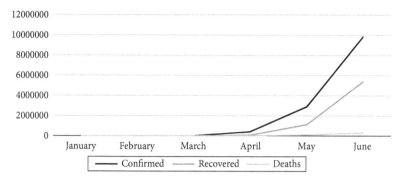

Figure 1.1: Trend of COVID-19 Cases in India
Source: Data hub compiled by Johns Hopkins University Center for Systems Science and Engineering.

the United States, Italy, Spain, and France. While no part of the country is insulated from the infections, Maharashtra is the worst-hit state in the country in terms of the total number of infections. Almost all major cities of the country including Mumbai, Chennai, Delhi, Hyderabad, Bengaluru, Kolkata, etc. have registered various phases of peak in COVID-19 in the past year. Despite nationwide lockdown in various phases that might have resulted in community spread of the virus, the different regions of India continue to witness new cases. Although the recovery rate for the country and states has shown visible signs of improvement and being hailed as one of the best in the world, it is premature at this stage to judge the nature and consequences of the fall-out of this pandemic on Indian economy.

Given high population density along with population clusters within megacities and large slums, the risks of faster spread of COVID-19 continued to be alarming. States such as Maharashtra, Delhi, and Tamil Nadu have emerged as epicentres of the outbreak in India. By end of October, NER reported 2,92,760 confirmed cases which constituted 3.6 per cent of total cases in India. Of this, 2,67,263 patients (91.2 per cent) have recovered. Fatality measured in terms of number of deaths has become less severe now than previous months (Ghani et al. 2005). For instance, unlike the region's share in recovery which hovered around 3.5 per cent since July, there has been a drastic fall in the region's share in country's total COVID-19 related deaths from 813.3 per cent in July to 42.2 per cent in October. However, the number of deaths for NER increased from 137 in July to 1,638 in October (Table 1.1). Assam being the largest state in the

Table 1.1: COVID-19 Situation in North-Eastern States

Category	April	May	June	July	August	September	October
Confirmed	62 (0.2)	1,803 (0.9)	11,986 (2.0)	53,041 (3.1)	1,40,030 (3.8)	2,44,040 (3.9)	2,92,760 (3.6)
Active	28 (0.1)	1,419 (1.4)	4,249 (1.8)	15,421 (2.6)	33,889 (4.0)	50,586 (4.9)	25,497 (3.5)
Recovered	34 (0.4)	384 (0.4)	7,737 (2.2)	37,620 (3.4)	1,06,141 (3.7)	1,93,454 (3.7)	2,67,263 (3.6)
Death	–	5 [150.0]	15 [200.0]	137 [813.3]	465 [239.4]	1,152 [147.7]	1,638 [42.2]

Source: Analysis by authors based on data from www.covid19india.org

Note: Figures in parentheses indicate percentages of India total. Figures in square bracket denote growth rate.

region has become the worst-hit state in the region. Assam contributes approximately 69 per cent of total reported cases in the region. Further, deaths have been reported in Arunachal Pradesh, Assam, Meghalaya, and Tripura as well (Figure 1.1).

Consistent with all-India average, NER experienced steady rise in recovery rates over time. Recovery rate has improved considerably from 64.5 per cent in June to 91.3 per cent in October in 2020. More or less similar trends were observed for individual states in the NER. For Assam and Tripura, the recovery rate was above 93 per cent, whereas it was still below 80 per cent for Manipur (75.4 per cent) and Nagaland (77.5 per cent). Interestingly, recovery from COVID-19 was quite unpredictable for the region in the month of July, which started improving during the September–October (Table 1.2).

As demonstrated in Figure 1.2, COVID-19 cases continue to rise in the NER. During the un-lockdown phase in June, cases in these states increased exponentially. However, the NER, compared to the rest of the country, could be able to contain the rapid spread of the virus fairly well which could be attributed to prompt action by the state governments, border guarding forces, and the local public, who supported the immediate closure of 5,000 km of international borders in the region. The state governments had taken strict actions to ban all tourism activities, interstate borders movement were sealed, and there were strict guidelines in place for all public health care units with respect to preparation for COVID-19 cases.

Table 1.2: COVID-19 Recovery Rate in North-Eastern States (%)

State	April	May	June	July	August	September	October
Arunachal Pradesh	100.0	25.0	32.5	57.7	70.2	70.3	85.6
Assam	67.4	13.9	67.2	75.4	78.4	80.5	93.8
Manipur	100.0	15.5	44.8	64.4	69.3	77.0	75.4
Meghalaya	0	44.4	79.2	26.1	49.1	70.5	84.3
Mizoram	0	100.0	76.2	60.5	58.3	80.5	85.8
Nagaland	N.A	0	36.6	37.5	77.4	81.5	77.5
Sikkim	N.A	0	56.8	36.1	74.1	75.8	89.4
Tripura	66.7	54.7	78.4	66.6	63.8	76.4	93.3
NER	54.8	21.3	64.5	70.9	75.8	79.3	91.3
India	26.0	48.2	59.4	64. 6	76.9	83.5	91.0

Source: Analysis by authors based on data from www.covid19india.org

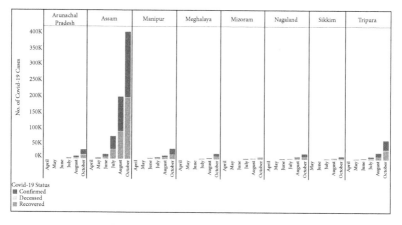

Figure 1.2: Number of COVID-19 Cases in North Eastern States
Source: Drawn by authors based on data from www.covid-19India.org.

Rising cases, strict lockdowns, and preventive measures imposed by central and state governments have undoubtedly impacted economic activity across the region in all sectors. The Ministry[1] of Development of North Eastern Region observed that the NER has emerged as the model[2] of corona virus management for the rest of the country to emulate.

[1] *The Times of India* (2020).
[2] Coronavirus: Northeastern states sound alert (2020).

Macroeconomic Impact of COVID-19

The novel corona virus has inflicted huge damage on economies around the world. The magnitude and severity of the outbreak has led the world to deal with the 'lives versus livelihood'. Almost all countries have imposed strict containment measures such as lockdowns, travel restrictions, and strict social distancing norms for past several months, leaving detrimental impact on the livelihood of people. Non-essential economic activities around the globe have come to a complete halt resulting in severe economic crisis. As per the International Monetary Fund (IMF) projections, global economy is likely to shrink by 4.9 per cent in 2020 which is the worst economic catastrophe since the Great Depression of 1930 (Bloomberg, 2020). India is no exception to this economic collapse. In fact, the anticipated loss of income and impoverishment of people in a country of India size could be massive. Despite having no option at hand, long periods of lockdown and social distancing rules have had adverse impacts on the economy triggering severe demand and supply shocks across the country. However, the imposition of strict lockdown has led to enhancement of health infrastructure in the country by pushing both the government and private sector to incur unplanned expenditure[3] of Rs. 300 crore on COVID-19 related health care services.

Indian economy is expected to face contraction of (-)23.9 per cent in 2020–2021:Q1 as compared to 5.2 per cent in 2019–2020:Q1. Given the heightened uncertainty and prolonged recession following drastic fall in induced consumption and investment, it is likely that Indian economy will contract by 10.3 per cent in 2020 as per the IMF October 2020 projections. During March–August, it was only essential consumption and government expenditure on health and essential services that constituted the core of economic activity in the country. With successive phases of unlocking in the months of September and October, business activities have picked up in some cities but may not be adequate to drive any significant economic turnaround in the coming months. Abrupt disruption in urban and rural activity has led to a steep fall in private final consumption expenditure (PFCE) from Rs. 19.92 trillion

---

[3] See Sharma (2000).

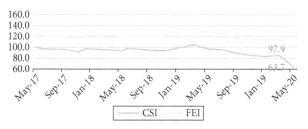

Figure 1.3: Consumer Confidence Survey 2020 Indices
Source: RBI, Consumer Confidence Survey, 2020.

in 2019–2020:Q1 to Rs. 14.61 trillion in 2020–2021:Q1. It is more likely that people will postpone non-essential consumption till assured sources of income are restored, mostly in private and informal sectors. Besides the actual impact, the perceived impact of the pandemic among the people is terribly high due to fear and uncertainty which would suppress consumption and investment in the next few quarters of 2020–2021. Data from the Reserve Bank of India reproduced in Figure 1.3 showed that consumer confidence collapsed in the month of May (RBI, 2020). The current situation index and the future expectations index were both below 100, indicating that consumers were pessimistic, as reading above 100 represents optimism.

Overall consumer spending remained afloat, mostly due to relative inelasticity in essential spending; consumers, however, reported sharp cuts in discretionary spending. Given the asymmetric nature of employment elasticity, post-crisis recovery would depend on degree of macroeconomic uncertainty and consumer confidence (Nag and Geest, 2020). The steeper decline in working hours would likely to cost 130 million full jobs globally as per the ILO estimate for 2020:Q1. Information compiled by the Centre for Monitoring Indian Economy and illustrated in Figure 1.4 shows that the unemployment rate in both rural and urban areas rose sharply in March when the lockdown was imposed. It remained relatively high in April, before showing signs of improvement starting in May and June when activities in certain sectors resumed.

The number of new Employees' Provident Fund (EPF) subscribers declined sharply from 13.9 million during 2018–2019 to 11.04 million

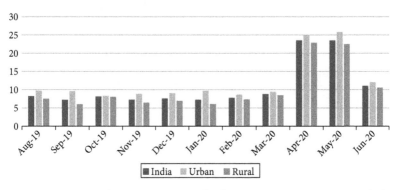

Figure 1.4: Unemployment Rate in India from August 2019–June 2020 (%)
Source: CMIE, 2020.

during 2019–2020. There was increase in number of members who ceased their subscription to EPF which would be due to job losses from 0.41 million in April 2020 to 0.44 million in May 2020. However, the fall in subscriptions was moderated to 0.29 million in June when restrictions in some sectors of the economy were partially relaxed. Although the contribution of total subscribers towards National Pension Scheme increased from 4.55 million in April 2020 to 6.14 million in June 2020, new subscribers added in June were lesser as compared to April and May with sharp decline of close to 20,000 subscribers from the previous month.

While all the states of India are witnessing similar economic impacts, the magnitude of shock could be disproportionately high for smaller states. For instance, since states in the NER are relatively small, they can be expected to face sharper economic downturn than the rest of India. NER as a whole was growing in double digits before the pre-COVID-19 period with enormous potential to expand its economic prosperity across agriculture, industries, and services. Given the strong natural resources and land borders with neighbouring countries such as Bangladesh and Myanmar, the region is important for India's 'Act East Policy', for strong regional connect with South Asia and Southeast Asia, and for integration of NER with regional production networks.

The most immediate impact of the COVID-19 pandemic in NER was on the progress achieved on various SDGs. Before the outbreak of the pandemic, the region has been in forefront for undertaking proactive policies and adopting localization for achievement of SDGs. Assam had emerged as a committed partner on SDGs and become the first state in the region to launch initial roadmap for successful implementation of the SDGs. The initial monitoring and evaluation of the SDGs by NITI Aayog India Index, 2019–2020 for states indicated that Sikkim has been a top performer in achieving SDG 7 (renewable energy) and SDG-15 (life on land), while Nagaland has been successful in achieving SDG-12 (responsible consumption and production) and Manipur has made considerable contribution towards SDG-15. Table 1.3 presented the NER performance as per the India index on SDG in 2019–2020. Due to limited fiscal space, the progress realized in SDGs was seriously impaired due to diversion of financial resources and capacity in government machinery towards mitigating the COVID-19 crisis.

Since precise data for measuring the impacts of the pandemic on different sectors, employment, migration, etc. are not available, the only way to assess the impact is to map the nature and scope of adverse effects by comparing it with the past trends. In essence, lockdown during March–July implied complete shutdown of economic sectors which makes is easy to approximate losses occurred due to COVID-19. In that perspective, the likely impact of the pandemic on different sectors of the north-eastern economies could be studied by looking at the composition of state output. By and large, all the states in NER have strong tertiary sectors except for Sikkim which contribute between 40 per cent and 70 per cent of their Gross State Domestic Product (GSDP) (Figure 1.5). It entails that services sectors such as banking and insurance, transport and logistics, education, health services, government services, tourism, hospitality, travel, and others which were badly hit during the pandemic would cause sharp fall in state gross domestic product (GDP) in 2020. In other words, the loss of jobs, incomes, and livelihood could be considerably high in the NER region.

Barring services sectors, the contribution of agriculture and industry to economies of NER is not negligible. Lack of labour affecting harvesting of crops and distressed sale of agriculture produce lowered income and purchasing power of the farmers and agriculture-dependent families. Likewise, closure of manufacturing units might have impacted employment of skilled and semi-skilled labour in different states of the region.

Table 1.3: NER Performance on SDGs in 2019–2020

NER	SDG 1	SDG 2	SDG 3	SDG 4	SDG 5	SDG 6	SDG 7	SDG 8	SDG 9	SDG 10	SDG 11	SDG 12	SDG 13	SDG 15	SDG 16	Composite Score
Arunachal Pradesh	34	66	50	58	33	88	74	52	31	38	43	67	31	71	62	53
Assam	48	39	44	44	33	78	70	62	46	67	40	68	47	90	52	55
Manipur	42	69	62	70	34	87	72	27	43	81	28	85	37	100	70	60
Meghalaya	68	35	53	55	34	70	52	65	22	76	22	60	36	99	59	54
Mizoram	67	75	52	61	37	81	81	42	8	66	33	50	45	75	63	56
Nagaland	56	70	29	47	42	75	70	28	23	61	23	100	51	94	84	57
Sikkim	65	66	59	58	49	79	97	68	27	64	74	60	38	100	69	65
Tripura	70	49	61	55	32	69	56	63	48	45	31	92	37	88	73	58
India	50	35	61	58	42	88	70	64	65	64	53	55	60	66	72	60

Aspirant (0–49)   Performer (50–64)   Front Runner (65–99)   Achiever (100)

Source: NITI Aayog (2020).

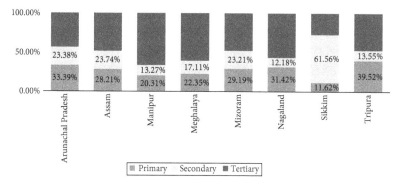

Figure 1.5: Sectoral Composition in GSDP of NER (2018-2019)
Source: Ministry of Statistics and Program Implementation, 2020.

Agriculture

Agriculture serves as a primary source of livelihood and economic security for a sizeable native population of the NER. Communities in the region are preponderantly agrarian and practise subsistence agriculture. Agriculture constitutes a significant portion (16 per cent–20 per cent) of state GDP for all the eight states in the region. Strict measures taken over the past five months to contain the spread of the virus have negatively impacted agriculture sector and considerably slowed down the rural economy in the region (IFPRI, 2020). Harvesting of Rabi (winter) crops which largely takes place in March and April was already underway in most of the states when lockdown was announced on 22 March 2020 by the Central Government. Farmers have complained that seasonal crops have been left to rot on the fields as villagers have been unable to work during the lockdown due to strict surveillance. Rough estimates by ICAR show that harvesting of around 10 per cent to 17 per cent of vegetables, 6 per cent of pulse crops, and 0.8 per cent of Rabi oilseeds was affected during the lockdown (ICAR, 2020). Further, the report claims that closure of weekly markets, unavailability of transportation, and shortage of storage facilities have all resulted in wastage of crops leading to a drastic fall in farm income for rural households.

Non-availability of labourers and closure of transportation during the lockdown affected pineapple production and sale in Tripura. The impact on agriculture in Sikkim was not necessarily less but was managed well. Supply of cardamom, turmeric, and other cash crops were resumed after initial disruption due to lockdown. The Sikkim Organic Mission through Sikkim State Cooperative Supply and Marketing Federation (SIMFED) and twenty-eight Farmer Producer Organisations (FPOs) managed the supply of essential vegetables and milk. Uncertainty among farmers to sell farm produce, shortage of agricultural and farm inputs, and pending loans have discouraged farmers from investing in new crops. Perceived fall in cultivation of crops is likely to have adverse impact on growth and yield of kharif crops in the region.

Further, sudden stop of tourism industry resulting in temporary closure of restaurants, hotels, and tourist spots coupled with high unemployment in the region has resulted in low demand for basic agricultural and dairy products. Poultry farmers have also incurred huge losses (~60 per cent) as the supply of feed for the poultry sector was predominantly dependent on states such as Kolkata and Hyderabad which were not accessible during the nationwide lockdown. Fall in demand for floriculture products proved disastrous for the sector as majority of them are marketed outside the region for religious and social ceremonies which were strictly prohibited during lockdown.

Tea industry, which is a major contributor to the rural economy in the region, has also taken a huge blow. The North Eastern Tea Association (NETA) has reported a loss of thirty million kgs of tea leaves due to the lockdown in March. The total revenue loss for the tea industry is expected to be more than Rs. 1,218 crore during the lockdown (The Economic Times, 2020). Contribution of the agriculture and allied activities to state GDP is expected to dip for all the eight states in the region in 2020. However, with adequate government support and incentives, agriculture sector may gain momentum in 2021. The pandemic coupled with natural disasters such as forest fires, floods, and droughts in the region is expected to further affect agricultural output in the upcoming months.

Manufacturing

Industrial sector in NER is relatively less developed than other parts of India. Small industries dominate industrial scenario in the NER (North Eastern Council Website). The industrial sector in the region constitutes between 10 per cent and 50 per cent of GSDP. Assam and Sikkim are the most industrialized states in the region with the sector contributing more than 25 per cent and 50 per cent to GSDP, respectively. Due to shutdown of manufacturing sectors, thousands of informal workers lost their jobs and mass exodus of internal migrant workers took place from urban to rural, areas particularly from construction and Micro, Small and Medium Enterprises (MSME) sectors. In absence of any means of livelihood, these daily workers were pushed into abject poverty during the pandemic. Thus, it is important to analyse the real-time impact on major industries of the region including agro-based and food processing, tea, petroleum, construction, and mining.

Generally, agro-based and food processing industries employ a major portion of the workforce in the region. These industries suffered from shortage of labour and liquidity constraints due to cessation of economic activities in all the eight states. Liquidity crunch and limited working capital and labour were the major concerns for the industries in the region. Paucity of working capital deterred procurement of agricultural produce, the negative effects of which were trickled down to the farming sector subsequently (The Economic Times, 2020). Tea industry, as discussed earlier, has faced huge losses. Delayed stiffing of tea leaves due to the lockdown has led to astronomical rise in prices of green leaves and fluctuating supplies for production ready factories (FirstPost, 2020). The khadi and village industry and the handloom industry combined employ approximately thirty lakh workers in the NER in a normal year, which was badly affected during COVID-19. The state-wise employment trends in khadi and village industries are presented in Table 1.4. In a situation of complete lockdown, the extent of job losses that could have happened in the past year can be assessed. These industries also faced unprecedented crisis due to non-availability of raw materials. Since transportation across states except essential supplies was restricted, there was great difficulty in delivering yarn to the weavers. As sale of yarn is not listed as an essential commodity, both its production and sale were completely stopped during the lockdown.

Rubber industry in the region also suffered heavily during the pandemic. In Tripura, the estimated loss to the industry was around Rs. 250 crore. The status of petroleum industry in the region was not different. There have been massive production cuts due to the fall in demand during the lockdown. Consumption of fuel products in India has declined by

Table 1.4: Cumulative Employment in Khadi and Village and Handloom Industries in NER (Lakh)

States	Khadi and Village Industries (2018–2019 Provisional)	Handloom Industries (2019–2020)
Arunachal Pradesh	0.20	0.95
Assam	5.59	12.84
Manipur	1.12	2.25
Meghalaya	0.62	0.43
Mizoram	1.27	0.28
Nagaland	0.97	0.43
Sikkim	0.27	0.01
Tripura	1.17	1.38
Total	11.21	18.55

Source: North Eastern Council Website.

more than 80 per cent resulting in troubled times for the petroleum industry of the North East (The Telegraph Online).

As a part of the North East Industrial Policy, all eight states ramped up investment in infrastructure resulting in increased construction activity before the pandemic (Ministry of DONER , 2020). However, the construction industry witnessed work disruptions due to the stringent lockdown, closure of brick fields, and closure of cement industry. Loss of income as well as diversion of government funds towards tackling the pandemic has severely hit the industry causing large-scale unemployment of daily wage workers in the region (Guwahati Plus, 2020). Mining industry is also faced by lack of demand from end-use sectors such as power, steel, and cement and non-availability of labour. Further, falling demand for minerals has had a profound impact on the employment and well-being of the local community (KPMG, 2020). Despite announcement of economic package by the centre, credit flows to MSME sectors did not pick up as expected signalling very high risk perception about future business prospects in states such as Tripura.

The SDG-9 score of NER which reflects on innovation, industry, and infrastructure has been considerably weak even after the launch of various flagship programmes by the union government such as Skill India, Make in India, and Startup India. The health crisis in the region and disruption of industrial activity can further degrade SDG-9 score for the states. Overall, adverse impacts of the pandemic on the industrial sector and unemployment in NER are likely to persist. However, with increased government incentives and economic support packages, a likely turnaround in production and sales may be expected. Further, short-run monetary measures to prevent further worsening of liquidity crunch and quick measures for insolvencies are important for protecting small investors and MSMEs in the region.

Services

The services sector of the north-eastern states is the second largest employer after agriculture and constitutes a significant portion of the formal sector economy in the region. The sector contributes between 25 per cent and 65 per cent to the GSDP across all eight states with the highest contribution in Manipur (~65 per cent) and Meghalaya (~54 per cent). While all services sectors were affected, we focus our attention on certain such as tourism, transportation, financial, and education services those were relatively more impacted. The vibrant tourism sector covering several wildlife, religious, cultural, and ethnic tourism spots had faced complete halt during the COVID-19 pandemic affecting jobs in organized and unorganized sectors. The whole tourism value chain across hotels, restaurants, resorts, travel agencies, tour operators as well as food businesses associated with the sector was disrupted.

Figure 1.6 shows the number of domestic and foreign tourists in the all eight states. Assam, Sikkim, and Meghalaya accounted for the highest number of tourist visits in 2018. These states in the past four to five months have also witnessed a stark rise in COVID-19 cases, forcing the state governments to impose strict containment measures affecting the sector, especially in Assam and Meghalaya. Overall, along with huge income and revenue losses, the pandemic is expected to leave a huge surge in unemployment rate in the sector (The Sentinel, 2020).

The Google mobility report which records movement of people to spaces such as shops, workplaces, parks, and other areas showed a sharp decline in overall mobility due to the lockdown. In other words, it indicated a stark downfall in profit earned through people's visits in these

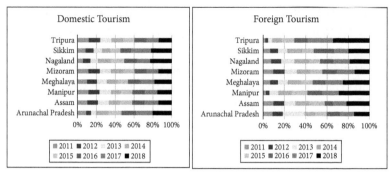

Figure 1.6: State-wise Number of Tourist Visits in NER
Source: North Eastern Council, 2020.

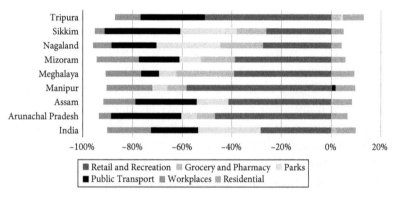

Figure 1.7: Mobility of People in North-Eastern Region (June 2020)
Source: Google LLC, 2020.

areas. Closure of tourism industry coupled with reduced movement of people, as shown in Figure 1.7, has negatively impacted the retail sector in the region. Transportation sector reports also reflect the same impact across the value chain.

Transportation services were completely shut in March 2020, when the nationwide lockdown was announced. Aviation industry was worst hit with forecasted loss of up to Rs. 25,000 crore in 2020 for the industry for India as a whole (CRISIL, 2020). Air, water, road, and rail commercial services were completely prohibited in the region, while permission for only essential services was granted resulting in huge revenue losses

Table 1.5: Network Status of NER (as on October 2019)

States	Telephone Exchange (Wireline) in nos.	Total Capacity (Wireline + Wireless) in Lakh lines	Total DELs (Wireline + Wireless) in Lakh	VPTs in nos.
Arunachal Pradesh	92	5.778	2.926	1,054
Assam	544	25.11	28.065	105
Manipur	43	3.942	1.583	418
Meghalaya	49	6.465	3.226	270
Mizoram	55	3.41	2.273	83
Nagaland	61	3.443	1.265	67
Sikkim	32	1.561	0.506	376
Tripura	82	8.697	4.269	222
Total	958	58.405	44.114	2,595

Source: Department of Economic Affairs (2020).

for the transportation sector coupled with disruption of supply chains of different businesses across the eight states (The Economic Times, 2020).

Education services are also adversely affected in the region. Educational institutes in all eight states were closed in March 2020. Like rest of India, NER was also affected with disruption in learning after the closure of schools and universities leading to tremendous pressure on access and ownership of smart phones and internet use among the children. The status of internet connectivity and its penetration in the region is shown in Table 1.5, as digital connectivity is not well developed in the region resulting in difficulties for students and teachers. The schools and colleges in the rural areas were worst affected. Further, students in rural areas and from lower income groups who do not have adequate access to smart phones and laptops could not properly avail the benefits of online education. While there were not many job losses or revenue losses in the education sector, the overall closure of the sector itself was a matter of concern.

The IT sector all over India is expected to suffer a decline in revenues by almost 5 per cent to 10 per cent due to reduced business activity during the lockdown. As of 31 December 2019, twenty-nine BPO/ITES units were planned to be set up in six NER (Nagaland, Assam, Meghalaya, Arunachal Pradesh, Tripura, and Manipur) under the North East BPO

Promotion Scheme (NEBPS). This is anticipated to suffer a delay due to this pandemic (See MeitY). As per the data by Department of Promotion of Industry and International Trade, the share of foreign direct investments (equity inflows) in the north-eastern states also declined from 0.02 per cent in (October–December 2019) to 0.01 per cent (January–March 2020) The stock markets in states of Arunachal Pradesh and Mizoram witnessed a steep decline in number of registered investors.

As per RBI Aizawl, the projected impact of COVID-19 on Mizoram's economy for the year 2020–2021 could be to the tune of Rs. 676,184 lakh for the primary sector, Rs. 629,439 lakh for the secondary sector, and Rs. 11,19,476 lakh for the tertiary sector. Migrant labourers were badly affected due to closure of economies for several months. Return of migrant labourers to their native places during the lockdown not only destroyed livelihood and income of the people in the country including the north-eastern states but also created complications for the local administrations to rehabilitate them and ensure their social welfare. For example, about 16,000 migrant labourers returned to Tripura and around 33,000 labourers from other states were stranded in the state.

Policy Measures Undertaken

COVID-19 pandemic has affected activity in all sectors of the Indian economy. All the states and union territories faced similar kinds of economic disruptions. In order to mitigate the adverse impacts on the economy, it was crucial for the governments in the NER to implement suitable policy measures which would ensure stability in the economy in the short-run and provide relief to the citizens. In this section, we highlight key measures taken by governments in the region to deal with the pandemic.

Liquidity Measures

Reserve Bank of India announced a Regulatory Package on 27 March 2020 to decrease the burden on Indian financial markets. As the RBI Governor's Statement on 22 May 2020, relaxation of repayments, mitigation of debt burden, and averting financial strain on the economy were the major focus areas to control the disruptions due to the pandemic (RBI, 2020). With an aim to ease debt burden and preserve liquidity with households, RBI has extended moratorium on loan repayments till 31 August 2020 applicable for all the commercial banks, financial institutions, cooperative banks, and non-banking financial companies. RBI has also relaxed the norms for provision of working capital finance. Lending institutions had the option of reassessing the 'drawing power' by decreasing the margins till 31 August 2020 and reassess the cycle of working capital. The lending institutions were asked to provide an Management Information System (MIS) for reliefs provided to borrowers lending Rs. 5 crore as of 1 March 2020. The recalculation of the drawing power would not be treated as a concession or any kind of change in the terms and agreements by the government. The rescheduling of payments would not be classified as default for the purpose of Credit Information Companies reporting (RBI, 2020).

The changes in the regulatory measures were to ensure expansion of liquidity for smooth functioning of the financial institutions. Ease of credit flows and financial strain, betterment of markets due to the increased volatility, are all taken care of by strengthening monetary transfers to deal with the pandemic. The policy repo rate was lowered from 4.4 per cent to 4 per cent, and reverse repo rate was cut from 3.75 per cent to 3.35 per cent. The bank rate was reduced from 4.65 per cent to 4.25 per cent (RBI, 2020). The central bank has also decided to increase the pre- and post-shipment export credit period to fifteen months from existing twelve months. The import payments on or before 31 July 2020 had also received an extension from six months to twelve months. RBI has relaxed the guidelines associated with the Consolidated Sinking Fund of the state governments. From coming up with a contingency plan for financial institutions to aligning a cut down in the rates for better economic performance, RBI undertook pragmatic measures to revive the economy and prevent the economy from hard-landing (RBI, 2020).

Preventive Measures

While measures related to revival of economy were given utmost priority, it was also crucial to undertake preventive health care measures by the state governments and the central government. The state governments launched mandatory health screening setups in the airports and border crossings. Every state issued its quarantine guideline policy in line with the central guidelines. There were restrictions imposed on visa renewal, public gatherings, and travel to limit the spread of the virus. Improving health infrastructure was given high priority by collaborating with schools and universities to turn them into COVID-19 testing centres. India became the second largest manufacturer of Personal Protective Equipment (PPE) kits across the globe in just a few weeks of COVID-19. The state governments started providing ration kits to the needful during the lockdown. The central government released Rs. 890 crore under the second instalment of COVID-19 Emergency Response and Health System Preparedness Package. In the month of April, the central government announced distribution of free ration under *Pradhan Mantri Garib Kalyan Anna Yojana*.

Policy Measures Undertaken by NER Governments

North-eastern states were quick to respond to the fight against the pandemic in early May with strict lockdown impositions, quick medical supplies, managing public distribution system, and optimizing use of health infrastructure facilities. The Government of Arunachal Pradesh followed strict quarantine restrictions and temporarily suspended foreign visits issuing Protected Area Permit. The state had set up an Economic Revival Committee to overcome the macroeconomic disruptions resulting from COVID-19. Social media platforms were given importance to spread awareness about the pandemic. Steps were taken towards making the state becoming self-reliant in supplies during the lockdown.

Assam has been worst hit not only in terms of the impact of pandemic in the state but also the devastating effects of the flood and forest fire. More than 90 per cent of the Kaziranga National Park was overwhelmed with flood adding anxiety to the affected people. The Assam government started four plasma banks in the state (All India Radio, 2020). The functioning of industrial units was permitted since 1 April 2020, and a committee was formed for monitoring fake news. Assam was the first state to independently import 50,000 PPE kits from China on

1 April 2020. COVAAS App was launched by the government to spread COVID-19 awareness and provide easy access to e-pass. The government requested private schools to cut down the fees by 50 per cent and launched a TV channel *Gyan Brikshya* for all the school students. Life insurance cover for journalists, job cards for migrant workers, and launch of *Dhanwantri* scheme for home delivery of medical supplies were some of those other initiatives undertaken by the Assam government (Government of Assam, 2020).

Manipur announced relief measures—provision for food and medical care on 29 March 2020 (CII, 2020). A surveillance system was set up to monitor the pandemic more effectively. A Memorandum of Understanding was signed by the Manipur Health Minister with seven public and three private hospitals to raise a dynamic health care infrastructure in the state for the implementation of Ayushman Bharat—Pradhan Mantri Jan AarogyaYojana (AB-PMJAY) and Chief Minister-gi Hakshelgi Tengbang (CMHT). On 28 May 2020, Manipur launched State Cine Policy 2020 for generating more revenues through its own creative entertainment (Government of Manipur, 2020).

Strict regulations concerning the entrants in the state has kept the number of COVID-19 patients in Meghalaya low. On 24 April 2020, the Government of Meghalaya filed Expression of Interest to disinfect and sanitize the Bethany hospital in Shillong. The workers were promised a fifty-day payment or for any day applicable based on the industrial shutdown period during COVID 19. The state has spent close to Rs. 100 crore in fighting the pandemic. The state provided Rs. 3,000 to around 24,516 registered construction workers and Rs. 2,100 to unregistered construction workers. Further, provisional kits were provided to 10,000 households costing around Rs. 2,000 crore.

Mizoram was recognized as the fifth state in NER to get a COVID-19 testing lab, and it provided financial aid to more than 40,000 construction workers. Section 144 was imposed for gathering of more than five people in certain districts of the state to control the pandemic. Nagaland established a state-level control room for issues related to COVID-19. The state banned imports of pigs on 26 April 2020. All the frontline and government workers were promised to be paid an ex-gratia amount of Rs. 10 lakh. In April 2020, the state announced increase in use of Point in Scale swipe machine to reduce cash transactions to deal with COVID-19 social distancing norms.

Sikkim followed stringent restrictions in the time of pandemic leading to zero cases in the state till May 2020. Even now the state has sealed three international borders and the border with West Bengal. The ASHA workers were provided with an honorarium of Rs. 5,000. The state came up with measures to dispose the bio-medical waste generated due to COVID-19. The state promoted IT sector for enhancing the education system during the pandemic. The permission for independent BSNL Administrative Control Centre for better connectivity to promote online education was announced by the state (Government of Sikkim, 2020).

Tripura has been distributing Vitamin-C rich fruits for free across the state to enhance immunity in its citizens as part of the Chief Minister's Public Immunity Campaign. The campaign was implemented by the National Urban Livelihood Mission, and Tripura has allocated one crore rupees towards this programme (Mathur, 2020). In addition, several initiatives were taken by the states to promote nutritional gardens in school premises. Due to the lockdown NER is focusing more on online marketing strategies engaging them in Digital India initiative.

Barring the policy measures announced by the union government, the state governments in the north-eastern region implemented some new measures/initiatives to mitigate the economic impacts of the pandemic and help restore normalcy in essential supplies. Table 1.6 presents the snapshot of the policy measures adopted by different governments in NER. For instance, in Tripura, the government provided credit linkage and handholding to local firms through joint liability groups. Primary agricultural societies opened multi-service centres to ensure decentralized procurement, storage, and distribution of agricultural produce during the lockdown. Likewise, Mizoram supported the local manufacturing units to farmers for increasing maize production, extended credit support to poultry farmers, piggery units, and small textile units. Sikkim also devised various ways of promoting credit off-take to support the local businesses and create income-generating activities. National Bank for Agriculture and Rural Development (NABARD) implemented several schemes in the NER in Assam, Arunachal Pradesh, and Tripura. The programmes such as Start-Up Manipur Initiative and Restart Meghalaya Programme are innovative steps to revive the economy in the region. Assam initiated measures to help the tea industry and rehabilitate the tea farmers during the lockdown. In a nutshell, the state governments in the

Table 1.6: New Policy Measures Undertaken for Mitigating COVID-19 Disruptions

State	New Measures
Tripura	• Provided free ration to 6.19 lakh poor families in April and enhanced availability of food grains • Transfer of Rs. 500 to each BPL household • Transfer of two months of advance social pension • Ensuring credit linkage and handholding to shopkeepers under the Mukhyamantri Swanirbhar Yojana • Joint support by NABARD and Tripura Gramin Bank in formation and linkage of 10,000 Joint Liability Groups for next two years • Five Primary Agricultural Credit Societies identified as multi-service centres to facilitate decentralized procurement, storage, and distribution of agricultural produce • Tripura Grameen Bank launched COVID-19 emergency products for dairy, piggery, poultry, and fishery sectors; financing of landless cultivators, and loans for agricultural pump sets, solar hybrid deep freezer for storage of milk, etc.
Mizoram	• Implementation of Emergency Guaranteed Credit Line Scheme was fast-tracked • 400 local designers and tailors were involved in design, stitching, distribution, and sale of masks (Committee on Promotion of Locally Manufactured Protective Gears) • Rs. 3 lakh support per unit to 220 beneficiaries to be given under Piglet Multiplication Unit and Piggery Fattener Units Schemes • Rs. 7,500 each to 2,591 identified beneficiaries under the project for Increased Maize Production • Rs. 1.5 lakh per unit to 440 poultry farms under the Rainbow Rooster Farming Scheme • Rs. 1.7 lakh each to proposed 110 Fly Shuttle Frame Loom Units • RBI Regional Office conducted financial literacy programmes
Sikkim	• Banks have been advised to increase crop insurance coverage under Pradhan Mantri Fasal Bima Yojana • MUDRA loan amounting to Rs. 7.92 crore were disbursed during April–June 2020 • From 2 June onward, every Wednesday and first Thursday, bankers and govt. officials would interact with farmers for matters relating pending loan applications; credit camps to spread awareness and generate credit proposals, etc. • Two Credit Facilitation Camps (Banker Borrowers' Meet) was held at Geyzing (West Dist.) and Namchi (South Dist.) on 28 and 29 August, respectively • 2,364 applications amounting to Rs. 44 crore were processed for working capital support to MSMEs

(continued)

Table 1.6: Continued

State	New Measures
Assam*	• Revival of tea industry: subsidy for shifting of production to orthodox tea, 3% interest subvention on term loans and working capital loans, constructing free houses for labourers of Assam Tea Corporation at Rs. 24 crore • Bamboo hospital furniture use was encouraged • SIDBI support to bamboo-based micro enterprises • NABARD financial assistance of Rs. 20 lakh through 1,000 women Joint Liability Groups to benefit 5,000 women in Jorhat and Sivasagar district • NABARD assistance of Rs. 14 lakh to Assam Gramin Vikash Bank for procuring mobile banking van • NABARD Rs. 29 lakh to 37 skill development, training, and capacity building programmes • Pahi self-help group members were given order of 3,000 masks at affordable prices • Assistance to MSME included 5% per annum for ventilator manufacturing units; 20% additional working capital term loan, etc.
Arunachal Pradesh	• NABARD schemes for employment generation, capacity building, and training of youth and women for entrepreneurship for income generation included (a) Micro Enterprise Development Programme: Rs. 264,850, (b) Livelihood and Entrepreneurship Development Programme: Rs. 14,68,000, and (c) Skill Development Programme: Rs. 95,500 for sectors such as mushroom cultivation, bakery and food processing, handloom and textile, detergent making, spices and aloe vera, and Tangsa bag making • Rs. 31, 09,000 grant support for setting up of Rural Marts and Rural Haats
Nagaland	• Rs. 372 lakh support to skilling of reverse migrants under Off Farm Development Programmes and Micro Credit Innovation Programmes
Manipur	• Marketing arrangement for handloom and handicraft products • Export and marketing arrangement for fruits, vegetables, and spices • Development of industrial estates and common facility centres • Launch of Start-Up Manipur Initiative • State Task Force for improving internet connectivity
Meghalaya	• Launch of Rs. 14,515 crore Restart Meghalaya Programme to support farmers, entrepreneurs, and promote basic infrastructure and services covering interest subvention of 2%, Rs. 4 crore to 400 entrepreneurs for purchase of power tillers, Rs. 10 crore Corpus Fund for loans to Producer Groups, Rs. 15 crore for setting up of modern markets, and Rs. 5 crore for setting up of small farm-gate infrastructure, etc.

Source: Inputs from RBI Regional Offices in North Easter Region.
Note: '*' applies to Arunachal Pradesh and Nagaland as well.

region tried to contain the severity of the economic downturn which had badly affected the livelihoods of the people in the region.

Conclusion

Like other parts of the country, the north-eastern states have faced the devastating impact of the COVID-19 pandemic. Although the number of infections in the region moderated subsequently, the region was not free from sudden disruption in supply chains and local businesses especially during the lockdown. With shutdown of economic sectors, unemployment in the states aggravated affecting the livelihoods of the people and lowering the prospects of achieving SDGs. The overall economic impact of the pandemic is similar in nature compared to other parts of the world even though the magnitude of disruptions could be proportionately low relative to other states of the country. Unlike industrialized states, the NER states are dependent on agriculture, small-scale industrial units, tourism, and other services sectors. A large number of migrant labourers have returned to the states during lockdown which has compounded the difficulties of the local administrations in engaging them in productive economic activity. Moreover, the migrant labourers working in the NER were also stranded for long.

Besides the economic packages announced by the union government, the states have introduced several new policy measures to contain the spread of the corona virus and support the ailing economic sectors. As per the *Garib Kalyan Yojana* scheme of the centre, the state governments distributed free ration and essential supplies managed through multi-service centres of primary agricultural cooperative societies. Credit linkage programmes were implemented by a number of state governments in NER with support from NABARD. The joint liability groups were supported to revive the local poultry, piggery, diary, and other agriculture and allied sectors. Services sectors were yet to pick up, but the overall loss of output, income, and livelihoods were massive. The progress attained in certain indicators of SDGs in the pre-COVID period has been seriously impaired, thereby affecting the development process in the region.

2

State Initiatives and Localization of SDGs

Introduction

India has been one of the strong votaries of pursuing Agenda 2030 with all its earnestness. Having already prepared its Voluntary National Review 2017, the country was getting ready to present its next Voluntary National Review (VNR) in 2020. Going by the experience of individual states in giving priority to SDGs as part of the sub-national policy action, it is encouraging to note that all the eight States comprising the North Eastern Region (NER) have made special efforts in drawing up state-level strategies and follow-up action plans that would enable localization of SDG targets. State level of ownership of SDGs holds enormous significance for a country of India's size and diversity where whole-of-society approach and cooperative federalism have gained currency in recent years. This fulfils the initial criteria of SDGs roadmap as it ensures coherent policy approach with focus on inclusive development and regional balance with local accountability. Such a policy paradigm also takes care of regional and local context, internalizes local aspirations and agro-climatic needs, focuses on specific fragilities and vulnerabilities, both for local communities as well as that of the environment, thereby forging natural and spontaneous partnerships among actors who have immediate stakes. The NER states, in the intervening period (commencement of the SDG implementation phase since 2016), have been able to produce valuable SDG vision/strategy documents, often supported by necessary legislative changes and budgetary provisions with additional plans for local self-governments and district administration. This chapter elaborates such initiatives for each State in NER. The following Table 2.1 gives a concise representation of the same.

Rise of the North East, RIS, Oxford University Press. © Research and Information System for Developing Countries 2023.
DOI: 10.1093/oso/9780192849342.003.0002

Table 2.1 Localization of SDGs—Initiatives by NER states

Arunachal Pradesh	Assam	Manipur	Meghalaya	Mizoram	Nagaland	Sikkim	Tripura
Guiding Document: Vision and Sustainable Development Goals of Arunachal Pradesh—An Eastern Frontier State of India (2016)	**Guiding Document:** Assam 2030 Initiative (2016)	**Guiding Document:** Vision 2030 (2019)	**Guiding Document:** Meghalaya Vision 2030: Towards Building State Capability, Enhancing Freedom and Accelerating Development (2019)	**Guiding Document:** Vision 2030 (2018)	**Guiding Document:** Vision 2030 (2016)	**Guiding Document:** Well-Being of Generations Act (bill proposed in State Assembly in July 2017)	**Guiding document:** Vision 2030, seven-year action strategy, three-year action plan, and indicator document
Nodal Office: Department of Finance, Planning and Investment—SDG Policy Cell	**Nodal Office:** Transformation and Development Department—SDG Cell Centre for Sustainable Development Goals	**Nodal Office:** Planning Department—Unit Cell	**Nodal Office:** Planning Department—SDG cell	**Nodal Office:** Planning & Programme Implementation Department—SDG cell (Research and Development)	**Nodal Office:** Planning & Co-ordination Department, Economic & Statistics Department—SDG Cell	**Nodal Office:** Planning & Development Department—SDG Cell	**Nodal office:** The Planning (P&C) and Planning (Statistics) Departments
Knowledge Partners: CSDG, UNDP, OKDISCD, Smart Village Movement	**Knowledge Partners:** Centre for Sustainable Development Goals, UNDP; UNICEF; OKDISCD, TERI, World Bank	**Knowledge Partners:** Manipur University, NITI Forum for NE, UNDP	**Knowledge Partners:** UNDP	**Knowledge Partners:** Mizoram University, ICFAI, ATI, State Institute of Rural Development and Panchayati Raj, UNDP	**Knowledge Partners:** UNDP	**Follow-up Action:** Stakeholder consultation for the proposed bill, International Conference on Biodiversity, Youth Summit on SDGs	**Knowledge partners:** UNDP
Budgeting: Aligned with SDGs	**Budgeting:** Aligned with SDGs	**Monitoring:** State Indicator Framework (under preparation)	**Monitoring:** State Indicator Framework, Block-level indicators (under process)	**Monitoring:** High Level Monitoring Committee, Technical Committee, District Level Monitoring Committee, District Indicator Framework and District-wise Index Score (in process)	**Monitoring:** Qualitative village-level indicators		**Monitoring:** The State Institute of Public Administration and Rural Development (SIPARD) High Level Monitoring Committee (HLMC)
Monitoring: Dashboard, State-level indicators, Real-Time Monitoring aided by geo-tagging system (under implementation)	**Monitoring:** State- and District-Level Indicator Framework, District-Level Dashboard	**Follow-up Action:** Sensitization at all levels	**Follow-up Action:** Mapping of Departments against SDGs, Workshops	**Follow-up Action:** Workshops, Sensitization through local and social media in local language, audio-video content for schools & colleges	**Follow-up Action:** Workshops		
	Follow-up Action: District-Level Manual for integrating SDGs, Single Synergized Holistic Initiative						

Source: Authors' compilation.

The federal governance structure of the country, complemented by layers of local self-governments at different levels, makes the need for localization relevant. The special status of the NER of the country in terms of their environmental and ecological importance—two of the thirty-six global biodiversity hotspots are located in this region—makes the argument for localization of Agenda 2030 all the more prominent. The present chapter looks at the efforts initiated by the states and further down the administrative structure in internalizing the SDGs through crafting of institutional mechanisms at local levels and linking them bottom up across the hierarchy.

Three common ingredients make meaningful contributions to the achievement of sustainable development goals (SDGs). They are: access to resources, access to participatory institutions, and ensuring multi-stakeholder participation. Such a triad of ingredients makes a case for localization of action all the more necessary. Access to resources and institutions is always better ensured if operationalized at a lower scale, i.e. if there are institutions designed at local levels to implement the desired actions. From the perspective of localization, partnership among stakeholders operating across different administrative and social levels is of immense importance. Such a partnership would ideally engage officials, academics, civil society, organizations communities, and other relevant actors right up to the level of citizenry.

An approach for the localization of SDGs would ideally involve a slew of steps not necessarily in the prescribed order. Creation of vision/strategy documents is considered as an early step in defining the contours of necessary actions. Establishment of a unit/cell/centre on SDGs can be an effective move in giving the necessary shape to the things to come. Identification of the nodal department is a very important milestone in traversing the road to sustainable development. The nodal department would facilitate mapping of efforts of all development-linked departments against the prescribed goals. Multi-stakeholder partnership that embraces citizens from all walks of life, often having conflicting interests, is a necessary condition to implement such mapped actions. A simultaneous alignment of the SDGs with the development schemes cannot be overlooked either. Once aligned in terms of actions, SDGs are also required to be aligned with allocation of resources in the state budget. Next, it is important to develop the State Indicator Framework—identification of state-level indicators—that would facilitate and streamline the process of localization of SDGs. Close on the heels of the first level of localization would be that at the second level—developing District Indicator Framework. The construction of indicator frameworks would also pave the way for developing an effective monitoring framework to ensure that the operational efforts are progressing in the desired direction. Preparation of outcome budget for the SDGs is another important process related to the whole exercise which would crucially depend on the monitoring framework in use. Effective localization of SDGs would be achieved with preparation of District-Level Manual for facilitation of extending Agenda 2030 to the Gram Panchayat (GP) level through establishment of GP-level indicators. It would help initiate inter-village and inter-district comparison of SDG indicators. Another important step in localization is linked to incorporation of SDGs into the Economic Survey document of the respective state and adoption of single holistic synergized approach towards SDGs. Efforts at enacting legislative tools for implementation of SDGs are also a welcome move. Finally, all these initiatives are to be ably backed by capacity building initiatives as may be necessary.

State-Level Initiatives

Arunachal Pradesh

The state has prepared a draft of the Vision 2030 Document: Vision and Sustainable Development Goals of Arunachal Pradesh—An Eastern Frontier State of India which provides a roadmap for the achievement of the goals for the state. Welfare of its people being the priority, the state has adopted a three pronged objective approach so that the vision is in alignment with SDGs. The three objectives for the state are as follows: (a) Develop Infrastructure, (b) Harness Potentiality, and (c) Provide Quality Life. A separate SDG Policy Cell has been created in the Department of Finance, Planning and Investment. The cell would be empowered with technical capacity for it to play a central role in the monitoring of the implementation of the SDGs. The Special Secretary (Planning & Investment) has been nominated as the nodal officer. A retired Principal

Chief Conservator of Forests has been appointed as a full-time Consultant Advisor (Land Resource & Sustainable Development) since November 2017 to work full time on the SDGs (Sinha, 2018). One Deputy Director and one Research Officer from the Planning Department would be assisting the consulting advisor. There has been a comprehensive mapping of each of the SDGs with the Departments of the State Government to ease the implementation and increase the accountability. For example, SDG 1 has been mapped with Health and Family Welfare Department, Rural Development Department, and Urban Development and Housing Department.

In a step towards multi stakeholder partnership for the realization of SDGs, the Planning Department is being helped by the Centre for Sustainable Development Goals (CSDG) Guwahati and the Regional Office of United Nations Development Programme (UNDP) Guwahati. The state was also expected to enter into Memorandum of Understanding (MoU) between the Omeo Kumar Das Institute of Social Change and Development (OKDISCD) Guwahati for revising the Human Development Index for the state (Sinha, 2018). The government signed an MoU with Smart Villages Movement (SVM) on 13 June 2018 to build smart scalable villages in the state. The SVM will work in the realms of energy and information communications technology, healthcare, education, agriculture, water and sanitation, livelihood, transportation, and safety and security in the villages to connect rural communities to global markets. The development interventions of the state have been aligned with the SDGs. For example, SDG 1 (No Poverty) has been mapped with the Mahatma Gandhi National Rural Employment Guarantee Scheme (MNREGA), Pradhan Mantri Awas Yojana—Gramin, CM's Rural Housing Scheme, Chief Minister's Adarsh Gram Yojana, Deen Dayal Upadhyaya Gramin Kaushalya Yojana, etc. Arunachal Pradesh bears the distinction of being one of the few states which has aligned its state budgetary allocations with the SDGs. Budget speech of 2019–20 by Chowna Mein, Deputy Chief Minister and Minister-in-Charge Finance on 8 July 2019 underscored Arunachal's commitment to the SDGs as the fulfilment of the goals were the axial point of the budget. The budget of 2019–20 of Arunachal Pradesh provides goal-wise financial allocation for each of the SDGs. Vision 2030 document of the state has delineated the indicator framework of the state for the realization of the SDGs; however, the source of the data for indicators do not find a mention in the document. But information on the baseline quantitative value for each indicator and target value for each indicator by the years 2019, 2022, and 2030 is provided along with the strategy for achieving them. A web-based real-time monitoring framework aided by satellite based monitoring and geo tagging systems have been proposed to be set up in the state (Sinha, 2018). Arunachal Pradesh becomes only the second NE state which has prepared an outcome budget for 2019–20 which provides the deliverables against the outlay of each of the mapped schemes.

Capacity building measures form a very important pillar for the realization of SDGs for the states. A regional workshop on SDGs was held for the North-Eastern states at Aizawl on 24 August 2018 with support from the North Eastern Council. The workshop was attended by the various stakeholders from UNDP, NITI Aayog, Ministry of Statistics and Programme Implementation, Institute of Chartered Financial Analysts of India (ICFAI) University, and representatives from the states of Arunachal Pradesh, Assam, Manipur, Meghalaya, Mizoram, and Nagaland. To increase the efficiency and seamlessness of the implementation of the SDGs, a sensitization workshop was organized in the Itanagar in 2016 which was attended by the Commissioners, Secretaries, and the Nodal Officers (Sinha, 2018). The attendees were sensitized with the draft of the mapping of the SDGs with the government schemes, developing a monitoring and evaluation framework for the SDGs and the concept of High-Priority Targets with their indicators (Sinha, 2018). To alleviate the capacities to take forward the SDGs in the state, in partnership with UNDP, a workshop was organized. There were five technical sessions in the workshop which focused on the relevance, institutional structure, monitorable indicators, localization, and implementation strategies for the SDGs in the state (Sinha, 2018).

Assam

On 28 December 2015, the Government of Assam through a government order launched 'Assam 2030 Initiative' which was effective from 1 January 2016. The improvement in Assam's prospects in SDGs is due to some of indigenous efforts which include having a separate think tank to work towards the realization of the SDGs. The Government of Assam established the Centre for SDGs in the Assam Administrative Staff College (AASC), Khanapara, Guwahati in January 2016. The nodal department for the implementation of SDGs in the state has been the Transformation and Development Department since January 2016. It also houses a separate SDG Cell to better coordinate the activities of the different departments. This institutional framework is aided by the SDGs Strategy Support Group (SSSG) that was created through a government order in 2017. SSSG comprises officials from different departments who share the Assam government's passion about the SDGs. For each of the SDGs, the Vision 2030 document provides information about the lead department, supporting departments and cross-cutting departments.

Multi-stakeholder partnership for the SDGs has taken place in the form of partnerships with UNDP, UNICEF and their associate agencies, OKD Institute of Social Change & Development, Coalition for Food & Nutrition Security, and Tata Energy Research Institute (TERI) North-East for collaborating on activities towards planning and monitoring of SDGs. Assam collaborated with the United Nations in India for the preparation of the *Assam Human and Sustainability Development Report 2019*. CSDGs and World Bank have come together to prepare an action and project monitoring dashboard for the state. The state has aligned its development schemes with the SDGs. For example, SDG 1 (No poverty) has been mapped with Axom Adarxo Gram Yojana, while SDG 4 (Quality Education) has been mapped with Gyanjoti Scheme. Assam became the first NE state to align its Budget document with the SDGs in 2016–17, and it has since become a norm. Draft of Assam Agenda 2030 has been prepared which lays down comprehensive strategies for the realization of each SDG through seven thematic divisions of the SDGs with detailed strategic interventions, fifty-nine major indicators from baseline of 2016–17, targets for these indicators till 2019–20, 2023–24, and 2030. In addition, the government has provided the source of data for these indicators. A district indicator framework has been prepared to increase focus on the SDGs at the district level. The Centre for SDGs under the World Bank Non Lending Technical Assistance is working on developing an IT-based Monitoring Dashboard for tracking SDG-related projects in the State. Since the outcome budget of 2017–18, the administration has taken up the practice of tracking the relevant components for each scheme/programme and outlay against the Assam Vision 2030. The Outcome Budget for the year 2019–20 has already been presented in the budget session of the legislative assembly.

The State released the district-level manual for the integration of SDGs to the districts, councils, blocks, and panchayats in March 2019. The manual will aid the officials to realize the crucial role institutional systems and monitoring mechanisms through the identification of key priorities in the districts/blocks/panchayats with respect to SDGs. The first phase of district-level trainings commenced in October 2017. It is worth recognizing that since 2016–17, the *Economic Survey* provides a detailed analysis of the SDGs and also the baseline status of different indicators. It projects current trends and required trends with respect to the targets which would help in prioritization of policies. The highlight of *Economic Survey of 2017–18* from the perspective of SDGs was the inter-district comparisons of each of the SDGs. Out of total of thirty-three districts, data were made available for twenty-seven districts. The policy makers of the state believe that the Millennium Development Goals (MDGs) could not be completely realized because they were not implemented as a single package with the responsibilities spread across different departments. This led to coordination problems, and ultimately the outcomes fell short of their targets. Rather than being a collection of individual goals, SDGs are seen as a singular package, and therefore they are being implemented as a Single Synergized Holistic Initiative. The Centre for SDGs had conducted ten programmes during the financial year 2016–17 collaboration with the Centre for Innovation & Future Studies, AASC, and UNDP. In line with the earlier efforts, the centre had conducted an Innovation Lab on Chief Minister's Samagra Gramya Unnayan Yojana. In 2016, in collaboration with NITI Aayog, United Nations, Research and Information System for Developing Countries and Vijnana Bharati, the centre had organized a two-day Regional Consultation on SDGs for Human Settlements in Himalayan Region.

Manipur

In 2017, The Centre for the Study of Social Exclusion and Inclusive Policy, Manipur University was tasked with the preparation of the Vision 2030 document. The Vision Document was released recently by the Hon'ble Chief Minister. The state houses a separate unit/cell for the implementation of the SDG Agenda (Jain, 2018). Nodal department for the SDGs in the state is the Planning Department headed by the Department's Director. The director is responsible for liaising with NITI Aayog and is assisted by a Joint Director and a Research Officer. The draft of the Vision 2030 included data generated by district-level interfaces. A four-day workshop was held in Manipur University in June 2017 where the data were discussed with representatives from the line departments to quantify the data into indicators. Manipur is at initial stages of conceptualizing a monitoring framework for the SDGs (NITI Aayog, 2019a). *The Economic Survey of 2019–20* for the state does not give specific details about the activities towards localizing the SDGs in the state, but it does provide a general understanding of NITI Aayog's role in the implementation of the SDGs in the country.

Meghalaya

Meghalaya has a Vision 2030 document which was prepared by the National Institute of Public Finance and Policy, New Delhi and was published on 18 December 2012. The vision document talks about sustainable development, but unlike the other states, it is not thematically aligned with the SDGs. A new document titled *'Meghalaya Vision 2030: Towards Building State Capability, Enhancing Freedom and Accelerating Development'* has been prepared recently and awaits finalization. According to the state administration, there is a separate cell which looks after the implementation of SDGs in the state, and it was formulated on 29 March 2018 (Government of Meghalaya, 2019). In an important step towards localization of the SDG Agenda 2030 in the state, the mapping of the departments of the state against the SDGs had been completed by 12 June 2018. For example, the departments identified with SDG 1 (No Poverty) are Social Welfare, Agriculture, Animal Husbandry, Urban Affairs, Community and Rural Development, Fisheries, and Disaster Management. To further streamline the implementation of the SDG Agenda, the existing governmental interventions have been aligned with the SDGs. Policy makers of the state have adopted interventions such as

Integrated Village Co-operative Societies (IVCS)—SDG 1, Integrated Farming—SDG 2, Megha Health Insurance Scheme—SDG 3, Meghalaya Basin Development Authority—SDG 8, Enterprise Facilitation Centre— SDG 8, 1917 iTeams—SDG 9, and Aquaculture Mission—SDG 12 (Government of Meghalaya, 2019). With the seventeen SDGs being divided into clusters of Social, Economic, Environment and Peace and Partnership goals, the state budget of 2019–20 mentions interventions in each of the areas; however, the budget is not explicitly aligned with the SDGs.

The state has recently come out with a draft set of State Indicator Framework. The different departments of the government had prepared action plans and formulated indicators in 2018. It should be noted that the state has developed quantitative block-level indicators for the villages of East Garo Hills and Khasi Hills with the baseline data of 2010. Meghalaya is cognizant of the need for improved capacities of the officials as a crucial aspect for the realization of the SDGs in the state. The government has been organizing Field-Level Leadership Development workshops since November 2016. The workshops aim to strengthen the connect between the field-level workers and the common citizenry so that a reciprocal relationship can be built which would aid the officials of the line departments for better delivery of goals (Government of Meghalaya, 2019).

Mizoram

Mizoram has earnestly started its plan to achieve the SDGs by 2030, and thereby it has formulated 'New Economic Development Policy (NEDP)— Comprehensive Growth Strategy for Mizoram'. The NEDP would serve as a framework for the economic policy and strategic driving force of the state's economy. Vision 2030 document for the state was published in July 2018 and is anchored within the NEDP framework. A cell for the SDGs has been created in the Research and Development Branch of Planning and Programme Implementation Department headed by the Principal Adviser. It has employed consultants to review and monitor the progress of the implementation of the SDGs in the state. According to the Vision 2030 document, the Planning and Programme Implementation Department is the nodal department for SDGs (2018). Mapping of the departments against the relevant SDGs has been done by the nodal agency. For example, the implementation of SDG 1 (No Poverty) is looked after by the Rural Development Department, Public Health Engineering Department, Urban Development & Poverty Alleviation Department, Social Welfare Department, and Health & Family Welfare Department (Government of Mizoram, 2018).

State administration has undertaken various efforts to establish multi-stakeholder partnership for the successful implementation of the SDGs. Partnerships for the achievement of the SDG Agenda have been forged at the international level. UNDP has been assisting the state in the technical matters. Mizoram University, ICFAI University Mizoram, Administrative Training Institute (ATI), and State Institute of Rural Development and Panchayati Raj (SIRD&PR) are institutional partners of the government who provide the implementors with technical support (Government of Mizoram, 2018). The state government has further tapped the colleges and schools to increase the sensitization towards the SDGs. Penetration of local media has been utilized by organizing talk shows on SDGs while short video clips in local language have been circulated on social media. This will help foster inclusive responsibility towards the realization of the SDGs.

In the Vision 2030 document, national interventions/schemes had been identified for aligning with the SDGs. For example, MNREGA and Atal Pension Yojana had been identified as the schemes which would be mapped with SDG 1 (No Poverty). The vision document details the allocation for the existing centrally sponsored schemes over the years after aligning them with the SDGs. A Technical Committee on the SDGs had been formed under the Chairmanship of Director, Economics and Statistics Department to identify the baseline data and targets. The Vision Document identifies the indicators for the targets of the SDGs. The source of data for the indicators has been provided. For example, for SDG 1 (No Poverty), the sources of the indicators would be BPL Survey, Social Welfare Department Records, Census. A baseline survey has been conducted which was monitored by a three-tier system; the State Level Monitoring Committee, District Level Monitoring Committee, and Village Level Committee. Mizoram is the only other state apart from Assam to have a district indicator framework which further localizes the SDG indicators. A High Level Monitoring Committee (HLMC) has been set under the Chairmanship of the Chief Secretary, Government of Mizoram and Secretary, Planning and Programme Implementation Department. The HLMC would monitor the progress of implementation of the SDGs by the respective departments which have been mapped to them. It would submit an 'action taken report' on a quarterly basis to the Planning and Programme Implementation Department. There has been a constitution of District Level Monitoring Committee under the Deputy Commissioner and Village Level Monitoring Committee under the President of the Village Council. The state has adopted the good practice of preparing district-wise index score for each of the SDG indicators. The availability of the average index score for each of the SDGs has enabled the districts to be ranked. *The Economic Survey of 2018–19* gives details about the implementation framework, monitoring framework, and landscape analysis of SDGs.

The administration has undertaken various capacity building initiatives in the form of workshops at state and district levels. On 29 January 2019, a state-level sensitization workshop on SDGs was held at Assembly Conference Hall. The workshop was attended by Members of Legislative Assembly, Nodal Officers from all line departments, District Authorities, and Village Councils/Local Councils Presidents/Secretaries. District-level sensitization workshop was held in the seven district headquarters from 31 January to 5 February 2019 (Government of Mizoram, 2018).

Nagaland

Vision 2030 document of Nagaland which was released on 11 December 2016 is based on the principles of 'Governance', 'Infrastructure', and 'Skilling the Youth'. The vision of the state acknowledges the inter-dependence between the three principles. Good governance would encourage the youth to be active participants for the realization of the Vision 2030, governance reforms would improve the infrastructure of the state, and the improved infrastructure capacities would provide better avenues for the youth. The government has made efforts to prepare short-, medium-, and long-term action plans (Choudhury, 2018). According to a presentation by the Planning Department of Nagaland submitted to NITI Aayog on 11 December 2018, SDG Cell has been set up in

Planning & Co-ordination Department headed by Principal Secretary & Development Commissioner (Government of Nagland, 2018). Planning and Co-ordination Department is the nodal department for the implementation of SDGs, while the Economic & Statistics Department has been appointed as a nodal agency which would ensure availability of data in real time along with facilitating monitoring and evaluation of SDGs dashboard. The state had briefed NITI Aayog in December 2018 that it had identified twenty-three departments which would be mapped with the SDGs (Government of Nagland, 2018). The Directorate of Economics and Statistics of the state has developed qualitative village-level indicators which can help in the creation of indicators for the SDGs. The state is working towards the creation of SDG Cell in each of the line departments which would not only aid in the data collection for the preparation of state-level indicator framework but also monitor the implementation of the SDGs. There was a two-day state-level workshop on building capacities for taking forward SDGs conducted in collaboration with UNDP on 13 and 14 November 2018, where discussions took place on the issues linked to (i) Contextual relevance of SDGs; (ii) Strategy and Action plan with timelines with respect to mapped departments; (iii) Developing an institutional structure for SDGs; (iv) Identifying monitorable indicators, and (v) Developing monitoring systems in the state.

Sikkim

Presentation made to NITI Aayog during 'Meeting with states/ UTs: Improving Implementation of SDGs' acknowledges the presence of an SDG Cell in the state (Jain, 2018). The government in its budget of 2016–17 buttressed Sikkim's orientation of policies along the lines of sustainability even before the Indian government became signatory to the pact in 2015. Sikkim had taken up the ambitious task of grounding the implementation of the SDGs in a legislation. The office of Sikkim's Member of Parliament, P. D. Rai proposed to table a bill in the state Legislative Assembly in July 2017. If the bill had become an act, it would have been called the Well-Being of Generations Act. The act was to be anchored in the principles of shared responsibility, precaution, transparency and participation, rights of citizens, integration

between economic, social and ecological needs and thresholds, inter-
and intra-generational equity, strengthening of local economies, and
valuation of social and natural capital. The consultancy process of the
bill included a diverse range of stakeholders such as the state's drug user
community, representatives from drug rehabilitation centres, farmer
producer organizations, urban local bodies, health professionals, education officers, teachers, as well as organizations such as the Swiss
Agency for Development and Cooperation, UNDP, World Wide Fund
(WWF) India, Development Alternatives (an advocacy-based Indian
non-governmental organization), independent experts as well as Cyril
Amarchand Mangaldas (a leading law firm in India), supporting as the
legal experts.

Tripura

Tripura began its efforts to come up with a Vision 2030, seven-year
strategy, three-year action plan, and indicator document on 26 October
2016 in consultation with the line departments. Vision 2030 provides
strategy for achieving the SDGs while simultaneously laying targets for
2022–23 and 2030–31. The Planning (P&C) and Planning (Statistics)
Departments is the nodal agency which is involved for preparation, implementation, and monitoring of SDGs. The department has undertaken
the mapping of the relevant departments with the SDGs. Towards developing a multi-stakeholder partnership for the realization of the SDG
Agenda, consultations have taken place with UNDP while State Institute
of Rural Development & Panchayati Raj (SIRD&PR) has been engaged
in facilitating adoption of SDGs at the rural level. Indicators for the SDG
targets have been identified along with their data source. An High Level
Monitoring Committee (HLMC) has been set up under the chairmanship of Chief Secretary to oversee the progress of SDGs (Government of
Tripura, 2018). The state aims to operationalize the SDGs in the districts
and urban local bodies while efforts are being made to integrate the SDGs
with the Gram Panchayat Development Plan. *Economic Review of 2017–18*
recognizes the importance of implementing the SDGs successfully by
achieving the Vision 2030 through effective implementation of seven-
year strategy and three-year action plan.

The state has put much emphasis on improving the capacities of its personnel which finds a mention in SDG India Index 2019–20. The State Institute of Public Administration and Rural Development (SIPARD) has been entrusted with training within the state, covering Panchayati Raj Institution bodies, districts, and blocks while learning from good practices from other states. In addition, all Additional Chief Secretaries/ Principal Secretaries/Secretaries and HODs are sensitized in different forums for localization and capacity building in the respective line departments for SDGs oriented monitoring.

Conclusion

The SDG India Index 2019–20 tracks the progress of all the States and UTs on a set of hundred indicators drawn from the National Indicator Framework and identified by the NITI Aayog, the primer think tank of the Government of India. The first version of the Index (SDG India Index 1.0) released in December 2018 was based on sixty-two indicators while the second one (SDG India Index 2.0) released in December 2019 is based on hundred indicators. Moreover, a number of indicators figured in SDG Index 1.0 do not find place in SDG Index 2.0. As such, a comparison of state performances based on two series of index is difficult.

In any case, a comparison between Index 1.0 and 2.0 indicates that almost all the NE States (except Mizoram) have performed better and improved their scores in 2019–20, even though Mizoram has slipped by three points from 59 in 2018–19 to 56 in 2019–20. Sikkim has shown a better performance in 2019–20 and find place in 'front runner' category from 'Performer' category in 2018–19. Assam has moved upward from 'Aspirant' category in 2018–19 with a score of 49 to 'Performer' category in 2019–20 with a score of 55. Other NE States maintained their 'Performer' category in both the years with upward trend in their scores in 2019–20 as compared to 2018–19. The improved performances give a clear message of concerted efforts of the State Governments towards achieving SDGs. However, a lot still needs to be done in this regard and to boost the implementation with improvement in service delivery mechanism and machinery particularly in hill areas.

Achievement of SDGs, however, cannot be solely attributed to the efforts at localization of the initiatives and institutionalization of the processes alone. A paradigm that intends to 'leave no one behind' within a stipulated period of time can be realized only when there evolves a seamless coordination among all stakeholders operating at all hierarchies. As the idea suggests, sustainable development echoes the age-old African philosophy of *Ubuntu* that means 'I am because we are'. The realization that development at the global level is difficult to achieve in the absence of development right down at the level of an individual creates the urge for and challenge to sustainable development. The largely inclusive process followed in arriving at the SDGs, unlike the way its previous avatar in MDGs were identified, makes it amply clear that the well-being of an individual located in a village in the state of Manipur cannot be fully realized without appropriate cooperation from someone located in the neighbourhood. Such idea of neighbourhood need not necessarily be confined within the village. SDGs and their fulfilment call for cooperative endeavour from individuals located beyond the village. The artificially determined politico-administrative boundaries have to be pierced to make sustainable development a reality. Each neighbouring village has to contribute to the process. Each neighbouring districts and states have to effectively cooperate with each other. Each country has to live up to the expectations of other countries, especially the neighbours. Finally, the global community, as a whole, has to share their resources with those in need—the spirit behind SDG 17. The Indian philosophy of '*Vasudhaiva Kutumbakam*' also attests to this idea of global neighbourhood. Sustainable Development cannot be achieved through administrative fiat alone. It requires an effective people-to-people connect to actualize the idea. Politico-administrative structure can only facilitate and fast-track the process in the desired direction.

Consequently, localization of SDG related actions is a necessary condition, but not a sufficient one. The reasons are not far to seek. Two politico-administrative units may well be part of two different governance mechanisms. However, they may share identical agro-climatic zones, ecological profile, topographic features, ethnic and linguistic profiles, and quite often, common resource and production bases. All these features are meaningfully linked to the development profile of a region. The capacity of a habitation to share and complement common developmental aspirations is seriously hampered by such governance differentials. They often undermine the role of communities in contributing to the process of sustainable development. Localization of SDGs is a means to identify the complementarities beyond the political boundaries. A village in District A adjacent to another village in District B within the same country, or, for that matter, a district in Country I sharing international border with another in Country II are expected to share identical features that may call for near similar and coordinated efforts towards their sustainable development. Localizations help identify such similarities.

The efforts by the NER states in localizing their SDG indicators right up to the village level (achieved in some cases, others following up) will be effective in identifying the potential development complementarities and facilitating the actions to be brought into operational focus. However, the extent to which such complementarities are put to an operational framework will determine the extent of success achieved.

The engagement of multiple stakeholders operating at several levels holds the key to success. Such bunch of stakeholders include the panchayat functionaries, block-level decision makers, district officials, line ministries at state and national levels, and above all, the NITI Aayog. Needless to add, their actions may often require looking beyond the administrative boundaries. Local economic institutions, for example, cooperatives, farmers producer organizations, self-help groups, and the likes are to be seamlessly engaged in the endeavour. The social institutions such as the civil society organizations, academia, and other peoples' organizations will also have to be functionally engaged.

Localization would provide the monitoring framework to ensure that such complementarities are in place and add significantly in identifying a detailed roadmap to sustainable development for the NER region. The local experiences, on a comparative foundation, are reflected in SDG indices being developed periodically by the NITI Aayog. A detailed perspective of the findings thereof has been provided in the Chapter 7. A consolidation of the localization efforts at several layers into generation of a national agenda would be the ultimate challenge for all concerned. NITI Aayog will have to shoulder considerable responsibilities in collating, analysing, and disseminating the results of the localization efforts to generate the big picture at the national level for onward transmission to the global decision-making process.

SDG 17 calls for an effective partnership for development. To reiterate, localization would provide the required building blocks necessary to tread the path to sustainable development. The identified complementarities are to be leveraged through coordinated actions to ensure that efforts put in are sufficient enough to achieve the SDGs in tune with Agenda 2030.

3

Drivers of Economic Prosperity and Sustainable Livelihood

Economic Prosperity in the North East Contributing towards India's Five Trillion Economy

India's nationally stated aspiration to emerge as a five trillion dollar economy by 2025 is founded on the agenda of economic transformation that the country has witnessed in the recent years. Economic performance at the national level is also critically dependent on the performance of individual states and overall progress of the regions. In this regard, North East India deserves foremost attention, where possibilities are immense for economic growth in the eight States in order to support their efforts in capturing larger share in the national income. The Gross State Domestic Product (GSDP) of the Northeastern states constituted 2.7 per cent of India's gross domestic product (GDP). It would be, therefore, pertinent to focus on the drivers of economic prosperity that could guide the aspirations and efforts of regions that seek rapid economic progress despite longstanding capacity challenges.

The growth of GSDP in the North Eastern Region (NER) has been quite encouraging in the recent years. Since 2014–15, NER has almost outpaced growth at the national level. As is clear from Table 3.1, the NER, which was lagging behind at 3.4 per cent and 5.9 per cent in 2012–13 and 2013–14, respectively, bounced back with 8.2 per cent in 2014–15. This lead has continued since then. In fact, deceleration in the national average has still placed the NER at a higher pedestal. As the last column in the same table shows, there is significant diversity in the per capita income as Sikkim (Rs. 2.1 lakh) and Mizoram (Rs. 1.05 lakh) are far ahead from the national average and also from the rest of the North Eastern states, viz.

Rise of the North East, RIS, Oxford University Press. © Research and Information System for Developing Countries 2023.
DOI: 10.1093/oso/9780192849342.003.0003

Table 3.1: GSDP in North Eastern States

States	2012–13	2013–14	2014–15	2015–16	2016–17	2017–18	Per Capita NSDP, in Rs. (2017–18)
Arunachal Pradesh	2.1	9.2	16.6	-1.0	2.7	7.3	89,217
Assam	2.9	4.9	6.9	15.7	6.0	8.4	57,099
Manipur	0.6	8.6	8.0	7.7	4.0	4.7	48,113
Meghalaya	2.2	1.8	-2.7	2.4	5.3	9.3	61,789
Mizoram	7.2	16.2	24.6	9.4	10.3	8.8	105,617
Nagaland	5.7	7.2	4.4	1.8	6.7	3.4	66,305
Sikkim	2.3	6.1	7.9	9.9	7.2	6.9	219,792
Tripura	8.7	9.3	18.2	-0.7	8.8	10.7	74,637
NER	3.4	5.9	8.2	10.6	6.2	8.1	–
All India	5.5	6.4	7.4	8.0	8.2	7.2	87,632

Source: National Statistical Office (NSO).

Arunachal Pradesh (Rs. 89 K), Tripura (Rs. 74 K), Nagaland (Rs. 66 K), Meghalaya (Rs. 61 K), Assam (Rs. 57 K), and Manipur (Rs. 48 K)

In 2018, exports from the region were 0.73 per cent of its GSDP as against 12 per cent for the country as a whole. Total exports of the region touched US$ 432.9 million, in the backdrop of India's strong focus on trade to reach US$ 5 trillion economy by 2025 and persistent focus on the 'Act East policy'. Spatial distribution of the registered companies in the North East, as reported by the Ministry of Corporate Affairs, shows that there are 2,777 companies in the corporate sector in India, of which 370 companies are located in the Northeast region. It is evident from the database that the distribution of registered companies is highly skewed in the North East where 76.2 per cent of the total number of companies is located in Assam followed by Meghalaya (Table A in the Appendix).

Revenue receipt of a state is also important for maintaining its macroeconomic stability. The tax bases of several NER states are relatively weaker than the other states of India. The situation is more apparent when the own-tax and non-tax revenues are examined separately as shown in Table B in the Appendix. Some states maintained high tax-GSDP ratio in the region such as Arunachal Pradesh, Assam, and Meghalaya, whereas a few other including Manipur, Mizoram, Nagaland, Sikkim, and Tripura had low tax/GSDP ratio in the range of 4 per cent to 5.6 per cent in 2017–18. Because of the limitations in the collection of tax revenue, public debt situation of the Northeast states deteriorated during the past decade. In the case of Assam, the public debt increased sharply about ten times between 2000–01 and 2013–14 (Baishya and Goswami, 2017). For neutralizing the resource constraints in the region, states are adequately supported by the Central assistance through various arrangements. In light of the preceding and in order to boost regional economic growth and leverage the region towards its full potential towards contributing to the national aspiration of a five trillion economy, it is pertinent to orient economic policymaking at the sub-national level towards facilitation and creation of 'drivers' of economic prosperity. This chapter identifies the most important growth drivers for the region and presents the roadmap on macroeconomic foundations, local production, trade, and competitiveness.

Drivers of Economic Prosperity: Literature and Local Context

The preconditions for growth and drivers of economic prosperity have received considerable attention in the economics discipline. However, such 'drivers' are not well defined in many cases and preconditions tend to vary across countries. Objective of policymaking, therefore, is to find the reasonable substitutes (suited to the local needs and context) for most widely used instruments that are considered 'effective' in stimulating economic growth. Rodrik (2005, 2004) suggests that institutional quality is critical to economic prosperity universally. While well-established economic principles supporting economic growth emphasize on the importance of protection of property rights and promoting competition, sound fiscal and monetary policies, it is imperative that these are embedded in institutional designs that are 'sensitive' to local opportunities and constraints. These studies go on to suggest that the latter may need special efforts over the longer term for strong institutional underpinning that could provide the economy with elements of resilience and maintain its productive dynamism. The importance of co-evolution of institutions along with rising economic prosperity has also been endorsed in the works of Ha Joon Chang. According to him, institutions also play a pivotal role in coordination and governance; learning and innovation; as well as in income redistribution and social cohesion that may, in turn, provide robustness to the economic growth profile (Chang, 2007, 2011). While role of trade as an engine of economic growth has been extensively studied in the economics literature, which has helped in closing the gap in per capita incomes and benefits accruing to developing and less developed countries in recent decades through deeper integration, one of the most powerful articulation on trade driving economic growth in resource poor regions came in the form of Lewis (1980). Similarly, the human capital component of endogenous growth theories as well as leveraging modern connectivity-driven competitiveness, innovation, and entrepreneurship has become hallmark of growth trajectories of countries experiencing very high economic growth. The seminal work capturing the origin and landscape of endogenous growth in economics literature by Paul Romer (1994) is an authoritative account in this regard. A wide body of literature has also looked into the extent of benefits that infrastructure investments bring to the economy (Esfahani and Ramı´rez, 2003; Munnell, 1992).

The chapter looks at the potential of the North Eastern states in achieving high economic growth (with a comparative understanding vis-à-vis the other states in India) from the perspective of contribution of the primary, secondary, and tertiary sectors to the economy and covers production, trade and market linkages for individual States while drawing out a comprehensive account of economic prosperity and sustainable livelihood for the region. Subsequent chapters of the report also look at other enabling factors of production such as human capital, communication, connectivity, and infrastructure for economic growth of the region.

In the context of the North Eastern India, the productive dynamism has been particularly low; even as institutional embeddedness through strong local governance institutions has faced staggered progress due to multiple factors. Despite decades of assistance from the Central government and numerous initiatives on their own, industrial activities in the Northeast region have not picked up in a desirable manner. Lack of quality infrastructure in the Northeast states has been among the key reasons for the sluggish growth in the industrial sector. To generate positive externalities and provide necessary impetus to production activities, Jena (2017) argued that cluster development approach should be adopted to boost manufacturing development in the rural areas. In the process, the firms in rural and household industries would come together as a network of firms in a cluster, contributing to sustainable livelihood of people who are involved in the process (Das and Das, 2011). Beyond industrial production activities, the services sector remains immensely important at the national level as a growth driver. In a recent study, Singh (2018) has observed that the services sector leads the sectoral contribution to GDP much ahead of agricultural and manufacturing sectors in the NER. Kolhe (2017) examined tax incentives policy of the Central government for the NER states to spur industrial growth by expanding various forms of incentives including income tax and excise duty for a period of twelve years, starting from 2004–05 to 2015–16.

Agenda 2030 explains sustainable development as an intricate and delicate interdependence among five Ps, viz., People, Prosperity, Planet, Peace, and Partnership. People's welfare and prosperity form important pillars of the agenda which have to be achieved in consonance with sustainable planet, peace, and partnership among all actors. Sustainable prosperity for people rests on key sectors. Sustaining agriculture to support income growth, crop diversification, access to world markets, self-sufficiency as well as reorienting agricultural practices to suit nutrition needs and climate challenges is part of the mandate of Sustainable Development Goal (SDG) 2. Rapid and durable economic growth as well as inclusive development is the key aspiration of SDG 8. The underlying targets cover issues of productivity through diversification, technological upgrading, and innovation, including through a focus on high-value-added and labour-intensive sectors. In terms of inclusive development, SDG 8 aims to promote formalization and growth of Micro, Small and Medium Enterprises (MSMEs), including through access to financial services in order to achieve full and productive employment and decent work for all by 2030.

The SDGs highlight the centrality of economic capacities at the sub-national levels to promote inclusive development. The SDG 8 emphasizes on economic growth for regions around the world that need accelerated pace of socio-economic development. The criticality of the North East in that regard cannot be overemphasized. The underlying targets cover a range of issues including emphasis on rapid economic growth in low per capita regions, productivity, Small and Medium Enterprises (SMEs), resource efficiency, decent jobs, etc. Hence, the progress of SDG 8 would have direct significance for achievement of SDG 1 that aspires to universally eliminate poverty by 2030. The SDGs have also laid substantial emphasis on governance parameters as a precondition to achieve inclusive and sustainable economic development. This relates to promoting conducive policy architecture and reforms that remove supply side bottlenecks supported by appropriate regulatory architecture.

To supplement the targets of SDG 8, there is need to widen the industrial base and creating more opportunities for value addition and employment generation two explicit targets under SDG 9. The target 9.2 mandates promoting inclusive and sustainable industrialization and, by 2030, significantly enhance industry's share of employment and GDP, in line with national circumstances (and double its share in least developed countries) which may be interpreted as localization and regional strategies and target 9.3 which suggests increasing the access of small-scale industrial and other enterprises, in particular in developing countries, to financial services, including affordable credit, and their integration into value chains and markets. The emphasis on integration into value chains and global markets naturally brings in the scope for strong trade orientation and competitiveness building efforts at the sectoral level.

Global elimination of poverty in all its forms is an uncompromising political commitment under the Agenda 2030, and the rest of all the SDGs are expected to work in unison to achieve SDG 1 in the stipulated timeframe. Quality of economic progress can ultimately be ascertained when poverty is driven to negligible levels through expansion of opportunities, protection of livelihoods at the bottom, provision of social security to cover for vulnerabilities, building capacities, skills and empowerment, increasing access to economic resources, and building resilience to climate change and disasters. Poverty elimination requires massive resource mobilization and reduction of regional disparities when it comes to economic development.

In the backdrop of the Agenda 2030 and its priorities for localization in the developing regions of the world, it would be pertinent to focus on production and trade keeping in mind the targets under SDGs 8 and 9 in the context of the North East. We note that key obstacles to growth in North East have been lack of rapid expansion in economic activities and lack of gainful employment in the region, despite having large potential for economic activities. There is a need for adopting 'big bang' approach for agro-processing industrialization to absorb production of local resources and meeting the rising demand for exports as well as domestic market. Similar activities concerning exports may be strategized for mining, manufacturing, and services sector. For making the export sector attractive, the sliding rank of ease of doing business (EoDB) in different NER states needs to be corrected when the global ranking of India in EoDB has been unprecedentedly skyrocketing during the past five years.

SDGs have outlined the expectations on agriculture (SDG 2) and industry (SDG 9). The services sector is spread across several other goals, more from a means to end perspective including health, education, professional services (as in finance, governance, administration, and law), tourism, etc. The underlying importance of services is across sectors with regional specificities with higher importance in high per capita regions. Agriculture and industry, on the other hand, are considered foundational stages of economic transformation paradigms across all regions globally and hence the exclusive focus as part of the Agenda 2030. In order to promote inclusive development, which allows business units to attain scale and widen their impact on the overall development of countries, it is important to ensure that competition is fostered and transparency, accountability, arbitration, and compensation are ensured. Such ideals are enshrined with some focus under SDG 8 and SDG 16. The EoDB indicators highlight in some measure the state of affairs in that regard. The World Bank's EoDB index comprises parameters such as starting a business, construction permits, power connection, registering property, getting credit, paying taxes, trading, and hiring.

During the past seven decades, development process of the NER has gone through a critical phase of ups and downs. Economic development of the region remained below that of rest of India despite high literacy rate, low density of population, high forest cover, sufficient cultivable land, and rich mineral resources. On the other hand, during the past three decades, India has emerged as one of the vibrant and resilient economies in the world. While India recorded an average growth rate of 7.9 per cent per annum, the global economy grew at the rate of 4.2 per cent during the period of global buoyancy (2003–07). India's growth performance was adversely affected during the period of recession like most of the economies in the world. Contrary to the experiences of several countries, India's average growth performance improved significantly during 2013–18 over its performance during 2008–12. In the second phase of the global recession, it emerged as the fastest growing economy among the large economies. Despite fluctuations in the growth performances, India's rapid economic growth is also credited to with significant reduction in absolute poverty and progress towards eradication of extreme poverty.

Gross Fixed Capital Formation (GFCF) is the key driver of growth in any region. North East India's contribution to India in GFCF was 1.22 per cent, and it was less than half of region's contribution of GSDP to GDP of India in 2018. In terms of region's share in India, Gross Domestic Value Added (GVA) was 2 per cent of India in 2018, showing high inputs cost of the region. In terms of macroeconomic indicators, viz., GDP, GFCF, and GVA, Sikkim stands out in comparison with other states. Relative performance of the North East states in comparison with other states of India is presented in Figure 3.1. The figure indicates that high per capita income states are not necessarily those with high economic growth. Some of the

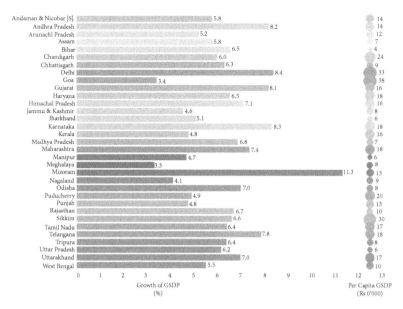

Figure 3.1: Inter-State Variations in GSDP State Growth Rate and Per Capita Income in 2018

Source: RIS database based on *Handbook of Statistics for India States*, RBI, 2019.

Note: The figures for the state of Jammu and Kashmir represent the region before bifurcation.

high-income states, such as Delhi, Karnataka, etc., are also having high average growth rate during 2001–18; on the contrary, some of the low to medium per capita incomes states, such as Andhra Pradesh, Odisha, Mizoram, etc., have high economic growth during the aforesaid period. A few states, such as Arunachal Pradesh, were affected by the economic slowdown, resulting in low growth performance amidst having high per capita income over a long period of time. Certain low per capita income states, such as Assam and Tripura, have maintained moderate level of growth during the period of recession. While two medium/high per capita income states such as Sikkim and Mizoram have registered high growth, certain low-income states such as Manipur, Meghalaya, and Nagaland have confronted with low level of growth performance. Therefore, there is no direct linkage between level of economic growth and per capita income in NER states. Since most of the regional states are not exposed heavily to the trade sector and overall Indian economy has expanded significantly, the trade induced shocks are likely to have least impact on NER states.

Drivers of Economic Prosperity

Macroeconomic Foundations

The NER states have large forest cover and manufacturing activities are relatively lesser than rest of the economy because of the topography of the region. The relative importance of the NER state in these broad economic activities with respect to other Indian states is shown in the Figure 3.2. Among the Indian states, largest contribution from the agricultural sector is observed in case of Nagaland. In the NER, other than Nagaland, Arunachal Pradesh received high contribution from the agricultural sector to the extent of 16 per cent in 2018–19. In other states of the region, contribution of agriculture to GSDP was in the range of 7 per cent in to 14 per cent in 2018–19.

States	Agriculture	Industry	Manufacturing	Services
Andaman & Nicobar |S|	5	23	1	71
Andhra Pradesh	16	31	14	53
Arunachal Pradesh	16	35	4	49
Assam	14	40	16	46
Bihar	12	20	8	68
Chandigarh	0	11	4	89
Chhattisgarh	12	51	21	37
Delhi	0	15	5	85
Goa	2	63	47	35
Gujarat	10	52	37	37
Haryana	11	33	23	56
Himachal Pradesh	8	48	32	44
Jammu & Kashmir	9	31	12	60
Jharkhand	9	38	17	54
Karnataka	6	27	18	66
Kerala	6	28	12	66
Madhya Pradesh	30	29	13	41
Maharashtra	6	35	23	59
Manipur	10	20	4	70
Meghalaya	11	24	10	64
Mizoram	9	33	1	58
Nagaland	41	28	4	31
Odisha	9	44	18	47
Puducherry	1	51	30	48
Punjab	18	28	17	55
Rajasthan	14	34	13	51
Sikkim	7	65	46	29
Tamil Nadu	5	39	26	56
Telangana	6	26	16	67
Tripura	13	30	6	56
Uttar Pradesh	15	31	16	53
Uttarakhand	4	56	43	40
West Bengal	13	31	16	56

Figure 3.2: Sectoral Share in GSDP for North East States in 2018 (%)

Source: RIS database based on *Handbook of Statistics for India States*, RBI, 2019.

Note: The figures for the state of Jammu and Kashmir represent the region before bifurcation.

It is important to note that within the industrial activities, non-manufacturing industrial activities are rather significant in most of these states. Manufacturing sector was contributing 46 per cent of the economy (GSDP) of Sikkim and 16 per cent of Assam in 2018–19. However, similar estimate for other NER states remained at 10 per cent or less in the aforesaid year. On the contrary, the non-manufacturing industrial activities ranged between 14 per cent and 32 per cent of GSDP; Arunachal Pradesh, Assam, Mizoram, Nagaland, and Tripura were some of the states having the contribution of non-manufacturing sector more than 23 per cent of GSDP. In sum, the contribution of manufacturing sector has been too insignificant as compared to non-manufacturing sector within the industrial sector contribution. Although construction, electricity, gas, etc. have high level of opportunities to generate employment and also contribute to GSDP, expansion of the manufacturing sector would put these states on a high growth trajectory. The service sector has dominant contribution to the economies of these North Eastern states. Among the states, contribution of services sector was the lowest for Sikkim (29 per cent) and largest for Manipur (70 per cent) in 2018. States from the region, with services sector income more than half of each state's GSDP, are Manipur, Meghalaya, Mizoram, and Tripura. In most of the states, public administration is one of the most important components in this sector. Therefore, there is 'no stylized facts' about the structural composition of the North Eastern states. Structural composition of the NER economies may not be appropriate consideration to explain the level of economic aspirations in certain states.

Thus, the services sector is the mainstay of the region where it contributes 30 per cent–70 per cent of GSDP of individual states. The agricultural sector is significant compared to national average in states such as Nagaland and Arunachal Pradesh. The non-manufacturing industrial sector is significant in many states and is in the range between 14 per cent and 32 per cent of GSDP. In the manufacturing sector, Sikkim and Assam are above national average in terms of the sector's contribution to overall GDP of the country. In the services sector, there are large variations in terms of contribution to the GSDP—with very high contribution for some NER states. The region is favourably placed in terms of availability of electric power. From conventional wisdom, availability of power is a precondition for industrialization. At present, power balance for India is largely negative, in other words, the power

Box 3.1: Leveraging Regional Cooperation for Achieving
the SDGs in the North East

The North Eastern Region of India is nested in an interesting geography that intimately connects it with India's eastern neighbours, namely Nepal, Bhutan, Myanmar, Bangladesh, and China. As has been highlighted, global and regional cooperation is foundational to the concept of the Agenda 2030 and the SDGs as the larger development and sustainability implications are not restricted to political boundaries of countries. In fact, cooperation among countries, which share similar regional specificities, remains the cornerstone for cross-border developmental aspirations in the context of the SDGs and global partnership connecting trade, finance, technology, and capacity building (SDG 17). The NER possesses less than 10 per cent of the total land area of the country, but the importance of the region grows manifold as it shares international borders with all most all of India's neighbours. Each of these eight states shares a portion of the international border. Arunachal Pradesh has international borders to the tune of 1,863 kilometres shared with Bhutan (217 kilometres) and China (1,126 kilometres), and Myanmar (520 kilometres). Assam shares an international border of 529 kilometres with Bhutan (267 kilometres) and Bangladesh (262 kilometres). Manipur has international border with Myanmar (398 kilometres), while Meghalaya's international border is linked to Bangladesh (443 kilometres). Mizoram experiences 828 kilometres of international borders with Bangladesh (318 kilometres) and Myanmar (510 kilometres). Nagaland borders Myanmar alone (215 kilometres), while Tripura has its border only with Bangladesh (856 kilometres). Finally, Sikkim shares an international border of 351 kilometres—China (220 kilometres), Bhutan (32 kilometres), and Nepal (99 kilometres). This particular characteristic of the NER makes it a strong candidate for engaging effectively in India's 'Act East Policy' and thereby contributing to its aspiration towards achieving the Sustainable Development Goals (SDGs). However, establishing such a linkage between 'Act East Policy' and achievement of Agenda 2030 has to negotiate a good number of unique characteristic features of NER—some of them having the potential to contribute positively while some others are capable of making the intents difficult to achieve.

With strong natural resource endowments and strategic locations on the long land borders with Bangladesh, Myanmar, Nepal, and Bhutan, NER presents a unique case for a new model of development path beginning with transport corridor, elevating to economic corridor with maturing of production, agglomeration and trade processes, and finally to growth corridor that links the region with rest of South Asia and Southeast Asia. By enabling better sourcing of local natural resources in the hinterland and smooth supply of finished goods and services to rural and relatively less developed areas, physical connectivity in terms of robust network of roads, railways, ports, and airports can help integrate NER with the regional production networks in South and Southeast Asia and promote cross-border trade with neighbouring countries such as Bangladesh, Myanmar, Nepal and Bhutan. The Union Government of India at different points of time has given special attention to the unique strengths of the North Eastern states and explored the possibility of leveraging those unique strategic advantages for promoting bilateral trade with neighbouring countries by shifting from 'Look East Policy' to 'Act East Policy'.

Source: Authors' compilation.

demand is much higher than the existing level of power production. Except a couple of states, with balanced supply–demand situation in power availability such as Goa, Haryana, Madhya Pradesh, and Punjab, other states face power deficit of varying degrees. In this regard, the NER states face power deficit of a low magnitude. Criticality of power shortage from its potential demand for power was somewhat significant in selected states such as Assam, Manipur, and Tripura. Otherwise, power situation in the region is positive, signalling favourable conditions for industrialization in the region. The states in the NER have high hydroelectricity potential which needs to be harnessed (Baruah, 2017).

The poverty profile of the NER is highly skewed, similar to other Indian states. Policies of the states and centre to combat poverty elicited different responses during the past two and half decades as shown in Figure 3.3. While some of the states, such as Sikkim, addressed the issue of poverty effectively, a few others states, such as Arunachal Pradesh, Manipur, and Assam, could do very little in this regard. Similar results are also found by Konwar (2015). States such as Mizoram and Nagaland were estimated to have moderate level of poverty as per the Tendulkar methodology. According to the same estimate, India had 26.98 crore people living below the poverty line, of which 1.3 crore people were in the Northeast region. As shown in Figure 3.3 that there is no relationship between size of population and people below the poverty line. The NER region's share of total population in the country was 3.78 per cent in 2011, while its share of population below poverty line stood at 4.89 per cent during the same reference period. It is argued that skewed distribution of land may be the key reason for high incidence of poverty in a region where large population is dependent on agriculture (Nair et al. 2013).

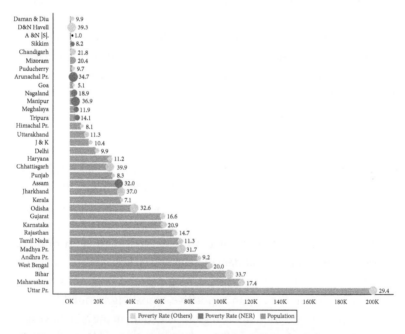

Figure 3.3: Population and Incidence of Poverty in Indian States in 2011

Source: RIS database based on *Handbook of Statistics for India States*, RBI, 2019.

Note: Poverty ratio is in percent. Red bubbles represent Northeast states.

The NER region has low level of workers' participation than several states in India. From the total workers of the country, the NER shared 2.1 per cent of it in 2016–17. Share of population of the region (3.78 per cent) was much higher than share of region's workforce (2.1 per cent), and such imbalance has to be addressed to encourage productive activities to proliferate. Several studies have outlined the causes for the low participation rate in the region and the manner in which such impediments can be addressed through state-level policies. With expansion of industrial activities in the region, large-scale migration can be prevented. Demographic dividend can be a major advantage for the region for the coming years. As per Periodic Labour Force Survey (PLFS) Annual Report 2017–18, among the North Eastern states, rural unemployment was maximum in Nagaland—21.6 per cent (also maximum among all the states), followed by Manipur—11.6 per cent, Assam—8.3 per cent, and Mizoram—6.5 per cent. Urban unemployment was higher than rural unemployment in five of the NE states, the gap being highest in Mizoram, followed by Meghalaya, Arunachal Pradesh, Sikkim, and Tripura. High urban unemployment is a concern for Nagaland—21.1 per cent, Mizoram—14.4 per cent, and Manipur—11.4 per cent, where the figures were all in double digit.

The state of EoDB for the NER states is presented in Figure 3.4. The regional profile of the NER states for the years 2015–16 and 2016–17 does not show encouraging results for the regional states with reference to other states of the country. Despite India's improvement in terms of its ranking in EoDB among other trading countries of the globe, NER states demonstrated deterioration of their ranks with respect to other states of the country. In Figure 3.4, each arrow represents change in the ranking of the state over the previous year. An upward arrow represents improvement in the rank of the state over the previous year and vice versa. When the rank of a state improves, the number presented on the arrowhead would be lower than the number near the nock of the arrow, and when ranking of a state declines over the past year, the number on the arrowhead would be larger than the number on the nock of the arrow. In Figure 3.4, EoDB ranking for the NER states is presented for the year 2015–16 and 2016–17. Among eight states in the region, half of them registered upward movement in their EoDB ranking in 2015–16, and they did so by improving their business environment. These States were Arunachal Pradesh, Manipur, Nagaland, and Tripura. All the important exporting

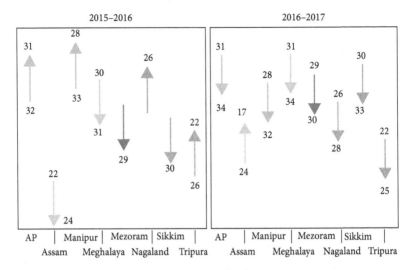

Figure 3.4: Movement of State-Level Rank of Doing Business
Source: RIS database based on *Handbook of Statistics for Indian States*, RBI, 2019.

states including Assam, Meghalaya, and Sikkim failed to maintain the pace of liberalization in comparison with other states in the region.[1]

Local Production

The industrial profile of the NER is extremely interesting as the latest Annual Survey of Industries (ASI) (Table 3.2), 2017–18 clearly shows the new off-take and energy in the region. The growth of industry in the NER was higher at 9.3 per cent as compared to 6.3 per cent at all India level. The double digit industrial growth is evident from Arunachal Pradesh, Assam, Manipur, Mizoram, and Tripura, while Meghalaya has recorded a negative growth. The number of factories in the NE region now stands

---

[1] The Department of Industrial Policy and Promotion (DIPP), Ministry of Commerce and Industry, in partnership with the World Bank Group, released the Business Reform Action Plan (BRAP) 2017 for implementation by States/ UTs. Assam - 84.75 per cent is the leading from the northeastern states that fall 2 levels below the Top-Achievers category, while all the other NE states are in the Aspirers group. Tripura—22.45 per cent and Nagaland—14.16 per cent follow Assam with a big lag, but in Mizoram—3.66 per cent, Manipur—0.27 per cent and Sikkim—0.14 per cent the index highlights the concern of non-supportive business environment. However, Meghalaya and Arunachal Pradesh may not have fulfilled all reporting requirements as evident from the available information.

Table 3.2: Select Features of Industries in North-Eastern Region States (Value Figures Are in Rs. Lakh and Others Are Numbers)

States	No. of Factories	Fixed Capital	Invested Capital	No of Workers	Total Output	Net Value Added
1	2	3	4	5	6	7
Assam	4,538 (1.91)	2,733,666 (0.83)	3,660,320 (0.82)	180,489 (1.48)	6,732,646 (0.83)	1,364,876 (1.10)
Sikkim	82 (0.03)	705,218 (0.21)	890,869 (0.20)	15,069 (0.12)	1,836,037 (0.23)	1,064,105 (0.86)
Meghalaya	133 (0.06)	361,974 (0.11)	495,077 (0.11)	10,758 (0.09)	568,899 (0.07)	122,400 (0.10)
Tripura	607 (0.26)	45,161 (0.01)	76,863 (0.02)	23,393 (0.19)	155,929 (0.02)	30,480 (0.02)
Nagaland	186 (0.08)	20,764 (0.01)	32,133 (0.01)	5,207 (0.04)	54,104 (0.01)	13,167 (0.01)
Arunachal Pradesh	117 (0.05)	19,343 (0.01)	33,113 (0.01)	26,71 (0.02)	99,998 (0.01)	12,206 (0.01)
Manipur	191 (0.08)	15,929 (0.00)	22,625 (0.01)	7,334 (0.06)	42,083 (0.01)	8,376 (0.01)
North Eastern Area	5,854 (2.46)	3,902,055 (1.18)	5,211,000 (1.17)	244,921 (2.00)	9,489,696 (1.17)	2,615,610 (2.11)
All India	237,684	329,341,000	446,846,553	12,224,402	808,167,115	123,812,856

Note: Figures in parentheses are percent share in all India.

Source: Annual Survey of Industries, 2017–18.

at 5,854 in 2017–18 which was only at 2,975 in 2009–10. Accordingly, the jump in this period in the all India share is from 1.7 per cent to 2.5 per cent, though the share in the fixed capital increased from 1 per cent to 1.2 per cent. This shows the low capital base of the new units that have come up in the region. It is also evident from the state-wise value of gross output, which has remained at 1.2 per cent of the national average from 2009–10 to 2017–18. The NER share in the invested capital increased from 1 per cent to 1.2 per cent in the same time period. However, in this period, share of state-wise number of workers increased from 1.8 per cent to 2 per cent.

Within the region, in the period 2009–10 to 2017–18, Assam shows the highest gain where the number of units in the same time period expanded from 2,247 to 4,538, while in Manipur, it expanded from 85 to 191; in Meghalaya, from 100 to 133; in Nagaland, from 90 to 186; in Sikkim, from 46 to 82; and in Tripura, from 407 to 607.

With the expansion of units, the fixed capital in Assam increased from Rs. 9,801 crore to around Rs. 27,336 crore. However, in other states, this increase was varying across states as in Manipur, the fixed capital increased from Rs. 34 crore to Rs. 159 crore; in Meghalaya, from Rs. 1,495 crore to Rs. 3,619 crore; in Nagaland, from Rs. 20 crore to Rs. 207 crore; and in Sikkim, from Rs. 908 crore to Rs. 7,052 crore. However, in case of Tripura, it declined from Rs. 664 crore in 2009–10 to Rs. 272 crore in 2013–14 and gradually increases from 2014–15 (Rs. 324 crore) to Rs. 451 crore in 2017–18. If we look at the invested capital, it is around Rs 14,667 crore to Rs. 36,603 crore in case of Assam. While in case of Manipur, it increased from Rs. 69 crore to Rs. 226 crore; in Meghalaya, from Rs. 1,876 crore to Rs. 4,950 crore, and in Sikkim, it increases from Rs. 1,289 crore to Rs. 8,908 crore. In case of Nagaland and Tripura, the invested capital declined from Rs. 335 crore to Rs. 321 crore and Rs. 835 crore to Rs. 768 crore, respectively. If we look at the employment sector, the number of workers employed has increased in Assam from 1.25 lakh to 18 lakh, followed by Manipur, where it increased from 2,000 to 7,000; in Meghalaya, from 4,000 to 10,000; in Nagaland, from 2,000 to 5,000, and in Sikkim, from 4,000 to 15,000, while in Tripura, it declined from 25,000 to 23,000.

Financial inclusion continues to be a major issue in context of NER. The credit deposit ratio has been significantly lower than the All India average. As Table 3.3 shows, even though there is recent uptake in some

Table 3.3: CD Ratio (Based on Utilization) of North Eastern States (Per cent)

	2018	2017	2016	2015	2014	2013
Arunachal Pradesh	25.0	24.0	29.0	26.8	23.7	21.8
Assam	42.6	40.3	42.2	36.7	37.7	37.2
Manipur	44.6	38.7	41.1	34.0	33.6	28.6
Meghalaya	27.2	25.9	24.8	25.9	27.4	24.0
Mizoram	35.8	36.4	40.1	37.8	37.8	35.3
Nagaland	34.7	31.5	34.1	32.7	31.0	28.4
Sikkim	26.6	27.4	28.0	25.6	26.5	27.2
Tripura	40.7	35.9	35.3	33.7	32.4	32.8
North Eastern Region	38.8	36.4	38.0	34.2	34.5	33.4
All India	76.7	73.8	78.4	77.1	79.0	75.8

Source: Handbook of Statistics on Indian States, RBI.

states such as Manipur, Meghalaya, and Tripura, while in other states, fluctuation is clearly evident. The financial inclusion efforts and banking outlets along with concerted industrialization efforts probably may help change the scenario to a great extent.

The NER is better placed in so far as distribution of clusters in India is concerned. While 3.57 per cent of India's population is residing in the region, more than 7.57 per cent of country's industrial clusters are located in this part of the country. A survey undertaken by Research and Information System for Developing Countries (RIS), meant for identification of clusters in India, has grouped these surveyed clusters into three broad categories, including industrial, handicraft, and handloom clusters in India. Each broad category of cluster is further sub-divided into a number of sectors. Location of each sector was identified with its state, district, geographical location, and specific manufactured products. The RIS survey results show that NER region has 333 clusters from a total of 4,103 clusters in Indian as shown in Table 3.4.

In each of these broad groups of handicrafts, handlooms, and industrial clusters, there are several sectors with intensive economic activity. In these broad categories of clusters, distribution of these units is not uniformly seen across various industry sub-categories. Of the total of 333 clusters in the Northeast region, 86.1 per cent belong to handicrafts, 7.5 per cent to handloom, and 6.5 per cent to the industrial sector. In comparison with all India figures, the Northeast region shares 10.3 per

Table 3.4: Distribution of MSME Clusters in Northeast Region: Broad Categories of Clusters (Number of Clusters)

Sector	AP	Assam	Manipur	Meghalaya	Mizoram	Nagaland	Sikkim	Tripura	NER	India	NER to India %
Handicraft	39	63	47	16	6	26	10	80	287	2,783	10.3
Handloom	3	7	4	1	2	4	1	3	25	196	12.8
Industrial	–	4	3	2	–	1	–	5	15	968	1.5
Others	–	–	–	–	–	–	–	6	6	156	3.8
Total	42	74	54	19	8	31	11	94	333	4,103	8.1

Source: RIS database based on RIS All India Survey of Clusters, 2019.

cent of handicraft clusters in India, 12.8 per cent of handloom clusters, and 1.5 per cent of industrial clusters in the country. The region is less endowed with industrial clusters as compared to the all India figure, but the sector is critical for export activities in the region. In India's overall exports, handicraft ranks low among other sectors. In order to improve export prospects of the region, there is a need for establishing more industrial clusters in this sector. With grassroot innovation capacity, effects of economies of scale, and indigenous efforts of firms, clusters can push these firms to move up in the value chain and can compete with the global market (Das, 2005; Humphrey and Schmitz, 2000).

There has been considerable level of asymmetry in the distribution of cluster among the eight NER states. Largest number of clusters exists in Tripura followed by Assam, Manipur, Arunachal Pradesh, Nagaland, Meghalaya, Sikkim, and Mizoram. The top three states, including Tripura, Assam, and Manipur, share two third of total number of clusters in the region. From the total of 287 handicraft clusters in the region, 80 per cent of them are shared by four states, namely Tripura, Assam, Manipur, and Arunachal Pradesh. Handloom clusters are dominantly present in Assam, but other states have moderate to low level of such clusters.

While top three states, namely Tripura, Assam, and Manipur, have acquired 80 per cent of total industrial clusters in the region, other regional states are poorly endowed with such type of clusters. Mizoram and Sikkim have no industrial clusters, yet in order to undertake cluster-type manufacturing activities, the NER has wide range of resources to feed in to broad sectors such as agriculture, construction, electric and gas, manufacturing and services. The region could be transformed into an industrial powerhouse and can be a leading source of exports once the region is prepared to move along a predetermined export path with clear export strategy in the medium term. A high-cost region cannot afford to engage with only raw agricultural products to achieve global competitiveness, unless it is strongly adhering to low-cost local raw materials. Similarly, the region's medium-term export strategy should focus on graduating from agriculture-based exports to manufacturing and services-based exporting economy.

Each state produces a variety of handicraft and industrial products and the inventory of such products varies significantly across these states. Under the handicraft category, there are as many as sixteen sectors existing in the region, and under each sector, there are several clusters, engaged in the production of varieties of products. Cluster categories and sectors across states are presented in Table C in the Appendix and Annex A. In the handloom sector, products are considered as homogenous since further details of different handloom sectors are not available for various clusters located in these states. In the handicraft and industrial cluster categories, information on further disaggregated sectors is available. These sectors can be broadly classified into textiles, wood products, leather, gems and jewellery, base metal, art and culture, and stone products in the NER. Although the region reports presence of wide range of handicraft sectors in the region, the number of clusters in each of these sectors is seem to be highly asymmetric in nature. Among handicraft clusters in the region, substantial number of clusters is engaged with the production of basketry, mat weaving, and cane articles. There are as many as 144 such clusters in this sector, comprising more than 50 per cent of the total handicraft clusters in the region.

Textile is the second largest sector in the handicraft clusters, sharing 17.4 per cent of the total handicraft cluster in the NER. Clusters engaged in woodwork are the third largest group of handicraft clusters. Metal ware and carpet and durries are emerging as important group of clusters within handicraft. Other important sectors within the broad category of handicraft are earthenware, jewellery, leather, pottery and clay, etc. among others. The region has several other groups of cluster, but the number of clusters in each of these sectors is relatively small compared to aforesaid sectors. Handloom clusters are twenty-five in number, but they form 12.8 per cent of total number of clusters in the country.

The Northeast region has exceptionally less number of industrial clusters as compared to the all India figure from the RIS survey. There are as little as fifteen such clusters in the region, sharing 1.5 per cent of total number of industrial clusters existing in the country. Such industrial clusters are present in various sectors including agro food processing, leather, non-metal mineral products, paper products, textiles, wood products, etc., among others. From the total of fifteen such clusters in the region, eight of them are in the agro food processing, and another three are in the textile sector. The remaining industrial clusters are thinly spread in different products in the region. Sectoral distribution of clusters varies widely across states, demonstrating sectoral specialization of states in the NER as presented in Table C in the Appendix. Sectoral specialization of states enables policy makers to take a view on scale economies of certain products for exports. Existing literature highlights that one of the major impediments of the region is economies of scale. This is because of the lack of large corporate firms in the region, possibly due to the topography and other constraints of the region. Hence, SMEs and clusters may be focused on large-scale quality production for boosting exports. Coordination of similar type of clusters in a state or across the region may be experimented in order to produce export quality products with economies of scale.

In states such as Tripura, Assam, Manipur, Nagaland, and Arunachal Pradesh, there are several clusters, producing similar nature of products such as manufacturing of basketry, mat weaving, and cane articles. Large number of cluster under textiles is operating mainly in three states, namely Assam, Manipur, and Tripura. Woodwork activities are dominant in number of states such as Tripura, Arunachal Pradesh, and Nagaland. There is clear-cut specialization of clusters in the production of specific products in the region. Considering large number of clusters existing in individual states and also in similar sectors, achieving scale economies may not be an issue for the domestic or export markets. In case of small production capacity of clusters manufacturing similar kind of products, two or more states can join together for mass production. The experience of the region demonstrates that it can go for large-scale production in sectors such as metal ware, earthenware, carpet and durries, jewellery, leather, pottery and clay, etc.

The NER states are specialized in certain lines of products, and such products are manufactured in sizeable number of clusters. This implies that in certain products, individual states can attain scale economies to meet large export order. In certain other products, where a state lacks capability in maintaining scale economies or unable to meet bulk export demand, some states can work collectively with their clusters to maintain scale economies. For example, Arunachal Pradesh has specialized in basketry and cane articles, carpet and durries, metal ware, and woodworks. Assam is specialized in basketry and cane articles, textiles and food processing clusters but has to collaborate with Manipur and other states for enhancing production base in food processing sector. Manipur has large number of clusters in producing basketry and cane articles and textile products. Meghalaya largely has clusters which are into basketry and produce cane articles and has emerged as the second largest producer of such products in the NER. Mizoram is specialized only in the production of cane basketry as handicraft products. Similarly, Nagaland is specialized in clusters such as cane basketry and woodworks; Sikkim in cane basketry and textiles; and Tripura in cane basketry, textiles, and woodwork. The experiences of NER states indicate that the scale factor can be managed by individual states in several handicraft and handloom products. However, in the industrial sector, the region is lagging behind significantly. There are several clusters in the region, producing monolithic manufacturing products, but these clusters are thinly distributed in different states. There are several industrial products manufactured in the region, but not many clusters produce similar products to join hands to achieve scale economies when demand arises in the region. In the textile sector, particularly, in apparel production Assam, Manipur, and Tripura can join their production capabilities to create a large production hub for exports with scale economies and export competitiveness.

Information gap is a major challenge in the region for fostering its development goals. Parameters covered in existing databases for the region is narrowly focused, limited to a few dimensions of the industrial development in the region. For understanding status of the industrial sector in the region, spotty evidences are collected from existing secondary databases such as ASI, Prowess, Indian economy statistics of RBI, cluster analysis, Directorate General of Commercial Intelligence and Statistics (DGCIS), Comtrade, etc. In the absence of proper harmonization between these databases, the state of affairs in the industrial sector of the NER are not properly depicted, and there is very little clarity about the manufacturing sector activities at the regional and sub-regional level (i.e. at the state, district, and further sub-regional level). For understanding the role of industrial sector in the NER, we have undertaken trade and production analysis at the disaggregated level, using the existing secondary statistics to focus on various dimensions of the industrial sector.

Top four states of the NER share 95.7 per cent of total number of corporate firms located in the region (Table 3.6). This implies that bottom four states account for less than 5 per cent of total corporate firms existing in the region. It is evident from the operations of large firms in the corporate sector in India that they are the primary driver of export activities and that the contribution of the SME sector has been at a lower level. When SMEs start exporting, they continue to export without putting much pressure on their capital requirements for exports (Mohanty and Arockiasami, 2009). Poor export performance of the states in NER is the outcome of small number of corporate firms located in the region. For promoting exports, the cost factor is the key element which is closely linked with the scale factor. Therefore, it is important to observe conglomeration of factories, producing similar product in a place to justify the possibility of scale economies in a region. Distribution of firms in each state, producing similar products is necessary to achieve scale economies. Coverage of firms in NIC 2008 at five-digit level in different states of the NER region is presented in Table D in the Appendix. In the CMIE database, industries are identified at the disaggregated level, using NIC 2008 at five-digit level. The identified corporate firms at five-digit level are regrouped into one-digit sectors and two-digit divisions for more meaningful analysis. In this scheme, distribution of corporate firms located in various industrial groups and states is presented. In case more firms are conglomerated around an industry at five-digit NIC 2008 in a specific state, this would imply possibility of achieving scale economy in the state for the specific industry. This would have a positive implication for having low cost through the scale factor and hence, possibility for higher exports. In case corporate firms are thinly spread across industries/states, it may indicate lesser possibilities for exports.

For the analytical convenience, we have grouped products at the level of division using NIC 2008 industry classification. In Table D, division 01 refers to agriculture; 05-08 as mining, 10-32 as manufacturing, 34-42 as electricity, gas, and other utilities, and construction sector. Division 45 and onwards refer to services sector. Taking into account these broad sectors, we can examine conglomeration of firms in different states in specific industries. We have three major findings from the present analysis: (a) most of the firms are located in Assam and Meghalaya, and some industrial conglomeration of firms can be seen in these two states; (b) the states in the NER produce wide range of products, but most of them are produced by single firm, indicating possibility of lack of scale economies in the region and (c) conglomeration of firms is centred around several industries in services sector. In the agricultural and mining sectors, there is no conglomeration of firms. In the manufacturing sector, there were sixty-five products in the region. Agglomerations of firm in the manufacturing sector were in specific products such as biscuits (3), mustard oil (3), processed tea (30), plywood (4), cement products (19 in two states), ferrosilicon (3), etc. It may be noted that figure in the parenthesis indicates number of firms in the industry category. There is agglomeration of firms in the electricity sector (4). In the construction sector, there is agglomeration of firms in number of industries, including real estate (4), core construction activities (6), and construction of industrial plants (3). Similarly, services sector observes agglomeration of firms around certain industries such as wholesale and retail trade, financial and insurance services, and several other allied services. Presence of corporate firms indicates that the region has been able to attract corporate firms in specific states, namely Assam and Meghalaya, in both goods and services. Corporate activities are more prominent in the services sector than in the manufacturing sector activities. For promoting exports, scale of production in specific product needs to be promoted by attracting more large firms with capabilities to exports. Scale economies would help in bringing down prices, and hence, competitiveness of the industry. Thin presence of several manufacturing activities can bring competitiveness in a gradual manner when more industries would join in these states.

Trade and Competitiveness

Export competitiveness is the key question while discussing challenges concerning exports. There are several apprehensions about the region's efficacy in exports. Several states produce and compete for same products in the export sector, resulting in crashing of prices to rock bottom level. Some argue that input cost, particularly labour cost per hour is so high that exports are uncompetitive for the regional states (Bose, 2019). There are several other issues relating to export competitiveness of the region. In Table E in the Appendix, export competitiveness of each state is compared by taking selected products at six-digit HS. The purpose is to examine the following: (a) Is there any evidence to show that multiple states engage in the export of a product at a disaggregated level? (b) While exporting a product by several states, is there any evidence to show that some states are competitive and others are not with respect to India's export prices?

The region exported 836 products at six-digit HS in 2018. From the total number of exported items of the region, 389 products were estimated as competitive with respect to average export prices of India with the rest of the world. Export price comparison is a sound basis for estimating export competitiveness (Viner, 1960). After examining export competitiveness, Arunachal Pradesh had 40 competitive products, Assam 289 products, Manipur 16 products, Meghalaya 21 products, Mizoram 15 products, Nagaland 19 products, Sikkim 59 products, and Tripura 30 products in 2018. Though the region posted several products as export competitiveness, only sixty of them were exported by two or more states in the region. This indicates that scale economies are not there as coordination between states is missing while undertaking export activities. Out of sixty commodities, where each product was exported by two or more states in the region, only one product was exported by seven states, two products by six states, two products by five states, six products by four states, nine products by three states, and forty products by two states in 2018. There is large potential for exports but current state of export activity is very poor. Goswami and Saikia (2012) observed that the 'Look East Policy' could be useful in exercising NER's natural advantage of trade with the neighbours and to develop several industries based on local natural endowments through inflow of Foreign Direct Investment (FDI). In a historical perspective, Chutia (2015) found merit in opening up of historic road, connecting Lido in Assam with Kunming in China via Myanmar. This would open up a new vista of trade opportunities between NER and South East Asian as well as East Asian countries. State and regional trade strategies need to be evolved to direct large and MSME firms to cope up with exports to generate more employment and contribute to livelihood security of people in the region. Availability of resources is required to improve GFCF of the region which is very low as compared to other states in India. Perhaps trade sector development would contribute to SDGs 8 and 17 in the NER.

Despite having strong resource endowments in agriculture and mining, the region has displayed dismal performance in the export sector during the past several decades. In the overall export performance of India, the NER holds a very small owing to non-leveraging of its abundant resource potentials. There is considerable level of asymmetry between NER states in their engagement with the world for exports. Manufacturing exports have been concentrated in a few states, whereas large number of states was deprived of such accomplishment. Export of the region in 2018 was reported

Table 3.5: North East Exports to World in Broad Economic Sectors, 2018 ($'000 USD)

State	Agriculture	Mining	Manufacturing	Total Exports
Arunachal Pradesh	545.8	288.8	1,377.9	2,212.4
Assam	289,579.0	47,654.1	24,603.4	361,836.6
Manipur	82.6	430.8	2,016.9	2,530.3
Meghalaya	935.4	51,042.7	1,432.6	53,410.7
Mizoram	543.0	201.3	348.6	1,092.9
Nagaland	381.6	195.5	2,085.1	2,662.3
Sikkim	2,367.1	1,158.1	4,091.6	7,616.8
Tripura	755.2	419.1	422.0	1,596.3
NER	295,189.6	101,390.5	36,378.2	432,958.3

Source: RIS database based on RIS estimate based on DGCI&S, 2019.

at $433 million, sharing meagre 0.13 per cent of India's total exports in 2018. Assam took the lion's share of 83.6 per cent of region's total exports to the world, followed by Meghalaya with 12.2 per cent and Sikkim with 1.8 per cent in the same year. Shares of other states were in the range of 0.3 per cent to 0.6 per cent of region's total exports. To be more precise, top two exporting states of the region shared 85.9 per cent and top three states shared 87.7 per cent of regions exports in 2018. Sectoral composition of trade by states is presented in Table 3.5. Regional exports in the broad economic activities indicates that agricultural sector shared the largest proportion of the region's trade, followed by mining and manufacturing, which is, in fact, contrary to India's overall experience in the export sector (Mohanty, 2014).

Assam is ahead in almost all broad sectors of exports. The agricultural sector contributed 68.2 per cent of region's total exports to the world in the aforesaid year. In the mining sector, the region shared 23.4 per cent of its exports, mostly concentrated in Assam and Meghalaya. Although contribution of the manufacturing exports was least to the region's exports as compared to agricultural and mining sectors, several states participated in the exports of the sector. Notable states participated in manufacturing exports were Assam, Sikkim, Manipur, and Nagaland. Tripura and Mizoram are almost non-starter in manufacturing sector exports in the region. Distribution of exports in broad sectors of NER indicates that certain states are better endowed in specific sectors than others. Therefore, state-wise specific sectoral focus may be emphasized to strengthen export capacities of states in line with their specialization. Empirical evidences indicate that Assam and Sikkim can specialize in agriculture; Assam and Meghalaya in mining; and Assam, Manipur, Nagaland, and Tripura in manufacturing, based on their respective comparative advantage in production. Even though manufacturing sector contributes marginally to the overall exports of the region, several states have the base for taking manufacturing activities forward in the medium run.

Further, sectoral disaggregation of exports by state demonstrates distinct specialization of individual states by sectors. Section-wise exports of products by NER states are presented in Table D in the Appendix. The export sector in the NER is highly skewed and three states, namely, Assam, Meghalaya, and Sikkim shared 97.7 per cent of the region's overall exports in 2018. Lion's share of the region was seized by Assam (83.6 per cent), followed by Meghalaya (12.3 per cent) and Sikkim (1.8 per cent). While Assam had significant exports in eight sectors, it was three sectors for Meghalaya and four sectors for Sikkim in the same years. In the agricultural sector, fruits and vegetable sector was the most dominant sector for exports in 2018. The sector is emerging important for several other states such as Arunachal Pradesh, Assam, Mizoram, and Tripura. In this HS section, Arunachal Pradesh specializes in edible fruits and nuts; Assam in coffee, tea, and cereals; Meghalaya in oil seeds and oleaginous fruits; Mizoram in edible fruits and nuts; and Tripura in edible vegetables and certain roots. In the processed food sector, Sikkim is relatively more specialized than rest of the states and specialization is mostly in preparation of cereals and other edible products.

In the mineral sector, the NER region shared 23.4 per cent of overall exports of the region. Most of the states in the region participated in the export activities of mineral products, but Assam and Meghalaya took the lead in the mineral export of the region in 2018. Both the states exported mineral products such as salt, sulphur, etc. as well as mineral fuels. While Assam was the leading exporter of mineral fuels, Meghalaya was a major exporter of salt, sulphur, and other mineral in 2018.

Manufacturing sector witnessed specialization of states in diverse sectors. The region was exporting mainly in selected sectors such as chemicals, textiles, footwear, cement, jewellery, base metal, machinery, precision instruments, and handicraft in 2018. In the chemical sector,

Sikkim was engaged in the export of pharmaceutical products; and Assam was engaged in the export of essential oils and pharmaceutical products. Base metal sector is becoming important for region's exports. Certain states such as Arunachal Pradesh, Assam, and Meghalaya are very active in the exports of iron and steels. Among other sectors, export of machinery products is becoming paramount for the region.

The structure of exports by end-use across NER states shows that primary (18.7 per cent), intermediate (10.4 per cent), and final goods sector (70.9 per cent) are contributing to the overall exports of the region in a manner, which is inconsistent with the experience of the Indian economy (Mohanty et al., 2019). In the intermediate sector, semi-finished products (8.5 per cent) and final consumption goods (69.9 per cent) in the final goods sector dominate region's export sector. The region is far away from the critical export sectors such as parts and component in industrial intermediates and final capital goods in final goods sectors. One needs to examine the existence or possibility of developing value chain/supply chain in various sectors within or/and between states.

The states in the NER have specialized in specific broad sectors other than Assam, which has been contributing significantly to all broad categories of the end-use classification. Primary exports were mostly shared between Assam and Meghalaya, semi-finished sectors between Assam, Meghalaya, and Nagaland, and finished consumer goods with Assam. In the product classification of technology intensive products, large volume of trade is falling in the categories of resource-based and medium technology, but commensurate contribution is not coming from other categories such as low technology and high technology. Exports of high-technology products were small in quantum, but mostly from Assam and Sikkim.

The reason for low quantum of exports of low technology may be due to high cost of labour (Bose, 2019) and implementation of several welfare schemes of both states and centre, running by these states.

The proceeding discussion has given a bird's eye view about the pattern of trade undertaken by the states in the region. Broadly, one can observe three trends in the export sector: (a) the scale of trade of the region is very low, (b) the states have production and export base for several products, and (c) these products have thinly spread across states where these products can be exported to several destinations with their significant competitive strength. Regional states are exporting large number of products to various destinations, but number of exported products varies from one state to another.

The region is currently engaged in exports in almost all sectors and with the neighbouring countries as well as beyond these countries. The regional exports are not only reaching to neighbouring Regional Trading Arrangements such as SAARC, ASEAN, BIMSTEC, BICM, and BBIN, but also to far-flung countries including North America. Varieties of commodities including both primary and non-primary commodities exported by these states are presented in Table 3.6 and Annex B. A large number of products are exported from the region covering most of the broad sectors including fruits and vegetables, chemicals, base metals, machinery, etc., from all regional states. In the production of animal products, Assam exports largest number of products among regional states, and these products are mostly in the area of fresh and brackish water fish and dairy as well as poultry products. Nagaland has several meat products to export. Fruits and vegetable are major sectors where the regional economies have many things to offer for exports, especially led by Assam. The state is also exporting several products in the category of edible vegetables, fruits and nuts, tea products, and cereals in recent years. Other states such as Arunachal Pradesh, Mizoram, Meghalaya, and Sikkim are also engaged in exports in these products categories. Assam is the only state in the region, exporting animal and vegetable fats and oil. Processed food is an important sector where Assam and Sikkim are the lead exporters of the region. Assam exported much voluminous processed food than Sikkim and participation of other regional states in the export of this product category has been negligible.

From export point of view, mining sector is important for the region where all states are engaged in exports, though number of export products is small for several states. Sarma (2008) found that certain states such as Assam, Meghalaya, and Mizoram are strongly endowed with mineral resources. Most of them are exporters of mineral fuels or its derivatives, but a few states are involved in the exports of stone plasters, cement, sulphur, etc. The region is an important exporter of chemical products including pharmaceutical products. Assam, Sikkim, and Manipur are the leading exporter of such products, but in terms of their specialization in exports, there is considerable level of variations between states. While

Assam's exports were concentrated on specific products such as pharmaceuticals, tanning extracts, essential oils, and organic soap, Sikkim's exports were concentrated on pharmaceuticals and essential oils, and Manipur's exports were concentrated on pharmaceuticals and tanning extracts.

Plastic sector assumes considerable level of importance in the state for exports and is mostly managed by Assam, Sikkim, and Tripura. Other sectoral exports such as leather, wood products, wood pulp, footwear, and cement are mostly dominated by Assam, though other states are also engaged in the sector marginally in the region. Among others, export interest of the region is significantly associated with the textile sector where most of the states are associated in diversified segments of the same sector. However, certain states such as Assam, Nagaland, Sikkim, Tripura, etc. are important players in the sector. Most of the states prefer to export certain products, which are falling in specific product segment apparel and clothing including both knitted and not knitted, made up textiles and other vegetable, textile fibres. Regional states are also engaged in the export of gems and jewellery, but product diversification in the sector is not pronounced. The region has critical interest in the exports of base metal products. All states are active in the sectoral export, but a few states including Assam, Arunachal Pradesh, Sikkim, and Nagaland are more important than others in terms of exporting several such products. Most of these leading states are having sector focus on products such as articles of iron and steel, and tool and implements for exports.

Assam and Sikkim are exporting precision instruments, but scale economies are very low. Since the NER states have large number of handicraft clusters, substantial exports in diversified products can be possible in the broad HS section on miscellaneous manufacturing. Although a large number of clusters exist in states such as Tripura, Assam, Manipur, Arunachal Pradesh, etc., substantial number of products for exports is not coming from these states. Moreover, presence of large number of clusters in the region has virtually no impact on export activities in the handicraft segment of exports. Handicraft sector needs to be focused to make it export oriented and to compete with not only other states within India but also with other countries in accessing global market. It may be noted that India is an emerging economy where per capita income of

Table 3.6: Number of Export Products of NER States to the World by HS Section in 2018

Section	Description	AP	Assam	Manipur	Meghalaya	Mizoram	Nagaland	Sikkim	Tripura	NER
1	Live animals	1	8		1	1	2	2	2	17
2	Vegetable products	18	82	7	13	13	12	19	16	180
3	Fats & oils		2							2
4	Prepared foodstuff	10	31	1	1			8	1	42
5	Mineral products	3	39	6	14	6	6	13	4	98
6	Chemicals	1	104	9	1	1		24	1	143
7	Plastics		87		1		1	14	7	111
8	Leather, etc.		6				1			7
9	Wood	1	19				2	2	1	25
10	Pulp of wood	2	17		1			4	1	25
11	Textile	9	42	7	4	4	12	22	18	118
12	Footwear, etc.	1	9				1			11
13	Cement	2	49	1	3	2	3	4	1	65
14	Jewellery	2	3	1	1	1	1	3		12
15	Base metals	14	141	1	2	3	5	9		175
16	Machinery	14	227	3	3	2	6	21	5	281
17	Automobiles	2	16					2		20
18	Photography	3	21	3				12		39
20	Misc. Mfg.	1	35		1			2	1	40
21	Works of art		1							1
	Total	84	939	39	46	33	52	161	58	1,412

Source: RIS database based on Estimation based on DGCI&S, 2019.

the middle class economy is expanding fast (Mohanty et al. 2019). With substantial income with the middle class, which can demand for quality products for their consumption. They do not discriminate between domestic or imported goods and hardly compromise with quality of products. Therefore, producers of MSME should not have different views in order to access domestic or export markets while maintaining quality of products. In the absence of quality of product, domestic protection may not be helpful in providing larger space for marketing in the domestic economy. With low-quality products, domestic producer may not access a wider market in the domestic economy. Export focus should be on quality, scale economies, and timely delivery of products. In the process of supplying to domestic market with quality products, they can access global markets. These firms in the clusters can gradually emerge as global players through global value chain.

There is a dominant view in the country that NER may not cope with the specific import demand of ASEAN countries and East Asian countries, because of supply constraints of the region. Moreover, it is a common perception that the NER countries are not sufficiently equipped with number of competitive products to access such large market. In a study, Barua and Das (2008) discussed the potential of 'Look East Policy' to create trade boom in the NER by accessing opportunities created in the expanding markets of the South East Asian and East Asian countries. Brunner (2010) observed that natural resources, economies of scale, skilled manpower, local advantages, trade enabling policies, and low transaction cost are the natural advantages of the region in trading with Bangladesh and Myanmar. Improvement in the trade-related infrastructure, customs checkpoints, use of port facilities, etc. could bring down cost of exports from NER to Bangladesh (Rahman, 2014). Recent evidences from the present study indicate that NER has as many as 836 products to export to the rest of the world including Southeast and East Asia and is exporting to all eight member states of SAARC, eight ASEAN member countries and to the rest of the world as presented in Table 3.7.

Apart from South Asia and South East Asia, the region exported to East Asia, Middle East in Asia; East Europe, West Europe, North and South Europe and entire Africa, Latin America and Caribbean, Oceania and North America in 2018. The region has the capacity to reach South

Table 3.7: Act East Policy Focus of North East States for Export: Profile of Export with the Rest of the World

State	Export Destinations			
	ASEAN	SAARC	Others	
Arunachal Pradesh	MYS	BGD, NPL, PAK, BTN	DEU, SAU, ZAF, USA, AGO, EGY, JOR, IRL, BHR, CAN, GBR	
Assam	VNM, SGP, MMR, THA, MYS, IDN, KHM	BTN, NPL, BGD, PAK, LKA, AFG, MDV,	IRN, RUS, GBR, ARE, CHN, DEU, USA, KAZ, JPN, NLD, EGY, SAU, IRQ, BFA, NER, IRL, UKR, TWN, POL, AUS, CAN, CIV, NGA, KGZ, TUR, BHR, SWE, FRA, KWT, MLI, AGO, MEX, QAT, BEL, HKG, ITA, TUN, AZE, TJK, TGO, NZL, COL, MAR, GHA, NOR, CZE, ESP, BRA, CMR, KOR, PRT, LBY, GEO, KEN, DJI, ISR, DOM, SOM, CHE, ETH, UZB, SLE, LVA, BEN, BDI, ZAF, ECU, VEN, MDG, UGA, DNK, SYC, ZMB, GRC, JOR, HUN, MUS, SWZ, TZA, DZA, SVN, BGR, FIN, BLR	
Manipur	MMR	NPL	CHN, CIV, DEU, NLD, USA, KOR, CHI, NGA, POL, GTM, SVN, GBR	
Meghalaya	THA, SGP, MMR	BGD, NPL, BTN, PAK, LKA	ARE, KOR, KWT, EGY, OMN, USA, GHA, SAU, BEL, GBR, HKG, FRA, DEU, CAN, JPN	
Mizoram	THA	BGD, NPL	USA, HKG, NLD	
Nagaland	MMR, VNM	BTN, NPL, BGD	TUN, GAB, USA, COG, ISR, GBR, JPN, AUS, ZAF, KOR, FRA, NZL, BEL, ARE, ESP	
Sikkim	THA, MYS, MMR, VNM, PHL, IDN, KHM	NPL, BTN, LKA, BGD, MDV	ARE, CZE, ZAF, TZA, DEU, LBN, USA, QAT, OMN, TUR, BHR, EGY, JAM, GTM, MUS, PER, LBY, MEX, ETH, T'TO, NGA, DNK, YEM, KEN, IRQ, FRA, UGA, CHN, ITA, KWT, ECU, COL, ZMB, TGO, SEN, NLD, JPN, BEL, BRA, GHA, SAU, GBR, MNG, SLV, MWI, FJI	
Tripura	SGP, THA	BGD, NPL, BTN	ITA, NLD, USA, FRA ISR, GBR, OMN, CHE, CHN	

Source: RIS database based on the estimate of DGCI&S database, 2019.
Note: Country code as per ISO 3166-1 alpha-3.

East Asian countries in the framework of India's 'Act East Policy'. There may be competition with the South East Asian countries for trade, but several products exported by the NER are also the products which are imported by the ASEAN countries. The region's exports have reached several ASEAN countries such as Indonesia, Malaysia, Myanmar, Thailand, Singapore, and Vietnam. The NER is yet to touch a few other member countries of the ASEAN region including Brunei and Laos.

The challenges before the NER states are not coverage of exportable products or access to the global destinations where these products are demanded. The key issues for them are: (a) scale economies, (b) managing export orders from different destinations, considering perishable nature of commodities originating from the region, (c) moving from primary to more value added products, and (d) overcoming the challenge of supply constraints of exportable products.

Studies show there has been specific support coming from the central government agencies to promote exports in the region. In this regard, Chongloi (2011) found that Export Promotion Council such as APEDA supported agricultural exports through specific schemes in the form of improving packaging of products and assistance for inland transportation of perishable products to major export centres such as Kolkata, Delhi, and Mumbai. Export of states in terms of intensity of trade and coverage of export destination varies significantly between them. These variations across individual states are presented in Figures 3.5 and 3.6.

Technology intervention is very much required to improve export capabilities of the NER states. A few states such as Arunachal Pradesh, Manipur, Meghalaya, and Tripura have exported to the United States, Latin America, Europe, East Asia, Middle East, and Africa but could not reach some of the ASEAN countries yet. Such phenomena could be difficult to explain, but further analysis is required to examine India's strategy in the light of the Act East Policy. The regional states should not only reach to all South East Asian and South Asian countries individually but also to improve their quality of products from primary to more processed ones. The regional states should evolve independent trade policies to foster their trade performances, especially in the export sector. Exports could be the key policy to support livelihood security and to eliminate poverty in these states.

Figure 3.5: NER Exporting to the World, 2018

Source: RIS database based on the estimate of DGCI&S database, 2019.

Figure 3.6: NER Exporting to the World

Source: RIS database based on the estimate of DGCI&S database, 2019.

Conclusion and Policy Recommendation

- The region contributed 3.78 per cent of India's population and 2.7 per cent of GDP. Other key indicators such as GVA and GFCF are also lagging behind as compared to the national average. Such macroeconomic imbalance has to be addressed.
- The services sector is much larger than manufacturing and agricultural sector, though forest cover is high in the region. Service sector potential in IT and ITeS, hospital, tourism, education, and repair services may be harnessed to spur development in the region.
- Industrial activities are much stronger than manufacturing activities in the region. Considering the natural potential of the region, non-manufacturing industrial activities in the industrial sector may be focused for the future growth of the region.
- The manufacturing sector has remained insignificant in the SDP of the region. Further consolidation of the manufacturing sector would put the states on a high growth trajectory.
- Most of the projects are centrally sponsored with 100 per cent financial support. Such resources do not percolated down to lower income people of these states. The system has to be made more transparent to bring equity and alleviation of poverty in the society.
- Poverty profile of the region is highly skewed. Income generation and employment creation possibilities can be achieved with radical focus on domestic market in the short run and external market in the medium term by focusing on demand pattern of middle-income group.
- Power situation in the region is better off than the rest of the country. Harnessing on its hydroelectricity potential, the region can support its industrialization process.
- The challenges of the region are profound, and a 'big bang' approach needs to be adopted to reverse the process of unabated underdevelopment.

Advantage in Agricultural Resources for Exports

- Considering topography of the region, production of food grains may not be suitable to all states. Food grain is possible mostly in plain areas such as Assam. Therefore, the region has the potentiality to boom productively in the cultivation of fruits, vegetables, plantations, roots, floriculture, spices, fisheries, meat, etc.

- As the region is the citrus depository of the country, it produces large varieties of fruits such as banana, guava, jackfruit, kiwi, lemon, litchi, orange, pineapple, plum, and strawberry which can be used in agro-processing. There are several fruits such as litchi, oranges, and other fruits produced in the region, having high share in India.

- Considering the large production base fruits, more food processing units can be launched to process these local resources efficiently for exports and also for domestic markets.

- On the basis of specialization of each state in terms of production of specific products, appropriate agro-processing centres may be created with scale economies. With appropriate support from the state, marketing mechanism for distribution of final products can be developed for the domestic economy and export markets.

- The region can be graduated to a processing hub for meat where the region commands a lead in the production of swine and cattle meat over India.

- Several states are engaged in the production of organic products as use of chemical fertilizers was low in the past. Such products are to be made SPS and TBT compliant as health consciousness is picking up in the domestic and the international markets with a definite price premium.

- Each state in the region is engaged in the production of large number of products, and each of them has acquired specialization in specific line of agricultural production. This may lead to large farming to meet the commercial needs, leading to industrialization in the rural sector.

- The states have a distinct advantage in the production of spices such as coriander, garlic, ginger, pepper, and turmeric. With agro-processing, the region can emerge as a regional spices hub in the country.
- Similarly, the region has locational competitiveness in the production of vegetables such as bitter gourd, carrot, cauliflower, cucumber, lady's finger, parwal, potato, radish, and tomato. Certain states can undertake a lead in supporting food processing to maintain scale economies in order to foster rural industrialization in certain crops.
- Each state has competitiveness in the production of selective crops, without competing much with the neighbouring states except Assam.
- Production of a specific crop is led by one or two states, thus presenting the possibility of rural industrialization through food processing activities. There is hardly any space for competition between states securing market for a crop.
- Individual states have specialized in specific products, and all states have not specialized in all products. Therefore, each state can be industrialized in agro-processing without facing the constraint of raw material shortage, thus enabling each of them to maintain scale economies in different crops, leading to exports.

Regional Spread of Clusters and Export Prospects

- Each state has to come out with its individual export strategy to transform its economy into an industrial powerhouse by making its clusters export oriented in order to move along the predetermined export path in the medium term.
- Export strategy of each state should focus on graduating from agriculture based exports to manufacturing and services based exporting economy in the medium term. Large presence of clusters in handicraft, handlooms, and industrial sectors may be used as the instrument for transformation of the NER economy.
- Each state in the region has shown its niche area of clusters specific products. With or without production integration in the specific manufacturing sector between them, each state can target at

specific sectors with scale economies for accessing domestic or export market to begin with. Subsequently, two or more states can join together for mass production for exports.

Production Capacity of Manufacturing Sector for Attaining Scale Economies

- Distribution of registered companies is highly skewed in the NER, mostly located in Assam which is followed by Nagaland and Arunachal Pradesh. Industrialization in other states should be expanded to spur growth in external and internal trade.
- The states in the NER produce wide range of products, but most of them are produced by single firm, indicating possibility of lack of scale economies in the region. Instead of promoting large firms in other sectors, there is a need for more firms in the same sector to expand scale economies with efficiency and utilization of local resources.
- Major firms are mostly concentrated around specific industries in the services sector. Certain services sectors need to be oriented for exports.

Global Competitiveness and Regional Trade

- Manufacturing exports have been concentrated in a few states where top two exporting states of the region shared 85.9 per cent and top three states shared 87.7 per cent of region's exports in 2018. Other states should be made more proactive in promoting trade. That needs a robust trade policy for each NER states based on their natural endowments.
- Share of manufacturing exports was lower than agricultural and mining sectors in the region. But more states participate in manufacturing exports than other sectors. The region has a natural tendency to engage in the manufacturing exports, and this trend needs to be promoted through state level export strategy.
- Certain states are better endowed in specific sectors than others. For example, Assam and Sikkim in agriculture; Assam and Meghalaya in mining; and Assam, Manipur, Nagaland, and Tripura in

manufacturing can specialize, based on their comparative advantage in production. Such strategic importance of individual states should be captured through trade policy.

- In the agricultural sector, fruits and vegetable sectors were the most important sector for exports for the region.
- Exports in the manufacturing sector are expected to grow in specific industries such as chemicals, textiles, footwear, cement, jewellery, base metal, machinery, precision instruments, and handicraft.
- Focus on industrialization in food and mineral processing can give a big leap to the region in export. In order to promote manufacturing sector in the export strategy, state-specific and sector-specific focus may be accorded to boost external sector performance.
- Export of the region is dominated by intermediate, semi-finished products and final consumption goods. In the export sector, the region has three broad trends: (a) the scale of trade of the region is very low, (b) the states have production and export base for several products, and (c) these products are thinly spread across states where these products can be exported to several destinations with their significant competitive strength. These concerns need to be addressed.
- The region has specialized in the exports of selected products such as fruits and vegetables, chemicals, base metals, and machinery items. Trade in such sectors to be promoted in the medium term.
- In the export of chemical products including pharmaceutical products, three states have taken the lead including Assam, Sikkim, and Manipur with considerable variations in them in the volume of exports.
- The handicraft exports are not flourishing in the North East despite having large number of clusters in the region. Handicraft sector needs to be focused to make it export oriented and to compete with neighbouring states of the region.
- With an expanding middle-income group, clusters cannot make a major headway in accessing domestic market unless quality of products is assured. Export focus should be on quality, scale economies, and timely delivery of products.
- The NER is exporting more than eight hundred products to the world including most of the countries in South Asia and Southeast Asia. The challenges before the NER states are not in respect of coverage of exportable products or access to the global destinations where these

products are demanded. The key issues for them are: (a) scale economies, (b) managing export orders from different destinations, considering perishable nature of commodities originating from the region, (c) moving from primary to more value added products, and (d) overcoming the challenge of supply constraints of exportable products.

- Exports of regional states in terms of intensity of trade and coverage of export destination vary significantly between them. Such asymmetry in exports may be addressed through evolving robust independent trade policies for each state.

- The NER region has export competitiveness for around four hundred products at the HS Sub-heading level, but distribution of competitive products varies significantly across individual states.

- Around sixty items are exported by two or more states. This shows lack of scale factor in export pattern of the region.

- The NER states demonstrated deterioration in the business environment in the regional states despite India's major strides in this area. To reverse the situation in the states, a thorough homework is needed to liberalize the policy environment to push the trade agenda and facilitating access to FDI by individual states.

Appendix

Table A: Number of Corporate Sector Firms in the Northeast Region (Number)

State	Number of Firms
Assam	282
Meghalaya	52
Nagaland	10
Arunachal Pradesh	10
Tripura	7
Manipur	5
Mizoram	3
Sikkim	1
NER	370

Source: Ministry of Corporate Affairs, Government of India.

Table B: Tax Sources Situations in Indian States, 2017

States	Own Tax (₹ Bn)	Non-Tax (₹ Bn)	Total Tax (₹ Bn)	Tax/GSDP Ratio
Andhra Pradesh	527.2	39.9	567.1	7.1
Arunachal Pradesh	7.5	7	14.5	7.2
Assam	97.7	64.1	161.8	6.4
Bihar	320	28.6	348.6	7.1
Chhattisgarh	202	77.2	279.2	9.6
Delhi	366	8	374	5.5
Goa	48.5	28.6	77.1	12.3
Gujarat	779.7	170	949.7	8.2
Haryana	446.9	109.8	556.7	10.2
Himachal Pradesh	73.8	21.4	95.2	7.0
Jammu and Kashmir	101.4	53.9	155.3	12.2
Jharkhand	184	112.6	296.6	11.6
Karnataka	855.9	68.3	924.2	7.0
Kerala	488.2	117.3	605.5	9.7
Madhya Pradesh	463.4	95.2	558.6	8.6
Maharashtra	1,649.8	216.7	1,866.5	7.5
Manipur	6.4	2.5	8.9	4.2
Meghalaya	15.6	5.1	20.7	6.9
Mizoram	4.8	3.2	8	4.5
Nagaland	5.7	2.9	8.6	4.0
Odisha	265.2	90	355.2	8.5
Puducherry	27.2	14.2	41.4	12.8
Punjab	354.9	51	405.9	9.5
Rajasthan	518.2	166.6	684.8	8.1
Sikkim	7	4.7	11.7	5.3
Tamil Nadu	912.8	107.7	1,020.5	7.2
Telangana	613.7	66	679.7	9.0
Tripura	14.7	4.4	19.1	5.6
Uttar Pradesh	949.6	175	1,124.6	8.2
Uttarakhand	134.5	24.8	159.3	7.4
West Bengal	454.8	31.7	486.5	4.8

Source: RIS estimate based on Handbook of Statistics for Indian States, RBI, 2019.

Table C: Major Cluster Categories and Sectors in the North East (Number of Clusters)

Row Labels	AP	Assam	Manipur	Meghalaya	Mizoram	Nagaland	Sikkim	Tripura	NER
Handicraft	39	63	47	16	6	26	10	80	287
Applique			1						1
Basketry, Mat Weaving & Cane Articles	10	38	23	9	5	15	4	40	144
Carpet and Durries	6	1	1				3		11
Earthenware								5	5
Folk Painting							1	2	3
Forest based			1			1			2
Horn & Bone		1							1
Jewellery	3		2						5
Leather				1				4	5
Metalware	10	3	4					2	19
Natural Fibre		4							4
Pottery & Clay	1		2	1		1			5
Stoneware			1	1					2
Textiles	2	12	10	1		4	2	19	50
Toys & Dolls		1	1						2
Woodwork	7	3	1	3	1	5		8	28

(continued)

Table C: *Continued*

Row Labels	AP	Assam	Manipur	Meghalaya	Mizoram	Nagaland	Sikkim	Tripura	NER
Handloom	3	7	4	1	2	4	1	3	25
Industrial		4	3	2		1		5	15
Food Products		3	2	1		1		1	8
Leather and Leather and Fur Products				1					1
Non-metallic Mineral Products								1	1
Paper Products and Printing								1	1
Textiles Products (Wearing Apparel)		1	1					1	3
Wood and Wood Products								1	1
Others								6	6
Grand Total	42	74	54	19	8	31	11	94	333

Source: RIS database based on RIS All India Survey of Clusters, 2019.

Table D: Distribution of Organized Sector Firms in North East: 2014–15 (Number)

NIC08 Industries	AP	Assam	Manipur	Meghalaya	Mizoram	Nagaland	Sikkim	Tripura	NER
Agriculture	0	3	0	1	0	0	0	0	4
Mining	0	1	0	2	0	0	0	0	3
Manufacturing	6	114	2	32	0	4	0	2	160
10. Biscuits		3							3
10. Mustard oil		3							3
10. Tea, processed	1	30						1	31
16. Plywood		4				2			7
19. Petroleum coke		3							3
23. Cement		8		11					19
24. Ferro silicon	1			3					4
32. Misc. manufactured art.	2	13	1	5					21
Others	2	50	1	13	0	2	0	1	69
Electricity & gas	1	9	0	6	1	0	0	2	19
34. Diversified		3							3
35. Conventional electricity		1		4	1				5
Other manufacturing		5	0	2	1	0	0	2	11
Construction	1	16	0	0	2	1	0	1	21
41. Real estate		4			1				5
42. Construction		6			1	1			8

(continued)

Table D: *Continued*

NIC08 Industries	AP	Assam	Manipur	Meghalaya	Mizoram	Nagaland	Sikkim	Tripura	NER
42. Construction of other industrial plants		3							3
Other construction	1	3	0	0	0	0	0	1	5
Services	2	143	3	14	0	5	1	2	170
46. Wholesale trade in agri.		3		1					4
46. Wholesale trade in coal		4		1					5
46. Wholesale trade in misc. mnf.		16		3					19
64. Financial services, leasing		16		2		2			20
64. Fund based financial ser.		18		1		1		1	22
64. Non-banking financial services		10	1						11
64. Other asset financing services		4							4
64. Securities investment services		19		3		1	1		24
77. Renting services		8		2					10
86. Hospitals, health care centres, etc.		4							4
Other services	2	41	1	1	0	1	0	1	47
Grand Total	10	282	5	52	3	10	1	7	370

Source: RIS database based on Prowess, CMIE Online, Extracted on 25 September 2019.

Table E: Engagement of Multiple NER States in Exports of Specific Products: Comparison between State Export Prices with Overall Export Prices of India

HS	Description	AP	Assam	Manipur	Meghalaya	Mizoram	Nagaland	Sikkim	Tripura	NER
030289	Fish, fresh, or chilled	Comp	Comp			Comp		Comp	Comp	4
070200	Vegetables; tomatoes, fresh, or chilled	Comp	Uncomp	Uncomp	Comp	Comp	Comp	Comp	Comp	6
070310	Vegetables, onions, fresh, or chilled	Uncomp	Uncomp	Comp			Comp	Comp	Comp	4
070999	Vegetables, fresh, or chilled	Comp	Comp	Comp		Comp	Comp	Comp	Comp	7
080430	Fruit, pineapples, fresh, or dried	Comp	Comp	Comp		Comp	Comp	Comp		6
081090	Fruit, fresh	Comp	Comp		Comp	Comp		Comp		5
100610	Cereals; rice in the husk (paddy or rough)	Comp	Comp	Comp				Comp	Uncomp	4
100630	Rice, semi-milled or wholly milled	Uncomp	Comp		Comp		Comp	Comp	Comp	5
100810	Cereals; buckwheat	Comp	Comp				Comp	Comp	Comp	4
120991	Vegetable seeds, used for sowing	Comp				Comp		Comp	Comp	3
140490	Other vegetable products	Comp	Comp			Comp				3
262190	Slag and ash	Comp	Uncomp			Comp		Comp		3
271119	Petroleum gases and other liquefied gas	Comp	Comp					Comp		3
284440	Radioactive elements, isotopes	Comp	Comp			Comp			Comp	3
390920	Amino-resins; melamine resins, in primary	Comp			Comp		Comp	Comp		4
482190	Paper and paperboard, unprinted	Comp	Comp						Comp	3
611490	Garments; of textile materials, knitted	Comp						Comp	Comp	3
630492	Furnishing articles; of cotton, not knitted			Comp		Uncomp	Comp			3
710239	Diamonds; non-industrial	Comp	Comp		Comp	Comp		Comp		4
854442	Insulated electric conductors	Comp	Comp		Comp			Comp		3

Source: RIS database based on RIS estimate based on DGCI&S database, 2019.

Annex A: Distribution of Organized Sector Firms in NER: 2014–15 (Number)

NIC08 Industries	AP	Assam	Manipur	Meghalaya	Mizoram	Nagaland	Sikkim	Tripura	NER
01. Plants	1			1					2
01. Tea		1							1
01. Tobacco for mfg. cigars, cheroots		1							1
05. Coal				1					1
06. Crude oil		1							1
08. Limestone				1					1
10. Biscuits	3								3
10. Fish		1							1
10. Ghee		1							1
10. Infant milk foods		1							1
10. Maida		1							1
10. Mustard oil		3							3
10. Oil cakes, meals, and animal feeds		1							1
10. Sugar		1							1
10. Tea, processed		30						1	31
11. Beer		1							1
13. Cotton fabrics		1							1
13. Cotton yarn		1							1
13. Jute textiles								1	1
13. Other coated/laminated textile fabrics		1							1

Item						Total
13. Textiles	1					1
16. Other wood products	1					1
16. Plywood	4	1	2			7
16. Railway sleepers	1					1
17. Bobbins, spools, cops, etc.	1					1
17. Paper products	1					1
17. Writing, printing paper			1			1
19. Hard coke	1					1
19. Light distillates	2					2
19. Petroleum coke	3					3
20. Acrylic filament yarn (AFY)	1					1
20. Ethanolamines	1					1
20. High density polyethylene	1					1
20. Hydrogen, rare & other gases	1					1
20. Methanol (formaldehyde)	1					1
20. Other synthetic filament yarns	1					1
20. Sandal wood oil				1		1
20. Soap	1					1
20. Tooth brush	1					1
20. Urea	1					1
21. Ayurvedic & unani medicaments	1					1
21. Drug formulations					1	1
22. Plastic film	1					1

(continued)

Annex A: *Continued*

NIC08 Industries	AP	Assam	Manipur	Meghalaya	Mizoram	Nagaland	Sikkim	Tripura	NER
22. Plastic laminated sheets		1							1
22. Plastic tubes		1							1
22. Reservoirs, tanks, etc.		1							1
22. Sheets, films, etc. of plastic, not reinforced		1							1
22. Tableware, kitchenware, other household articles		1							1
23. Ordinary Portland cement		2							2
23. Asbestos-cement products		1							1
23. Cement		8		11					19
23. Cement clinker				2					2
23. Cement pipes	1								1
23. Ordinary Portland cement				1					1
23. Portland slag cement		1							1
24. Bars & rods		2							2
24. Bars & rods				1					1
24. Clad, plated, or coated flat rolled products				1					1
24. Ferro manganese		1							1
24. Ferro silicon	1			3					4
24. Finished steel (non-alloy steel)	1								1
24. Iron & steel				1					1

24. Semi-finished steel		1				2
24. Stainless steel angles, shapes & sections		1				1
24. Tubes & pipes						1
25. Articles of iron & steel						1
25. Sheet piling of iron & steel						1
26. Clocks & watches			1			1
27. Electrical machinery other than electronics		1				1
27. Transformers				1		
32. Misc. manufactured articles	2	13	1	5		21
34. Diversified		3				3
34. Diversified manufacturing		1				1
35. Biomass-based electricity		1				1
35. Conventional electricity		1	4			5
35. Gas-based thermal electricity					1	1
35. Hydroelectricity	1	1				2
35. Power distribution services		1				1
35. Power transmission services		1			1	2
35. Thermal electricity		1	1			3
41. Real estate		4	1			5
42. Infrastructure construction		2				2
42. Construction		6	1	1		8
42. Construction of other industrial plants		3				3

(continued)

Annex A: *Continued*

NIC08 Industries	AP	Assam	Manipur	Meghalaya	Mizoram	Nagaland	Sikkim	Tripura	NER
42. Construction of roads, bridges, tunnels, etc.		1							1
42. Infrastructure construction								1	1
42. Other infrastructure construction	1								1
45. Wholesale trade in automobiles		1							1
46. Wholesale trade in manufactured products		2							2
46. Commission agents services		1							1
46. Non-financial services		2							2
46. Trade & commissioning agents' services		1							1
46. Wholesale trade in agricultural crops		3		1					4
46. Wholesale trade in apparels (readymade garments)		1							1
46. Wholesale trade in cement, asbestos, abrasives, etc.		2							2
46. Wholesale trade in coal, lignite and peat		4		1					5
46. Wholesale trade in computer systems and peripherals	1								1
46. Wholesale trade in drugs, medicines & allied products		1							1
46. Wholesale trade in fertilizers		1							1

46. Wholesale trade in finished steel (alloy and non-alloy)		1				1
46. Wholesale trade in food & agro-based products		1				1
46. Wholesale trade in miscellaneous manufactured articles		16	3			19
46. Wholesale trade in non-metallic mineral products				1		1
46. Wholesale trade in power & electricity					1	1
46. Wholesale trade in stones, nec		1				1
46. Wholesale trade in tea		1				1
46. Wholesale trade in textiles & apparels		2	1			3
46. Wholesale trade in wood products		1				1
47. Retail trade		1				1
47. Retail trade in agricultural crops		1				1
49. Gas pipeline		1				1
49. Road freight transport services		1				1
50. Shipping services		1				1
52. NG storage & distribution services		1				1
52. Storage, warehousing & distribution services		1				1
55. Hotels, resorts & restaurants	1	2				3
58. Newspapers, journals, & periodicals		1				1

(continued)

Annex A: *Continued*

NIC08 Industries	AP	Assam	Manipur	Meghalaya	Mizoram	Nagaland	Sikkim	Tripura	NER
61. Cable television broadcasting media	1								1
62. Software services	1								1
64. Banking services	1								1
64. Financial services including leasing		16		2		2			20
64. Fund based financial services		18		1		1		1	22
64. Housing finance services			1						1
64. Non-banking financial services		10	1						11
64. Other asset financing services		4							4
64. Securities investment services		19		3		1	1		24
66. Development financing services		2							2
66. Financial consultancy & advisory services		1							1
71. Technical consultancy & engineering services	1								1
77. Renting services		8		2					10
79. Travel agencies and tour operators		1							1
82. Other business services		1							1
85. Education		2							2
86. Hospitals, health care centres, etc.		4							4
86. Medical & health services		1							1
Grand Total	10	282	5	52	3	10	1	7	370

Source: RIS database based on Prowess, CMIE Online, Extracted on 25 September 2019.

Annex B: NER Exports to World in HS Chapters, 2018 (in Number of HS Lines)

Sec/Chp	Description	AP	Assam	Manipur	Meghalya	Mizoram	Nagaland	Sikkim	Tripura	NER
1	**Live animals and animal products**	1	8		1	1	2	2	2	17
2	Meat and edible meat offal						2			2
3	Fish & crustaceans, molluscs	1	5		1	1		2	2	12
4	Diary produce: birds, eggs		3							3
2	**Vegetable products**	18	82	7	13	13	12	19	16	180
6	Live trees and other plants bulb				1	1			1	2
7	Edible vegetables & certain roots	5	26	4	1	3	4	5	6	54
8	Edible fruits & nuts: peel or melon	7	14	1	4	4	2	6	1	39
9	Coffee, tea, mate, and spices	1	28	1	6	1	4	3	2	46
10	Cereals	3	7	1	1	1	2	4	4	23
12	Oil seeds and oleaginous fruits	1	3		1	1		1	2	9
14	Vegetable plaiting materials	1	4			2				7
3	**Animal or vegetable fats & oils**		2							2
15	Animal or vegetable fats & oils		2							2
4	**Prepared foodstuff, beverages, etc.**		31	1	1			8	1	42
17	Sugars and sugar confectionery		3	1				1		5
19	Prep. of cereals, floor, starch, etc.		10					1		11
20	Prep. of vegetables, fruit, nuts, etc.		7					1	1	9

(continued)

Annex B: *Continued*

Sec/Chp	Description	AP	Assam	Manipur	Meghalya	Mizoram	Nagaland	Sikkim	Tripura	NER
21	Miscellaneous edible preparations		8					3		11
22	Beverages, spirit & vinegar		2		1			1		4
23	Residues & waste from food industries		1					1		2
5	**Mineral products**	**10**	**39**	**6**	**14**	**6**	**6**	**13**	**4**	**98**
25	Salt, sulphur, earths & stone plaster, etc.	3	13	2	8	1	2	3	1	33
26	Ores, slag and ash	1	2			1	1	1		6
27	Mineral fuels mineral oils and products	6	24	4	6	4	3	9	3	59
6	**Products of chemicals**	**3**	**104**	**9**	**1**	**1**		**24**	**1**	**143**
28	Inorganic chemicals compounds, etc.	1	5	2	1	1			1	11
29	Organic chemicals		5	1				2		8
30	Pharmaceutical products		15	3				19		37
31	Fertilizers		1							1
32	Tanning or dyeing extracts		14	3						17
33	Essential oils and resinoids	1	27					2		30
34	Soap, organic surface active agents, etc.		17							17
35	Albuminoidal substance; modified		3							3
36	Explosives: pyrotechnic products		1							1
38	Miscellaneous chemical products	1	16					1		18
7	**Plastics & articles thereof**	**1**	**87**		**1**		**1**	**14**	**7**	**111**
39	Plastics and articles thereof	1	42		1		1	11	3	59

Code										Total
40	Rubber and articles thereof		45						3	4	52
8	Raw hides & skins, leather, etc.		6						1		7
42	Articles of leather, saddlery & ham		6						1		7
9	Wood & articles of wood	1	19				2	2	1		25
44	Wood & articles of wood	1	16				1	2	1		21
46	Manufactures of straw, of esparto, etc.		3				1				4
10	Pulp of wood or of other fibers	2	17			1		4	1		25
48	Paper and paperboard	1	15			1		4	1		22
49	Printed books, newspapers, pictures	1	2								3
11	Textile & textile articles	9	42	7	4	4	12	22	18		118
50	Silk		6								6
52	Cotton	1	3			1	1				6
53	Other vegetable textile fibers; paper	1	3		1	1	1	1			8
54	Man-made filaments		1								1
55	Man-made staple fibres		2				1				3
56	Wadding, felt and non-wovens; special		3								3
57	Carpets & other textile floor covering							1			1
58	Special woven fabrics; tufted textile							2			2
59	Impregnated, coated, textile fabrics		1		3						4
61	Articles of apparel & clothing knitted	2	3	7			3	11	18		44
62	Articles of apparel & clothing not knitted		9			1	2	4			16

(continued)

Annex B: *Continued*

Sec/Chp	Description	AP	Assam	Manipur	Meghalya	Mizoram	Nagaland	Sikkim	Tripura	NER
63	Other made up textile articles		11	2		1	8	2		24
12	**Footwear, headgear, and umbrella**		9				1			11
64	Footwear, gaiters & like; parts of article		6							7
65	Headgear & parts thereof		3							3
67	Prepared feathers & down & articles						1			1
13	**Articles of stone, plaster, cement**	2	49	1	3	2	3	4	1	65
68	Articles of stone, plaster, cement, etc.		28		1	1	1	1	1	33
69	Ceramic products	2	11	1	2	1	2	3		22
70	Glass and glassware		10							10
14	**Natural or cultured pearls, jewellery**	2	3	1	1	1	1	3		12
71	Natural or cultured pearls, Jewellery	2	3	1	1	1	1	3		12
15	**Base metals & articles of base metal**	14	141	1	2	3	5	9		175
72	Iron and steel	2	41		2	1				46
73	Articles of Iron or steel	3	52	1		1	5	5		67
74	Cooper and articles thereof		3							3
76	Aluminium and articles thereof		5					2		7
82	Tools, implements, cutlery, spoon, etc.	8	23					1		32
83	Miscellaneous articles of base metal	1	17			1		1		20
16	**Machinery & mechanical appliances**	14	227	3	3	2	6	21	5	281
84	Nuclear reactors, boilers, machinery	11	136	1		2	3	10	5	168

Code	Description									
85	Electrical machinery, equipments, & parts	3	91	2	3		3	11		113
17	**Vehicles, aircraft, and vessels**	2	16					2		**20**
86	Railway or tramway locomotives		1							1
87	Vehicles other than railway or tram	1	15					2		18
88	Aircraft, spacecraft and parts therof	1								1
18	**Optical, photograph, & cinematography**	3	21	3				12		**39**
90	Optical, photographic, cinematograph, etc.	3	21	3				11		38
92	Musical instruments; parts & access		1							1
20	**Miscellaneous manufactured articles**	1	35		1			2	1	**40**
94	Furniture; bedding, mattresses	1	12					2		15
95	Toys, games, & sports, requisite		6							6
96	Miscellaneous manufactured articles		17		1				1	19
21	**Works of art collectors' pieces**		1							1
97	Works of art, collectors' pieces		1							1
Total		84	939	39	46	33	52	161	58	1,412

Source: RIS database based on India's Trade, DGCI&S, Kolkota, 2019.

4

Climate Adaptive Agriculture and Diversification

Introduction

As we discussed earlier, agriculture has a preeminent position in the states of North East. There is hardly any agricultural produce in the non-food grain category, where the North Eastern Region (NER) is not engaged in production. However, considerable level of disparities exists among regional states in terms of agriculture production. Because of the particular topography of the region, cultivation of fruits, vegetables, plantations, spices, fisheries, meat, etc. is of considerable importance for the region. There are a number of products such as pineapple, kiwi, and a large number of non-timber forest produce (NTFPs) or Minor Forest Produces (MFPs) such as Sugandhmantri tubers, Sonpatha, cinnamon/tejpat, which are majorly produced in the region. The region also has a large forest cover (one fourth of all India) and is part of two out of four biodiversity hotspots of the country. The region also serves as catchment area for major inland water bodies. It has high ecological fragility, and the intricate interdependence among agriculture, livestock, forestry, and natural resources such as water which is of immense significance for sustainable economic growth. Agriculture in the region faces multiple challenges due to its geographical characteristics and remoteness; in addition, the influence of climate change has implication for long-term economic benefits and livelihoods. It is important that a comprehensive strategy for the sector is adopted allowing for state-level variations towards climate adaptability, even as specific interventions are made for value addition, processing, and exports.

The agricultural sector in the NER, however, is a composite mix of paradoxes. While the region accounts for a large chunk of India's forestry

Rise of the North East, RIS, Oxford University Press. © Research and Information System for Developing Countries 2023.
DOI: 10.1093/oso/9780192849342.003.0004

resources, a considerable amount of such land is also used for shifting cultivation, especially devoted to paddy-based subsistence monocropping. Even though the average cropping intensity in the eight states together at 139.07 compares favourably with the national average of 141.55, states such as Manipur and Mizoram buck the trend and record cropping intensities of 100, indicating total monocropping. Incidentally, both these states engage in shifting cultivation to a considerable extent as indicated by the 2015–16 data made available by Bhuvan, the geo portal maintained by Indian Space Research Organization. On the other hand, Tripura (189.41) and Sikkim (176.62) exhibit a high degree of intensive agriculture, with very insignificant area under shifting cultivation. The rest of the states lie in between in terms of their recorded cropping intensities, with Assam's cropping intensity higher than the national average and states such as Arunachal Pradesh, Meghalaya, and Nagaland lower than the said average.

It may be noted that out of the 169 targets under the 17 Sustainable Development Goals (SDGs), one target is fully devoted to sustainable agriculture practices. SDG target 2.4 calls for actions from the national governments and other stakeholders including sub-national governments and local governments to ensure full implementation of sustainable food production systems and implement resilient agricultural practices that increase productivity and production and help maintaining ecosystems and strengthening capacity for adaptation to climate change, extreme weather, drought, flooding, and other disasters. The policies, strategies, and actions need appropriate reorientation in the light of ongoing and deepening adverse impact of climate change and its consequences. Climate change severely affects food and nutrition security, soil, and water management— impacting livelihood security. The North East Region is more vulnerable to climate change due to its fragile geology, high and skewed rainfall, necessitating forward-looking climate mitigation and adaptation initiatives.

Agriculture Resource-Based Development in the North East

The pace of expansion in Gross State Domestic Product (GSDP) is equally evident in the agriculture sector, where the total quantum of agriculture and allied activities, as a share in all India average, has hovered around

Table 4.1: State-wise Share of Agriculture and Allied Activities in North-Eastern Area (Per cent)

	2012–13	2013–14	2014–15	2015–16	2016–17	2017–18
Arunachal Pradesh	8.48	8.67	8.89	8.24	6.63	6.51
Assam	59.58	56.79	54.39	55.82	55.71	54.89
Manipur	4.97	5.12	4.87	4.47	4.63	4.81
Meghalaya	5.65	5.77	6.21	5.85	5.93	5.71
Mizoram	2.60	2.80	5.41	5.44	5.60	5.55
Nagaland	7.12	7.70	7.49	6.81	7.27	7.05
Sikkim	1.70	1.72	1.66	1.68	1.78	1.98
Tripura	9.89	11.42	11.08	11.69	12.39	13.51
North Eastern Region	17.69	18.56	18.68	19.67	18.56	18.73
Share of NER in All India	3.65	3.52	3.76	3.81	3.66	3.64

Note: Data have been restricted till 2017–18 as for most states data for 2018–19 is not available yet.
Source: NSO.

4 per cent. Within the NE States, Assam is the dominant player in the agricultural sector with 55 per cent of the total share in NER in 2017–18. This is followed by Tripura with 14 per cent; Arunachal Pradesh with 7 per cent; Nagaland with 7 per cent; Meghalaya with 6 per cent; Manipur with 5 per cent; Mizoram with 6 per cent; and Sikkim with 2 per cent. Table 4.1 clearly shows that over the years, dominance of Assam in the total share has declined from 60 per cent to 55 per cent which is being captured by Tripura which has gone up from 9 per cent to 14 per cent. However, contributions from all other states have largely remained at the same level in past six years.

Within the production pattern of agriculture crops, the latest data for 2016–17 show that NE region accounts for 3 per cent share in the total national production of food grains and 1.21 per cent in the total national oilseed production. Within this, rice accounts for almost 6 per cent in the total national production, while the share of jute is around 9 per cent. As Table 4.2 shows, the share of wheat, pulses, coarse cereals, and sugarcane is extremely limited. Rice is a major crop in Assam and Tripura, and jute is a crop widely linked with economic sectors across states of Assam (with largest production of 824 thousand bales) followed by Meghalaya with

Table 4.2: Production of Principal Crops in North Eastern Region 2016–17 (in '000 Tonnes)

State	Rice	Wheat	Coarse Cereals	Pulses	Total Food Grains	Total Oilseeds	Sugarcane	Jute*
2016–17								
Arunachal Pradesh	220	7.7	102.5	13.1	343.3	36.6	37.3	0
	(3.23)	(17.23)	(18.46)	(5.44)	(4.49)	(9.67)	(1.98)	
Assam	4,727.4	23.5	94.1	107.5	4,952.5	204.3	1,207.2	824.1
	(69.38)	(52.57)	(16.94)	(44.66)	(64.70)	(53.99)	(64.22)	(87.95)
Manipur	430.4	5.6	58.8	30.3	525.1	32.3	348	–
	(6.32)	(12.53)	(10.59)	(12.59)	(6.86)	(8.54)	(18.51)	
Meghalaya	203	0.9	44.4	11.8	260	14.9	0.4	94.7
	(2.98)	(2.01)	(7.99)	(4.90)	(3.40)	(3.94)	(0.02)	(10.11)
Mizoram	61.5	–	8.9	4.8	75.2	2.5	50.5	–
	(0.90)		(1.60)	(1.99)	(0.98)	(0.66)	(2.69)	
Nagaland	336.7	6.2	149.5	44.5	536.9	68.9	192.4	7.9
	(4.94)	(13.87)	(26.92)	(18.49)	(7.01)	(18.21)	(10.23)	(0.84)
Sikkim	19.7	0.3	75.9	5.5	101.4	6.4	–	–
	(0.29)	(0.67)	(13.67)	(2.29)	(1.32)	(1.69)		
Tripura	814.6	0.5	21.3	23.2	859.6	12.5	44.1	10.3
	(11.96)	(1.12)	(3.84)	(9.64)	(11.23)	(3.30)	(2.35)	(1.10)
N E Region	6,813.3	44.7	555.4	240.7	7,654	378.4	1,879.9	937
	(6.21)	(0.05)	(1.27)	(1.04)	(3.04)	(1.21)	(0.61)	(8.55)
All India	109,698.4	98,510.2	43,772.1	23,130.9	251,541.6	31,275.6	306,069	10,962.4

Source: RBI.

95 thousand bales. Tripura produces 10,000 bales followed by Nagaland, which produces 8,000 bales.

The focus of the chapter is to examine the potential of the regional states in agricultural and non-agricultural products. In the context of North East and rest of India, we have considered seventy-one agricultural crops for comparison of the region's production profile with that of the rest of India, particularly, in major crop categories such as food grains (3), fruits (25), live stocks (9), plantation (3), spices (8), and vegetables (23).[1] For exports, scale economies are important, depending much on local production to feed into the export system. As discussed earlier, population of the NER is 3.78 per cent of India's total population. We have considered those products where the region's production share is 4 per cent or more than that of India in 2015 as shown in Table 4.3. It provides the region's product-wise share in the country where the production share for each of these products is 4 per cent or more at any point of time during the period of 2005–15. The purpose of the analysis is to examine scale economies in the production of different products in the region.

To a large extent, the agricultural activities in the states are of a subsistence nature, and the products are mostly organic by default. This will be evident from the fact that use of chemical fertilizers in this region has been estimated to be 61.77 kg per hectare compared to a country-level average of 128.02 kg/hectare (Agricultural Statistics at a Glance, 2018: 318). According to Roy et al. (2015), the indigenous plough is still the main farm-level implement (95.7 per cent), while irrigation covers only 11 per cent of net sown area. Area under high-yielding variety (HYV) paddy is 9.50 lakh ha (35 per cent). The HYV seed replacement rate is extremely low, and 4.31 lakh farmers possess Kisan Credit Cards. Such subsistence practices cast a doubt about the sustainability of the livelihood of the population of the region under review. That concern is further evident from Nair et al. (2013) who estimated the extent of poverty across the seventy-two districts of NER and found that many of them exhibit significant incidence of poverty. Any effort towards achievement of SDGs would require consideration of strategies that can create sustainable livelihood opportunities in this region. Mission Organic Value Chain Development for North Eastern Regions (MOVCDNER) can be an effective vehicle to create a roadmap to move in the desired direction. It is evident from Table 4.2 that the region commands comparative advantage in production of rice among the varieties of crops under food grains.

Fruits: In fruits (Tables 4.3 and 4.4), the region is traditionally better placed in the production of banana, guava, jackfruit, kiwi, lemon, litchi, orange, pineapple, plum, and strawberry. The region is the citrus depository of the country, producing large numbers of fruits and vegetables (Deka et al 2012). In terms of the domestic share, the region had a very large segment of production in specific fruits such as kiwi (96.7 per cent), pineapple (47.6 per cent), strawberry (40.3 per cent), and jackfruit (28.5 per cent) in 2015. The region is persistently maintaining very high share of these crops for the past several years. The region represents the diversity of major fruits and vegetables (De, 2018). The region maintains high share in the production of several other fruit crops such as litchi, oranges, and other fruits in the country. There is high demand for these fruits in the domestic market and also in a number of export destinations. More food processing units can be launched to process these local resources efficiently for exports and also for domestic markets.

Research and Development: Assam Agricultural University (AAU), Jorhat

Rice being the staple crop, much emphasis was given to close the technological gap in rice cultivation in Assam during the past five decades through extensive research on plant breeding and genetics. AAU developed 113 crop varieties along with two animal varieties and one poultry breed with desirable traits catering to the needs of diverse farming communities which were adaptable to the six agroclimatic situations of the state with several in the pipeline for release or notification. Out of the total AAU-bred crop varieties, fifty-five varieties belong to rice, seven each to green gram and black gram, two each to lentil, sesame, jute, and forage, eight each to toria and sugarcane, and as many as twenty vegetables. This may have important implications.

Source: Assam Agricultural University.

Meat: Meat production share of the region is relatively very high. The NER is a major producer and consumer of swine meat. Its relative position in the production of swine meat has been much higher than that of the rest of India. Similar is the case in the production of cattle meat. In 2015, the production share of the region in the country was 18.6 per cent in the production of bovine meat. There is a large potential in the production of poultry meat in the region (Tables 4.3 and 4.4)

Vegetables: In the production of vegetables, the region carves out a special place in the country. Production of cabbage and radish from the region contributed more than one-tenth of country's production in 2015. Several other vegetable products shared significant proportion of the total production in the country, and some of these vegetables were bitter gourd, carrot, cucumber, mushroom, and parwal (pointed gourd). There were a few other vegetable products such as bottle gourd, capsicum, cauliflower, sitaphal (pumpkin), and sweet potato, which were important for the region's production of vegetables. Production profile of agricultural products in the state demonstrates that the region is well placed in the production of several agricultural commodities without the use of chemical fertilizers. With more state incentives and appropriate marketing outlet including exports, the region can achieve greater heights in producing organic products. Such products and their processed derivatives can be of great support to India's expanding domestic market, increasing urge for indigenization of import and intensifying supply base for promoting export in the medium term (Tables 4.3 and 4.4).

Spices: Production of spices is a major distinction of the region where the region has specialized in a number of spices with strong aromatic qualities. Not the quality of the products but also the scale of production of such products has been substantial as compared to rest of the country. Among the major spices produced in the region, crops such as large cardamom, chilies, cinnamon/tejpat, coriander, garlic, ginger, pepper, and turmeric are important. The region produced 99.4 per cent of cinnamon/tejpat, 39.5 per cent of ginger, and almost 100 per cent of cardamom in the country in 2015. Production shares of other spices such as coriander, turmeric, chillies, and pepper are significant in the country. In the plantation sector, the region produced almost one-fifth of country's total areca nut in the aforesaid year (Tables 4.3 and 4.4).

Table 4.3: The North East as a Leading Agricultural Producing Region: Production of Selected Products (%, Share of NER in India)

Sector/Product	2005	2006	2007	2008	2009	2010	2011	2012	2013	2014	2015
Agriculture											
Rice	4.0	3.2	3.6	4.2	5.1	4.9	4.3	4.9	4.5	4.9	4.9
Fruits											
Banana	4.2	4.3	4.1	4.7	5.0	3.8	4.7	5.2	4.9	5.0	5.2
Guava	4.6	4.4	4.2	3.6	3.6	4.2	4.1	3.5	2.6	2.4	2.7
Jackfruit							43.4	42.2	31.7	24.0	28.5
Kiwi							97.3	92.2	98.5	96.8	96.7
Lemon							7.9	8.9	7.8	7.7	9.8
Litchi	12.6	11.9	11.6	11.7	11.7	11.8	11.1	12.3	12.5	14.1	13.4
Mandarin (M. Orange, Kinnow, Orange)							8.5	13.3	12.1	11.4	15.9
Other citrus	4.5	5.1	4.8	4.3	5.3	6.8	22.2	16.2	20.0	26.2	1.0
Other fruits				7.0			0.2	3.9	5.3	10.8	12.0
Pineapple	39.1	39.6	42.9	45.4	48.4	47.3	53.4	53.6	54.5	48.3	47.6
Plum							1.5	4.2	6.0	6.7	3.8
Strawberry							0.0	74.8	47.2	22.4	40.3
Live stocks											
Cattle meat			21.6	25.5	29.9	31.1	23.2	20.5	15.9		18.6
Poultry meat			1.4	1.6	1.4	1.5	1.4	25.3	2.1		1.5
Swine meat			14.3	19.6	19.7	17.5	19.9	18.8	23.3		19.7
Plantations											
Areca nut							18.2	17.5	18.2	15.5	18.0

Spices											
Cardamom							31.7	29.0	24.4	22.9	22.9
Chillies							6.1	3.0	2.6	2.6	6.4
Cinnamon/Tejpat							99.2	99.0	99.0	99.0	99.4
Coriander							8.5	9.5	17.0	11.7	9.5
Garlic							5.6	5.5	5.6	5.0	5.0
Ginger							48.7	55.4	56.5	54.0	39.5
Pepper							5.9	5.0	5.5	4.7	6.4
Turmeric							6.6	8.2	6.5	10.3	10.8
Vegetables											
Bitter gourd							9.4	9.0	10.8	11.1	8.2
Bottle gourd							2.3	2.2	2.6	5.5	4.4
Cabbage	0.6	1.4	1.5	10.1	10.8	10.0	10.2	9.9	12.0	13.1	13.4
Capsicum							5.5	4.5	4.5	6.5	4.1
Carrot							7.4	7.6	9.5	10.9	8.0
Cauliflower	0.2	0.7	0.8	5.0	0.8	5.8	6.2	7.4	6.0	8.3	7.1
Cucumber							12.3	13.7	13.6	15.1	8.6
Mushroom									35.4	11.8	7.6
Parwal/Pointed gourd							0.0	2.3	3.1	1.7	8.8
Radish							10.9	10.9	11.7	16.4	11.1
Sitaphal/Pumpkin							3.2	7.8	9.2	3.5	2.6
Sweet potato	5.1	4.5	4.4	4.6	4.9	5.3	5.7	6.4	6.5	6.0	4.2
Tomato	0.1	0.4	0.5	3.2	3.6	2.8	2.7	2.8	3.1	3.6	3.2

Source: RIS database based on APEDA.

State-Specific Products: It is important to understand how regional states are placed in the production of agricultural commodities and whether these states have developed any specialization in the production of various agro-products. State-wise performance of the NER in different agricultural products is presented in Table 4.2. Share of NER States in the total national production in different agro-products show production capabilities of the region in mitigating supply gap of several agro-products in the domestic economy. Two important observations are emerging from the empirical analysis: (a) Each state is engaged in the production of large number of products, and (b) each state has acquired specialization in specific line of agricultural production. It is clear from the empirical finding that all states can undertake large farming to meet the commercial needs of the agricultural sector, leading to industrialization in the rural sector. On the basis of specialization of each state in terms of production of specific products, appropriate agro-processing centres can be built in different parts of the region. It would also require appropriate support from the state—towards marketing mechanism for distribution of final products in the domestic economy and to cater to the export needs.

The results show that the number of specialized products with large-scale production varies from one state to another. The number of such crops ranges from six to ten in each state except for Assam and Sikkim as shown in Table 4.4. Arunachal Pradesh has six specialized products, based on its share in the production of those products nationally. Those products are in sectors such as fruits (i.e. kiwi, orange, and pineapple) and live stocks (i.e. cattle meat and swine meat). In ginger production, the state has significant advantage.

Assam, being the largest state in the region, has specialization in twenty-four crops, spreading over broad categories of agriculture including food grains, fruits, vegetables, spices, etc. In the entire Northeast region, Assam has the advantage of producing rice and the state leads the region in the production of food grains. In the fruits sector, Assam has a significant production advantage in specific crops such as jackfruit, litchi, orange, and pineapple, where the state enjoys scale advantage in production. On account of lumpiness of production, it can undertake independent fruit processing activities without depending on the other states for supply of raw materials to its anticipated processing units. Other specialized fruit products of the state are banana, lemon, papaya, and other

Table 4.4: Share of NER States in the Production of Various Agricultural Products in India: 2015 (%, Share in India)

Sector/Product	Arunachal Pradesh	Assam	Manipur	Meghalaya	Mizoram	Nagaland	Sikkim	Tripura	NER Share
Agriculture									
Rice		4.9							4.9
Fruits									
Banana	0.1	3.0	0.3	0.3	0.5	0.4	0.0	0.5	5.2
Jackfruit	0.1	11.4			0.0	0.1		16.8	28.5
Kiwi	56.8				9.6	22.9	7.4		96.7
Lemon	0.0	4.5	2.3	0.4	1.1	0.5		1.2	9.8
Litchi		8.9			0.3	0.6		3.6	13.4
Mandarin (M. Orange, Kinnow)	5.3	5.1	1.1	1.0	1.0	1.3	0.4	0.8	15.9
Other fruits	0.1	1.5	3.8	5.1	0.6	0.2	0.0	0.7	12.0
Papaya	0.0	2.6		0.1	0.5	0.3	0.0	0.7	4.1
Passion fruit			74.0		2.7	23.1	0.0		99.8
Pineapple	1.9	14.8	6.7	6.4	1.7	6.6		9.4	47.6
Strawberry				18.3	22.0				40.3
Live stocks									
Cattle meat	2.9	1.0	2.6	7.2	1.2	3.5	0.3		18.6
Swine meat	1.3	4.5	1.7	2.9	1.9	4.4	0.1	2.9	19.7
Plantations									
Areca nut	1.2	10.5		3.7	1.0	0.3		1.4	18.0

(*continued*)

Sector/Product	Arunachal Pradesh	Assam	Manipur	Meghalaya	Mizoram	Nagaland	Sikkim	Tripura	NER Share
Spices									
Cardamom						5.9	17.1		22.9
Chillies	0.5	1.3	0.3	0.1	0.6	3.3		0.2	6.4
Cinnamon/Tejpat		9.4		99.4					99.4
Coriander				0.0	0.0	0.0			9.5
Garlic	0.0	4.8	0.0	0.1	0.0	0.2			5.0
Ginger	5.1	14.7	0.3	5.9	2.9	5.0	5.0	0.7	39.5
Pepper		4.8		1.3	0.0	0.1		0.3	6.4
Turmeric	0.4	1.8	1.7	1.7	2.9	1.0	0.6	0.7	10.8
Vegetables									
Bitter gourd		4.7		0.6	1.9	0.0	0.2	0.8	8.2
Carrot	0.0	5.2		1.7	0.1	0.4	0.2	0.4	8.0
Cauliflower	0.0	5.5	0.4	0.3	0.0	0.1	0.0	0.8	7.1
Cucumber	0.1	6.0	0.0	0.4	0.2	0.4	0.0	1.5	8.6
Mushroom	0.0					1.4		6.2	7.6
Okra/Lady's finger	0.0	3.1	0.0	0.1	0.4	0.0	0.1	0.3	4.1
Parwal/Pointed gourd		6.7	0.0	0.4				2.2	8.9
Potato	0.0	2.4	0.0	1.0	0.0	0.1	0.1	0.3	3.4
Radish	0.0	7.7			0.1	0.2	0.2	1.9	11.1
Tomato	0.0	2.4	0.2	0.2	0.1	0.1	0.0	0.3	3.2

Source: RIS database based on APEDA.

fruits. In the meat sector, Assam is the largest producer of swine meat in the Northeast. The state has a distinct advantage in the production of spices (i.e. coriander, garlic, ginger, pepper, and turmeric) and vegetables (i.e. bitter gourd, carrot, cauliflower, cucumber, lady's finger, parwal, potato, radish, and tomato). Considering the scale of production in the state, Assam can undertake food processing on a large scale to foster rural industrialization in certain sectors and work together with other states in selected other crops to maintain scale economies for processed agro-products.

Manipur has seven specialized products which mostly fall under the categories of fruits and live stocks. Its production share is very significant in crops such as passion fruit and pineapple. Manipur produced 74 per cent of country's total production of passion fruit and was an important producer of pineapple in the region in 2015. In these two products, the state can achieve scale economies. In other important crops such as lemon and other fruits, the state can collaborate with other neighbouring states for achieving scale economies in raw materials. It has strong production capabilities in the production of turmeric as well.

Meghalaya is the second largest exporting state in the NER, next to Assam. It has ten specialized crops where it has production advantage in the country and in the region as well. It has scale economies in the production of fruits, live stocks, plantation, and spices. In the fruits sector, the state has a very large production capacity in crops such as strawberry, pineapple, and other fruits. In the production of cattle meat, the state is the leading producer in the region. It has a strong production stake in swine meat. The state has absolute monopoly in the production of cinnamon/tejpat in the country where contribution of the state is close to 100 per cent. The state has scale economies in the production of ginger, areca nut, turmeric, and carrot.

The state of Mizoram has nine special products that are broadly located in sectors such as fruits and spices. The scale of production of the state is very high for strawberry and kiwi among major fruits produced in the state. Production is relatively high in fruit crops such as passion fruits and pineapples in the state. Like other NER states, production of swine meat is significant in the live stocks sector. Other specialized products of the state are ginger and turmeric. The state produces significant quantities of bitter gourd.

Nagaland has specialized in nine crops, but their export has remained low. It has specialized in the broad categories of fruits, meat, and spices. In case of two fruit crops, namely, kiwi and passion fruit, the state has significantly large production profile in the country. In the production of pineapple, it is one of the leading producers of the region. As far as meat production is concerned, Nagaland has a large contribution in the production of cattle and swine meat in the region. It is also a leading producer of several spices including cardamom, chillies, and ginger.

In the production of agricultural products, Sikkim has been maintaining a low profile compared to other states in the region. Contrary to its experience in maintaining scale in production of agricultural products, it was the third largest exporting state in the Northeast and was a major producer of three specialized crops including kiwi, cardamom, and garlic in 2015. The state is engaged in the production of several products, but the scale factor is not at play in many such cases. Instead of focusing on crop production, the state has been engaged in organic farming and food processing. This has given the state a big leap in catching up with export activities.

Although the state of Tripura produces several agricultural commodities, it specializes in eight crops which are mostly in the domain of fruits and vegetables. In the fruits sector, the state has an outstanding record of production in jackfruit and pineapple in the country. Besides, it is the second largest producer of litchi in the region. The state is mostly engaged in the production of swine meat. Production of bovine meat in the state is insignificant. In the vegetable sector, Tripura is the most visible state next to Assam. It is the largest producer of mushroom in the region. Large production is also noticed in several vegetable crops including cucumber, parwal, and radish.

Several horticulture crops and spices such as kiwi, pineapple, orange, turmeric, ginger, and large cardamoms are being cultivated in large quantities in the NE States. But marketing the produce has been a major challenge. The farmers are not getting the appropriate remuneration for their produce. Hence, there is an urgent need for food processing and packaging units in the NE region along with marketing facilities to boost the income of the local people and overall economy of the region.

In certain cases, most of the regional states are into the production of multiple commodities. Almost all states are significantly engaged in selected products such as pineapple, swine meat, and ginger. In most of these cases, one or two states have a substantial share of the region's output of specific crops/products. For example, production of several fruit crops is dominated by one or two states, namely, banana, papaya, jackfruit, lemon, litchi, orange, and strawberry. As a staple food, meat production is undertaken by most of the states in the region. Production of most of the spices is dominated by a state in spices such as cinnamon/tejpat, chillies, coriander, garlic, and pepper. Ginger, turmeric, and cardamom are significantly produced by more than one state in the region. Interestingly, production of vegetable crops is dominated by one or two states in the region. While production of cauliflower, lady's finger, potato, and tomato was led by a single state, production of crops such as bitter gourd, carrot, cucumber, mushroom, parwal, and radish was dominated by two states. Production trend in the region indicates that individual states have specialized in specific products. All states have not specialized in all products. The implication such a trend indicates that food processing can be easily undertaken in the region for a wide range of products without facing the constraint of raw material shortage. Specialization of in certain crops by the states can help in augmenting the level of raw material production to facilitate food processing activities in the Northeast region.

Fisheries as Key Sector for Food Security and Trade in NER

Fishery has emerged as a major sector in contributing to the various economic activities in the NER states including food security, aquarium fish trade, and high altitude fish sports for tourism. The sector has high potential to contribute to the regional economy, particularly to food security and livelihood security through trade. In the region, indigenous small fresh water fish species can play a key role in supporting the local people in achieving nutrition and livelihood security, especially for low-income households in some communities. Small fisheries assume importance for food and trade of ornamental fish in the domestic market and also in the international market. Such species have immense relevance for nutritional and livelihood security. The sector may be important in eliminating malnutrition among the poor. For this reason, local people follow the practice of pisciculture by engaging family members in fishery activities. In Assam, family-based fishery ponds, known as *Bari*, are popular to undertake fishery production along with other allied activities. They are used as part of the family farming system to undertake numerous activities including horticulture, plantation, and other livestock activities along with fish cultivation (Borah and Barman, 2019).

The region has a large freshwater fish biodiversity and vast water resources for growing fish varieties. Moreover, the regional agro-climatic conditions are also conducive for production of fresh water fisheries. Often high-altitude fish cultivation is undertaken in various parts of the region to promote fish sports, in order to promote tourism. However, the region has several challenges for improving fish production. The production of fish is not commensurate to the growing demand for fish in the domestic sector for consumption. Despite having strong preference for fishery as a staple food, there are issues relating to accessibility and affordability of fish for consumption by the local people.

The region has large fish diversity in terms of diverse flora and fauna. North Eastern region has two biodiversity hot spots namely, 'Indo-Burma hot spot' and 'Himalayan hot spot' (Kundu *et al.* 2019). NER is also part of 'Himalayan hot spot' which is rich in fresh water fish germplasm. Because of richness of fresh water fish biodiversity, the region produces several varieties of small and ornamental fish spices. Identification of fish varieties is a major problem in the region. Often DNA bar coding and morphological approaches are deployed to identify different fish species. The region has a large potential to export ornamental fisheries. It may be noted that ornamental fisheries trade is one of the most important fishery trade industries in the world. Taking in to account regional and global demand for ornamental fisheries, the sector could be an important one for generation of income for the fishery community in the region. Certain studies indicate that the NER has 422 fish species belonging to 133 genera and 38 families, contributing substantially to freshwater fish production in India. Nearly 128 ornamental fisheries are exported from the region (Dhar and Ghosh, 2014). Trade in ornamental fish has downside risk since 80 per cent of such species are sourced from the wild catch. As a result of over fishing of such species, several of them are conferred the status of threatened species by the International Union for Conservation of Nature.

Box 4.1: Food Processing in the North East

Prosperity and livelihoods of the region crucially depends on value addition on the wide range of agricultural, dairy products, and meat products from the region, and hence the need for strong push for the food processing industry. It is pertinent to note that, even with existing scale of operations, in aggregate, this sector in the North East possesses better competitiveness scores compared to the rest of the country in terms of lower input to value addition ratio. Illustrative policy push for this sector in recent times by two states is captured in the following.

Food Processing in Tripura

Food processing activities have been identified as a 'Thrust sector' by the State Government. Additional subsidies are being provided for food processing industries under Tripura State Incentive scheme.

Favourable agro-climatic conditions for growing various fruits and horticultural crops.

Major Fruit Crops—Pineapple, Jackfruit, Orange, Litchi, Cashew, Coconut, Mango; Major spices—Ginger, Turmeric, Chilli.

Queen Pineapple of Tripura has been declared as the 'State Fruit'. Pineapples and Oranges renowned for their unique flavour and organic nature of produce.

Potential for rice milling sector with modern technology. Already two Modern Rice Mill units are functional. Also, few more rice milling projects are in the pipeline.

During recent years, a number of food processing units have come up in Tripura. Some examples are: Modern Flour Mill, Cashew processing, Iodized salt, Ice slabs/Ice candy/Ice cream, Soya nuggets, Spice manufacturing, Bakery/Biscuits manufacturing, Groundnut processing, Salted snacks, Cold storages, etc.

The first Mega Food Park by the name of Sikaria Mega Food Park Pvt. Ltd. in village Tulakona, Agartala was inaugurated last year. The Mega Food Park has been set up in fifty acre of land at the cost of Rs. 87.45 crore. The Government of India has accorded approval of a financial assistance of Rs. 50.00 crore to the project. The food park has several facilities which includes a fully operational Dry warehouse and material handling of

5000 MT, Pineapple canning and Pulping line of 2 MT/Hr each, Packing Unit, Ripening Chambers of 40 TPD, Cold Storage of 5000 MT with Frozen Storage of 1000 MT, Quality Control, Research & Development Centre, etc. It also has fully developed industrial plots for setting up processing units and Standard Design Factory (SDF) Sheds to provide ready to move in facility for micro and small enterprises. The Park also has a common administrative building for office and other uses by the entrepreneurs and 5 PPCs at Sonamura, Hrisyamukh, Chandipur, Manu, and Budhjung Nagar with facilities for primary processing and storage near the farms. The Mega Food Park will leverage an additional investment of about Rs. 250 crore in twenty-five to thirty food processing units in the park and generate a turnover of about Rs. 450–500 crore annually. The Park will also provide direct and indirect employment to 5,000 people and benefit about 25,000 farmers in the CPC and PPC catchment areas.

Meghalaya Jackfruit Mission

The final Mission document of Mission Jackfruit was launched by Hon'ble Chief Minister of Meghalaya on 1 October 2018. With a view to leverage and make use of this tremendous and abundant natural resource, the five-year mission was launched with the following objectives and actions:

- To catalyse and promote sustainable rural and urban livelihoods through the processing and value addition of jackfruit by small-scale and nano enterprises.
- Creation of a value chain for jackfruit products and generating employment opportunities along the value chain for unemployed youth.
- Addressing food security and nutritional issues of the state in the long run.
- Protection and preservation of catchment areas through promotion of the widespread cultivation of jackfruit for its food, timber, health and soil amelioration benefits.
- Providing an additional source of income for rural and urban families through the commercialization of its processing and value addition.
- Developing the markets for jackfruit and its value-added products through a focused and professional go to market and field to fork strategy.

- Promoting the establishment of fifty SMEs in jackfruit processing through a credit-linked startup fund.
- Promoting the establishment of two hundred nano jackfruit processing/brining enterprises at village level through a credit-linked nano startup fund.
- Conduct hands on training for 10,800 entrepreneurs/master trainers in the incubation centres over the next five years.
- Conduct village-level Go Mobile trainings on plant management and minimal processing for 69,300 partners over the next five years.
- Development and creation of IEC materials, training manuals, publications, Z-cards, etc. Organization of Jackfruit Melas/awareness camps in all eleven districts every year for the next five years.

Source: Compiled from official sources.

Box 4.2: Major Network R & D Programmes on Bioresource-based Applications & Secondary Agriculture: Jackfruit and Citrus Fruits

In this project, 107 local Jackfruit genotypes for table purpose and 43 local genotypes for vegetable purpose have been identified. Budding technique in Jackfruit for multiplication of elite planting materials has been standardized; technology for preparation of ready-to-cook tender jackfruit for vegetable purpose has been developed. The process protocols for preparation of value-added products such as chips, pulp utilization for jam, squash, peda, and ice cream has been standardized.

In the project on value addition from Citrus produce, protocols have been developed for ready-to-serve drinks, fizzy carbonated drinks, squashes, and fruit juice concentrates from NER citrus fruits including Assam Lemon, Kachai Lemon, mandarin, and sweet orange. The protocol has also been developed for extraction of peel oil and pectin NER Citrus. Pilot testing and upscaling facility has been established at Medziphema, Nagaland.

Source: Department of Biotechnology, Government of India.

Box 4.3: Facilitating Sericulture in the North East

The Government of India has given special emphasis for consolidation and expansion of Sericulture in all the North Eastern States with critical interventions from host plantation development to finished products with value addition at every stage of the production chain. Under The North East Region Textile Promotion Scheme (NERTPS)—an umbrella scheme of Ministry of Textiles, the Government of India has approved thirty-eight sericulture projects in all North Eastern States in the identified potential districts under three broad categories, viz., Integrated Sericulture Development Project, Intensive Bivoltine Sericulture Development Project, and Aspirational Districts. A total of thirty-eight projects covering Mulberry, Eri, and Muga silk are implemented in all the NE States. Total cost of these projects is Rs. 1,106.97 crore, of which GoI share is Rs. 955.07 crore. The objective of these projects is to establish sericulture as a viable commercial activity in the NER by creating necessary infrastructure and imparting skills to the locals for silkworm rearing and allied activities in the value chain. The projects are proposed to bring around 38,170 acres of plantation under mulberry, Eri, and Muga sectors and expected to contribute additional production of 2,650 MT raw silk during the project period and generate employment for 316,000 persons.

Considering the potential for sericulture development in the NER, Ministry of Textiles has approved 14 new projects for implementation from 2018–19 onwards with a total cost of Rs. 284.02 crore, of which the GoI share is Rs. 261.30 crore to cover 17,141 beneficiaries resulting in the production of 366 MT of silk during the project period covering 7,160 acres of plantation from Mulberry, Eri, Muga, and Oak Tasar sectors. Besides, three new Eri spun silk mills will produce 165 MT of Eri spun silk yarn per annum. Further, the Government of India has initiated development of silk industry in the Aspirational Districts in one/two blocks per district covering Mulberry, Eri, Muga, or Oak Tasar as per the potential of the district with the involvement of State Governments. The projects are as follows:

(1) Establishment of Eri Spun Silk Mill in Assam,
(2) Establishment of Eri Spun Silk Mill in Bodoland Territorial Council (BTC),
(3) Establishment of Eri Spun Silk Mill in Manipur,
(4) Large-Scale Eri Farming in Arunachal Pradesh,
(5) Integrated Eri Silk Development Project for Sustainable Livelihood to Women folk of BTC through Tapioca plantation,
(6) Bivoltine Sericulture Development project through Women Empowerment in Wokha district of Nagaland,
(7) Sericulture Development in Aspirational District of Mizoram,
(8) Sericulture Development in Aspirational District of Nagaland,
(9) Sericulture Development in Aspirational Districts of Assam,
(10) Sericulture Development in Aspirational Districts of BTC,
(11) Sericulture Development in Aspirational District of Meghalaya,
(12) Integrated Muga Silk Development for Sustainable Livelihood in Arunachal Pradesh,
(13) Eri Silk Development Project through Women Empowerment in Chungtia of Mokokchung district, Nagaland, and
(14) Intensive Bivoltine Sericulture Development Project in Sapahijala in Tripura.

Source: Ministry of Textile, Government of India.

The region takes the lead in the export of India's aquarium fish. Ornamental fish trade has a large global market (Tlusty et al., 2013). It was estimated that 80 per cent of the total exports of ornamental fish from India is contributed by the NER (Mohapatra et al, 2007). The region has also specialized in the production of dry fish. Jagiroad, an industrial town in Assam, has emerged as Asia's biggest market for dry fish. Although the market is in its infancy, it can be graduated to a commercial hub for dry fish in the region. The existing bioresources in the region could generate huge wealth for the region, but appropriate regulatory framework needs to be put in place to arrest unsustainable practices of exploiting wild catch. However, fishery sector could be an important source of livelihood and food security for the region.

Minor Forest Produce and Medicinal and Aromatic Plants

An important source of livelihood for tribal people are Non-Wood Forest Products (NWFP), generally termed 'Minor Forest Produce (MFP)' means all NTFP and includes canes, fodder, leaves, broom grass gums, waxes, dyes, resins, and many forms of food including nuts, wild fruits, honey, Lac, Tusser, etc. There are about 7,500 MFPs found in different forests of India. Most of them have medicinal value. There are about 1,200 MFPs traded and 300 of them traded in higher quantity, i.e. more than 100 metric ton per annum.

The MFPs provide both subsistence and cash income for people who live in or near forests. They form a major portion of their food, fruits, medicines, and other consumption items and also provide cash income through sale. Collection and sale of MFP supports the livelihood security of hundred million forest dwellers (most of them tribal). MFPs provide 35 per cent of the income of tribal household in India. Small-scale forest-based enterprises are mostly based on MFP which provide up to 50 per cent of income for 20 per cent–30 per cent of the labour forces in India. Ministry of Tribal Affairs started giving minimum support price for ten MFPs in nine PESA States and increased it in phases. At present, forty-nine items are covered, and the coverage was also increased to the whole country under the scheme on 'Mechanism for Marketing of Minor Forest Produce (MFP) through Minimum Support Price (MSP) and development of value chain'.

Pradhan Mantri Van Dhan Yojana (Scheme) was launched by the Prime Minister of India on 14 April 2018. The main objective behind this scheme is to help increase tribal income through value addition. This is an initiative of the Ministry of Tribal Affairs and TRIFED. The Van Dhan Vikas Kendra is being established for providing capacity building training and skill upgradation and value addition facility and for setting up of primary processing.

North Eastern States are rich in forests, and these forests are repositories of large varieties of NWFP and medicinal and aromatic plants. Further, a study reveals that rural people are heavily dependent on the NWFPs for their subsistence and livelihood. The processing and value addition facilities are generally non-existent. Low return to the gatherers

---

Box 4.4: Promoting Bamboo in the North East

The North Eastern States along with West Bengal account for more than 50 per cent of the bamboo resources of the country. In early 2005, the North Eastern Council launched the North East Regional Bamboo Mission. Under the provisions of the North East Bamboo Mission, the Cane and Bamboo Technology Centre (CBTC) was identified as a Special Purpose Vehicle to implement the North East Bamboo Mission and an Action Plan was also drawn up, in which key areas requiring intervention were identified. The Department of Science and Technology, Government of India launched the National Mission on Bamboo Application, especially for technology application in the bamboo sector. The restructured National Bamboo Mission was approved by the Cabinet Committee on Economic Affairs on 25 April 2018. The Mission aims to promote holistic growth of the bamboo sector by adopting area-based, regionally differentiated strategy and aims to increase the area under bamboo cultivation and marketing. Under the Mission, steps have been taken to increase the availability of quality planting material by supporting the setting up of new nurseries and strengthening of existing ones. To address forward integration, the Mission is taking steps to strengthen marketing of bamboo products, especially those of handicraft items.

Source: Cane and Bamboo Technology Centre (CBTC), National Bamboo Mission, India State of Forest Report (2019).

---

due to unreasonably low prices paid to them is a matter of concern. Economically viable cultivation and sustainable field collection of medicinal plants gives India a huge comparative advantage in quality raw materials at internationally competitive prices for AYUSH Industry, nutraceuticals, herbal extracts, herbal cosmetics, pharmaceuticals, perfumes, etc. The processing of these plant products presents a great opportunity for sustainable employment. Moreover, a new segment of their extracts has made the sector more attractive by increasing the shelf life and with easier standardization.

From the analysis of data on the growth of the medicinal plants sector in volume and value given in Tables 4.5 and 4.6, respectively, and growth of export of AYUSH and medicinal plants products, it may be seen that though demand of medicinal plants has grown 55.55 per cent in terms of volume, the growth in terms of value was 553.6 per cent, indicating accelerated growth in demand and constraints in supply. Large quantities of many medicinal plants are being sourced from the region. Many countries like to get uninterrupted supply of Indian organic herbs with proper standards and traceability even at a premium price.

Many positive developments have taken place in the North Eastern States in the medicinal plants sector. All North Eastern States have constituted State Medicinal Plants Board. They are also implementing schemes of Ministry of AYUSH, viz., National AYUSH Mission and Central Sector Scheme on Conservation, Development and Sustainable Management of Medicinal Plants. Few industrial units of medicinal plants and traditional medicine have also come in the region. Dabur has established its manufacturing unit at Tejpur, Assam. It had also signed MoUs with four Forest Division in Manipur in 2016 to purchase ten medicinal plants at agreed price. Emami also has established a unit, mostly for Herbal Cosmetics in Guwahati, Assam. There is a need to give boost to the sector by attracting

Table 4.5: Growth of Medicinal Plants Sector in Volume from 2005–06 to 2014–15

Sl. No.	Estimated Annual Demand of Botanical Raw Drugs	2005–06 (Dry Wt. in MT)	2014–15 (Dry Wt. in MT)	Growth (Dry Wt. in MT)	Percentage
1.	Herbal Industry	177,000	195,000	18,000	10.16%
2.	Rural Households	86,000	167,500	81,500	94.76%
3.	Exports	56,500	134,500	78,000	138.05%
4.	Wastage	–	14,910	–	
Total		319,500	511,910	177,500	55.55%
5.	No. of Botanicals	1,289	1,622	333	42.92%
6.	Total no. of species traded	960	1,178	218	22.7%
7.	Number of species trader in high volume	178	242	64	35.95

Source: Goraya and Ved (2017).

Table 4.6: Growth of Medicinal Plants sector in Value from 2005–06 to 2015–16 (Rs. in Crore)

Sl. No.	Estimated Annual Demand of Botanical Raw Drugs* (Dry Wt. in MT)	2005–06	2014–15	Growth in Value	Growth in %
1.	Domestic Herbal Industries	627.90	1,950	1,322.1	210.56
2.	Rural Household	86	1,675	1,589	1,847.67
3.	Wastage		149	149	
4.	Exports	354.80	3,211	2,856.2	805.02
5.	Total	1,068.70	6,985	5,916.3	553.60

Source: Goraya and Ved (2017).

capital investment. The availability of quality raw material can be further enhanced with pure plantation of appropriate species of medicinal plants or their plantations in agro-forestry.

High Significance of Climate Adaptation in Agriculture in the North East

The regional setting of the NER displays the presence of as many as six different/diverse agro-climatic zones, thereby enabling the production of diverse agricultural crops. On the other hand, the physiographic barriers imposed by the lofty mountains, plateaus, hills, and perennial river systems and the locally generated needs of more than two hundred different ethnic groups with unique rights, rituals, and food habits hold the basis for practicing subsistence mode of agricultural production. This explains production of large varieties of crops for meeting wide-ranging requirements of each ethnic group. It is also indicative that the agricultural production system in the region is resilient to various adversities of nature by ensuring production of some crops at the event of failure of few others. It is imperative that climate adaptive agriculture is pursued with sub-regional/state-specific focus mostly in non-food categories of crops. However, out of the limited cultivable land available, paddy cultivation predominates the NER agriculture, which happens to be quite vulnerable to climate change. Further, seen from the lens of specific non-food grain sectors, the climate change poses larger threats to diverse livelihood activities such as tea/rubber plantations, spices, floriculture and fisheries, etc.

Non-availability of scientific data remains an unresolved challenge leading to sub-optimal vulnerability assessment and thus restricting choice of appropriate evidence-based interventions and impacting risk management. The Ministry of Statistics and Programme Implementation brings out an annual publication titled *'EnviStat'* in two volumes, which provides aggregated statistics on some indicators related to climate change, extreme events and disaster. The information covered needs to be further spruced up on the basis of Framework for Development of Environment Statistics adopted by the UN Statistical Commission in 2013, to undertake proper assessment of vulnerability over the years caused by climate change. The Government of India is also implementing the scheme of 'Establishment of an Agency for Reporting of Agricultural Statistics (EARAS)' in some states including the NE States of Arunachal Pradesh, Nagaland, Sikkim, and Tripura for generating estimates of area and production of principal crops and land-use statistics, which also would prove useful in tracking climate change led impact.

In a study of the NER to identify the strategies adopted by 120 paddy growers of Senapati district of Manipur and East Sikkim district of Sikkim, Rymbai and Sheikh (2018) argue that adaptation is crucial to curb down the negative impact of climate change particularly on the agricultural sector. They add that some of the widely adopted strategies could be the change in transplanting and harvesting times, in response to the scarcity of water.

Deforestation for timber harvesting and also for shifting cultivation increases soil degradation. Horticulture of variety of citrus fruits, sericulture, and contour farming are the tested options to contain soil erosion. But the promotion of agro-forestry models are not vigorously pursued in spite of the potential, especially in combination with traditional fruit trees, horticulture of short rotation small fruit trees and other suitable crops. Some of the Krishi Vigyan Kendras, ICAR based in Shillong have evolved such models.

Clustering of states or areas within states based on the similarity of geography and economic activities and customary practices, e.g. Mizoram, Manipur, and Tripura Hills and Nagaland share similarities in lifestyle due to shifting cultivation may prove to be useful. Plains of Assam and

Manipur valley share similarities in agriculture, rice cultivation, etc. Such kind of mapping of similarities is necessary to expand the area under specific crop or any other similar livelihood activity.

Hilly states such as Mizoram have large potential of converting Wetland Rice Cultivation (WRC) areas in the valleys. These areas form the most suitable sites for rice terraces due to the fertility of the soil and assured water sources originating from the forests in the upper side. In Mizoram, there is a potential of 3.54 per cent of the total geographic area of the state to be converted into WRC areas (Lallianthanga et al., 2013), Conversion of WRCs would be an important adaptation mechanism. Erratic rainfall and longer dry spells would not have immediate impact on the rice cultivation due to strategic location of the rice cultivation sites in the form of WRCs. It will not only enhance the rice production and self-sufficiency of Mizoram but also boost the creation of jobs at the local level and utilize the local knowledge and skills. Mizoram government's New Land-use Policy document could be of interest in the context of WRCs.

A large number of policy and programme responses of the Central and State Governments are under implementation, many of which directly or indirectly strengthen the mitigation and adaptation measures and to double farmers' income. The Annual Report for 2018–19 of the Department of Agriculture, Cooperation & Farmers Welfare states that to achieve the target of doubling farmers' income, a number of schemes and programmes are being implemented by the Government of India through State Governments, i.e. *Pradhan Mantri Krishi Sinchayee Yojana (PMKSY), Pradhan Mantri Fasal Bima Yojana, Paramparagat Krishi Vikas Yojana, Soil Health Scheme, Neem Coated Urea, and e-National Agriculture Market.* National Mission for Sustainable Agriculture (NMSA) aims at making agriculture more productive, sustainable, remunerative, and climate resilient by promoting location-specific integrated/composite farming systems; soil and moisture conservation measures; comprehensive soil health management; efficient water management practices; and mainstreaming rain-fed technologies. On-Farm Water Management aims at enhancing water use efficiency by promoting technological interventions such as drip and sprinkler technologies, efficient water application and distribution systems, secondary storage, etc., subsumed under the 'Per Drop More Crop (PDMC)' component of PMKSY. NMSA also focuses on Integrated Farming System for enhancing productivity and minimizing risks associated with climatic variability. Under it, cropping is integrated with activities such as horticulture, livestock, fishery, vermi-organic compost, green manuring, apiculture, etc. to enable farmers to maximize farm returns for sustained livelihood and mitigate the impacts of drought, flood or other extreme weather events with the income opportunity from allied activities. Reforestation and afforestation with community participation through customary institutions such as Village Councils, Biodiversity Management Committees, forest departments and Joint Forest Management Committees (not in all states), Self-Help Groups (SHGs), Civil Society Organisations (CSOs), can strengthen resilience for better adaptation interventions. Climate adaptive agriculture approach needs to internalize the socio-economic factors and environmental diversity, and its effective implementation requires identification and promotion of climate-resilient technologies and practices to harness the intersection of agriculture-water—energy-land ecosystem at all levels with special emphasis on the needs of the coming generations.

Soil Mapping in the North East: ICAR's National Bureau of Soil Survey and Land-Use Planning

The Regional Centre, Jorhat is engaged in conducting research on soil survey and mapping, fertility mapping, and land-use planning in collaboration with relevant institutions and agencies.

Soil resource mapping of North Eastern Region at state level (1:250,000 scale),

Soil resource mapping for district planning (1:50,000 scale),

Soil nutrient status mapping for Assam and Tripura States,

Soil erosion assessment for monitoring soil degradation status,

Characterizing the soil resources in fluvial landforms of Majuli Island for land use using remote sensing and GIS,

Mapping and assessment of nutrient status of soils in River Island Majuli, Assam,

A sustainable cropping system for rice fallows of Brahmaputra valley of Jorhat district of Assam,

Soil resource mapping of Kamrup district (1:50,000) of Assam for
  land-use planning,
Studies on infiltration, hydraulic conductivity, and moisture storage of
  some soils of Jorhat district, Assam,
Detailed soil survey of regional rain-fed lowland rice research station
  farm, Gerua, Kamrup district, Assam,
Soils of Bhareli River Basin for Land-Use Planning.

Source: ICAR.

Initiatives taken by NITI Aayog for the Himalayan States

All the North-Eastern States are fully part of Indian Himalayan Region
(IHR) except Assam in which only three hill districts namely Dima
Hasao, Karbi Anglong, and West Karbi Anglong are part of this region.
The unscientific exploitation of natural resources is leading to environmental degradation. Other challenges in this region includes high rate of
poverty, high outmigration rate, poor social and physical infrastructure,
market conditions, and lack of biodiversity data sets for development
planning. The States in NE region have thousands of springs which are
the main source of water for drinking as well as irrigating the agriculture
lands. Several of these springs have either dried up or become seasonal.
The reduction in the discharge of many springs is also being felt. This issue
is of great concern for the water security of several villages/habitations.
Besides this, shifting (jhum) cultivation is another issue which is mostly
prevalent in the North-Eastern States. Due to shortening of shifting cultivation cycle, the productivity of such lands is decreasing. The Ministry
of Agriculture & Farmers Welfare, Government of India has recently
advised all the States to include the shifting cultivation lands in various
schemes of the Ministry for conservation of natural resources, sustainable agriculture, and better livelihood options to the jhum cultivators.

   NITI Aayog prepared the reports on each of the five thematic areas for
Sustainable Development in the IHR namely—(i) Inventory and Revival
of Springs in Himalayas for Water Security, (ii) Sustainable Tourism in
IHR, (iii) Shifting Cultivation: Towards Transformation Approach, (iv)

Strengthening Skill & Entrepreneurship Landscape in Himalayas, and (v) Data/Information for Informed Decision Making. These reports were released on 23 August 2018.

1. NITI Aayog also constituted the 'Himalayan States Regional Council for Sustainable Development in Indian Himalayan Region' on 8 November 2018 to monitor the implementation of the action points in the earlier reports besides providing the hand holding to the Himalayan States. The Secretaries of the concerned Central Ministries and the Chief Secretaries of all the Himalayan States are the members of this Council.
2. NITI Aayog has initiated the process of mapping and revival of springs in Himalayan States in close coordination with Department of Water Resources and Department of Land Resources, Government of India.
3. Mapping of lands involved under Shifting Cultivation through North Eastern Space Application Centre, Department of Space to work on a policy to tackle the issue of shifting cultivation.
4. A Consortium of Central Universities in Himalayan States has been formed to study some of the important issues such as enumeration and valuation of the economic impact of female labour in the hills.
   • Agro-ecology in Himalayan States with special emphasis on marketing.
   • Development of eco-friendly and cost-effective tourism in hills.
     • Opportunities of livelihood to check migration from hills.
     • Water conservation and harvesting strategies.

Conclusion

Sustainability of livelihoods cannot be ensured by improved and efficient agricultural production alone. Given the topography of this region and the associated risks of ecological fragility, efforts in enhancing value addition to agricultural sector have to balance the concerns for sustaining the planet as well. Forests in this region play a significant role in contributing to environmental sustainability not only at a regional level but also at the global level. Recent estimates by the India State of Forests Report

2019 reveal that the region accounts for about 30 per cent of the country's total forest carbon stock, which works out to be 123.52 metric tonnes per hectare of forests. The figure is higher than the Indian average at 100.03 metric tonnes per hectare. At the state level, Sikkim (171.04) and Arunachal Pradesh (157.65) are the significant contributors to carbon sinks in this region. The global average carbon stock per hectare of forest, to give a comparative perspective, is estimated at about 162 metric tonnes (Pandey, 2012). Continuous accumulation of carbon stock through forests is key to play a meaningful role in contributing to the reduction of atmospheric concentration of greenhouse gases and mitigate global warming and climate change. The region also hosts multiple biodiversity hotspots that are home to numerous species, many of whom are endemic to the region.

Needless to add, efforts to enhance the agricultural might of the NER in a sustainable manner, cannot afford to be at the cost of dwindling forest cover. Further, it is now well documented that agricultural practices also contribute to the emission of GHG gases. An estimate for the NER region suggests that the emission of CO_2 equivalent in this region from livestock population is 10.946 Tg (teragram, 1 teragram = 10^6 kilogram) per year. Manure management activities emit 342.03 Gg per year (gigagram, 1 gigagram = 10^3 kilogram). Methane emission from rice cultivation accounts for 5,746 Gg per year. Annual emission due to shifting cultivation is estimated at 1,237.065 Gg. Thus, the total emission from all sources works out at 19.5503 Tg per year. Considering the fact that the existing land-use pattern in the region helps sequester 17.341 Tg of CO_2 equivalent (as in 2015), agricultural practices, even in its present subsistence dominated avatar is net carbon negative (Sharma and Sharma, 2018).

Under such circumstances, it is imperative that many more efforts are necessary to add value to the agricultural products generated in this region through off-farm mechanisms. Some well-researched crop substitution that may not jeopardize the existing carbon balance further is to be identified. More efforts are needed to go for processing of the available agricultural products including livestock and fisheries. An important and welcome addition towards this endeavour would be to add to the existing cold storage facilities of .04 metric tonnes per hectare of cropped area. The comparable figure for India as a whole is 0.18. The communities located in this region are also highly vulnerable to climate change impacts.

Climate change has the potential to impact human life through changes in temperature, precipitation, atmospheric composition, and climate variability and extremes. The impacts of climate change are of importance in connection with the overall water regime and with hazards out of natural calamities such as draught and floods. It also impacts the biodiversity profile of the region in terms of introducing changes in floral and faunal distribution and in disturbing the prevailing inter-species interactions.

5

Nutrition, Health, and Well-being

Introduction

The concept of 'well-being' enshrined in Sustainable Development Goal (SDG) 3 espouses the principle of integrated development as it includes nutrition, physical and mental health of individual and community, and sustainable environment and climate, all factors contributing to health and well-being. The traditional life styles of the people of the North East had recognized this. Nutrition is necessary for health and is derived from food obtained from nature or produced by agriculture. To that extent, SDG 2, which is aimed to 'End hunger, achieve food security and improved nutrition and promote sustainable agriculture', remains the foundation of SDG 3. It aims to provide nutritious food for all sections of the society; to end malnutrition through doubling agriculture productivity, enhancing income of small growers and using traditional knowledge for preservation of genetic diversity. To achieve these objectives, the goal recognizes the need for increased financing, regulation of global market for price stabilization for agriculture commodities and liberated global trade of agriculture produce. SDG 3 on good health and well-being is meant to 'Ensure healthy lives and promote well-being for all at all ages'. It aims for providing universal health coverage (UHC) at an affordable cost to reduce mortality, undernutrition, communicable diseases (CDs), non-communicable diseases (NCDs), neglected tropical diseases, and also to prevent and treat substance use, reduce injuries and deaths from road accidents, hazardous chemicals, pollution, etc. To achieve these objectives, it recognizes that the global partnerships would be helpful in conducting R&D activities, health financing, and developing capacities of health personnel and to reduce health risks. This befits the current approaches to health and well-being that is holistic and not limited to morbidities or pathogenesis, as in the Indian traditional medicine

Rise of the North East, RIS, Oxford University Press. © Research and Information System for Developing Countries 2023.
DOI: 10.1093/oso/9780192849342.003.0005

that balance of physical, mental, spiritual, social, and ecological dimensions is good health. Interconnections between SDG 2 and 3 are deep, as achievement of either of these is contingent upon achievements on the other. For example, the achievement of SDG 2 is critical in ensuring good health, i.e. SDG 3 as it requires agricultural policies conducive to nutritious and healthy diets. Moreover, these are critical to achievement of all other SDGs.

Provision of better health and nutrition services and improved education conditions are considered to be crucial for attaining higher levels of human development and well-being. It can lead to more effective social and economic empowerment. Furthermore, there exists considerable evidence that improved nutrition, healthcare, education, and gender equality make the workforce more productive and better numerated. The healthcare sector presents a complex picture in the North-East Region (NER), although on the whole it is doing better than most of the other regions of the country. There are areas where some States are doing very well and a few are lagging. The number of female per thousand male populations is higher as compared to the national figure except in Nagaland. It is perceived that the status of women in the tribal society is comparatively better population of which is much higher in the NER.

Nutrition and Health in the North East: An Overview

Although the targets under SDGs 2 and 3 do not adequately reflect the integrative nature of the two and does less than adequate justice to 'well-being', the current availability of data is limited to them. The National Family Health Survey-4 (NFHS-4) data for the year 2015–16 show the incidence of malnutrition reduced across NE States during the ten-year period since NFHS-3, among the children below five years of age and pregnant and lactating women. Status as per NFHS-4 is shown in Figure 5.1 covering the NE States and India.

As per NFHS-4, the proportion of children under five years, who were stunted (height-for-age below minus 2 standard deviations), was a high 38.4 per cent in India, against which the NER had lower levels except in Meghalaya (43.8). The remaining seven NE States, namely, Tripura (24.3), Mizoram (28.1), Manipur (28.9), Nagaland (28.6), Sikkim (29.6)

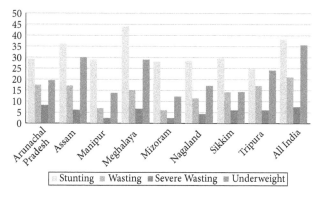

Figure 5.1: NER: Nutritional Status of Children under Five Years (%)
Source: RIS database based on NFHS-4.

Arunachal Pradesh (29.4) and Assam (36.4), had lower yet varied levels of stunting.[1]

Proportion of children under five years who were facing wasting (weight-for-height below minus 2 standard deviations) in all the eight states of NER was lower than the national average of 21.0 per cent. In fact, Mizoram (6.1) and Manipur (6.8) had less than one third and Nagaland (11.3) less than half of the national level, while Sikkim (14.2), Meghalaya (15.3), Assam (17.0), Tripura (16.8), and Arunachal Pradesh (17.3) also had significantly lower though varied levels. In terms of children under five years facing severe wasting (weight-for-height below minus 3 standard deviations are by definition a sub-set of children facing wasting), against 7.5 per cent children below five years in India, Arunachal Pradesh (8.0) had a higher proportion. On the other hand, Manipur (2.2) and Mizoram (2.3) had less than one third of the national level (similar to wasting), with Nagaland (4.2), Sikkim (5.9), Assam (6.2), Tripura (6.3), and Meghalaya (6.5) recording severe wasting below the national level.

Against 35.8 per cent underweight children (weight for age below minus 2 standard deviations) in India, all the NE States had lesser proportion ranging from Mizoram (12.0), Manipur (13.8), Sikkim (14.2),

---

[1] Figures in brackets are the levels in percentage terms—Source NFHS-4, 2015–16.

and Nagaland (16.7) which had less than half of the national level, to Arunachal Pradesh (19.4), Tripura (24.1), Meghalaya (28.9), and Assam (29.8), all below the national average.

Therefore, on prevalence of stunting, underweight and wasting among children (< 5 years), the position of North Eastern States was relatively better as compared to all India levels but still a lot needs to be done in this regard.

The status of anaemia (below 11 gram/dl) among children of age six to fifty-nine months and pregnant women (also below 11 gram/dl) of age fifteen to forty-nine years is shown in Figure 5.2 for the NE States and India. The position is better compared to India (58.6) on anaemia among children, and in fact Mizoram (19.3), Manipur (23.9), and Nagaland (26.4) had less than half the national proportion of anaemic children, whereas Assam (35.7), Meghalaya (48.0), Tripura (48.3), Arunachal Pradesh (54.2), and Sikkim (55.1) ranged almost three-fifth to the national level. In terms of anaemia among pregnant women, compared to India (50.4), Sikkim (23.6), Manipur (26.0), and Mizoram (27.0) had less than or around half the proportion of level in India, whereas Nagaland (32.7), Arunachal Pradesh (37.8), Assam (44.8), Meghalaya (53.3), and

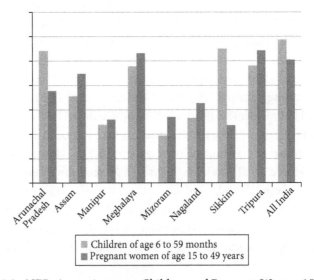

Figure 5.2: NER: Anaemia among Children and Pregnant Women 15-49 Years (%)

Tripura (54.4) ranged almost two-third of the national level, with the last two states being above it.

Importantly, although undernutrition parameters in NER are slightly better than the rest of India, a lot of concrete steps need to be taken to attain National Nutrition Mission (NNM) targets.

Further, as per NITI Aayog's SDG India Index and Dashboard 2019–20,[2] on SDG 2 compared to the national score of 35 the scores of all the NE States were better or equivalent. On SDG 3 compared to India's score of 61, Manipur (62) performed slightly better, Tripura (61) was equivalent, while the score of other NE States exhibit the need to make more efforts.

In matters of health indicators such as life expectancy, infant mortality rate and maternal mortality rate, the NER compares well with the other regions of the country. Most states do better than the national average. However, Assam's status raises concerns since it lags behind not only the other NE States but also most other states of the country.

Owing to the dominance of tribal population and heterogeneous culture, wider gender empowerment is visible alongside almost non-existent incidences of dowry, female foeticide, and female infanticide. On the contrary, it is observed that intermittent episodes of instabilities in the NER have severely affected the normal lives of the population, in particular of women and girl child (Mahanta and Nayak, 2017). Further, only 15 per cent of Sikkim's women in the age group of twenty to twenty-four years were married before the age of eighteen years as against the national average of 27 per cent. Sikkim is the best among all the NE States as there are only 3 per cent teenage pregnancies. With regard to the safe delivery mechanisms, in household decisions making, ownership of land, cell phones, and in terms of operation of bank accounts, Sikkim and Meghalaya's performances are also considered to be the best among NE States.

Policy Priorities

The major challenges are affordability and access to nutritious food, especially among the people in lower deciles of income. Notably, SDG target

[2] NITI Aayog SDG India Index and Dashboard 2019–20, figures in brackets are scores.

10.1 on reducing inequalities, in its domestic component, emphasizes on sustained income growth of the bottom 40 per cent population at a rate higher than national average. The problem among these deciles is compounded by inadequate awareness and sub-optimal functioning of related institutions. The situation is further aggravated to an extent by other related aspects of development such as lack of safe drinking water and sanitation, lack of healthcare facilities, limited availability of land for cultivation, low production and productivity, haphazard or unorganized plantations, heavy rainfall, extreme weather events, extensive soil erosion due to floods/flashfloods, environmental degradation, prevalent land tenurial systems, lack of proper markets, storage, agro-processing facilities, finance, infrastructure and connectivity, poor post-harvest management, limited availability of agriculture extension services, inadequate genetic improvement, etc. In the health sector, there are challenges that are common for the entire region, and there are new concerns which, in their intensity, vary from state to state. The aspirational yearning for faster industrialization, means for quicker economic development, also poses its own challenges for health and well-being, on account of environmental degradation and pollution.

In the matter of disease burden, like other parts of India, the NER also has the triple burden of continuance of CDs, such as malaria, and emerging challenges of NCDs, such as cancer, and mental health problems. Disease category-wise, communicable maternal, neo-natal, and nutritional diseases contributed 32.1 per cent of total deaths in the NER; NCDs account for 58.8 per cent and injuries 9.1 per cent. In case of CDs, etc., the percentage is more than the national average of 27.5 per cent. As far as specific causes of death are concerned, the NER has higher averages than all-India in diarrheal diseases (65 against 59), stroke (80 against 55), lower-respiratory diseases (43 against 38), tuberculosis (TB) (37 against 33), preterm birth complications (13 against 11), rheumatic heart diseases (8 against 5), hepatitis (14 against 5), lung cancer (6 against 5), other cancers (8 against 5), cirrhosis (9 against 5), and drowning (7 against 5) (Indian Council of Medical Research (ICMR) ., and Central Bureau of Health Intelligence (CBHI)).

Among the CDs, dengue cases have been showing an upward trend from virtually negligible number of cases in 2014. This draws attention to the need for increased attention to vector-borne disease control. Under the National Health Policy (NHP), premature mortality from NCDs is to be reduced by 25 per cent by 2025. Cancer incidence rates are double the national average in the NER, and the worst ones are Mizoram, Arunachal Pradesh, and Nagaland. The average stroke-related deaths for the NER are 80, way above the all India figure of 53 (CBHI).

Child and maternal malnutrition, unsafe water and sanitation, and unhealthy diet are major disease-causing factors. It is necessary to improve these in order to prevent persons falling sick. Immunization is the most pro-active preventive healthcare measure. The specific target under the NHP 2017 is to completely immunize 90 per cent of new born children by 2025 and all unimmunized and partially immunized children by 2020. When one looks at the available statistics, one feels that the NE States also have a lot of ground to cover.

Prevention is possible in case NCDS though it may not be adequate. The National Programme for the prevention of NCDs including cancer is focused on promoting a healthy lifestyle.

New Initiatives

Government initiatives have been aimed at addressing promotive, preventive, and curative healthcare, enhancing medical R&D and reducing financial burden on patients. The major programme under preventive healthcare is in nutrition. The Government of India launched the flagship programme named, National Nutrition Mission (POSHAN Abhiyan) in March 2018 aiming to improve the nutritional status among children, adolescent girls, pregnant women, and lactating mothers. The Abhiyan has focused on sensitizing people on healthy eating for addressing the twin burdens of malnutrition (undernutrition and obesity/overweight). The implementation strategy of the Poshan Abhiyan is based on intense monitoring and convergence based action plan right up to the grassroot level. It has been rolled out from March 2018 in phases to cover all district of the country. It targets to reduce stunting, undernutrition, anaemia (among young children, women, and adolescent girls), and low birth weight by 2 per cent, 2 per cent, 3 per cent, and 2 per cent per annum, respectively. Although the target to reduce stunting is at least 2 per cent p.a., it strives to achieve reduction in stunting from 38.4 per cent (NFHS-4) to 25 per cent by 2022 ('Mission 25 by 2022'). In fact, ICDS was launched earlier as a flagship programme with the objective to promote child development and to reduce the incidence of mortality, morbidity, malnutrition, and school dropout. Under it, supplementary nutrition is provided to children, pregnant women, and lactating mothers and also immunization and pre-school education facilities, etc. to the children in the age group 0–6 years. In order to cover the school children, mid-day-meals (MDM) launched later is a unique scheme designed to improve nutritional status and health of school children in the age group of 6–14 years under the Sarva Shiksha Abhiyan. It is the largest meal scheme under which children are served free lunch every day. Greater participation of local community and involvement of philanthropic/charitable institutions/civil society are sought and promoted. In addition, the government has enacted National Food Security Act 2013 which is operationalized through a scheme called Targeted Public Distribution System, under which legal entitlement was granted to poor households to get food grains at an affordable price. Technology-based reforms have been introduced by some states including linking with Aadhaar for better identification of beneficiaries and plugging leakages of food grains.

Linked with nutrition and health, and which have high impact on well-being, are the programmes on Swachh Bharat Abhiyan and National Water Mission, safe water and basic sanitation are being the essential ingredient of the primary healthcare as per the Alma Alta Declaration.

Apart from general nutrition, there have been focused programmes such as the National Iodine Deficiency Disorders Control Programme which achieved remarkable success with the consumption of adequately iodized salt at household/community level. In the NE States now, the proportion of households which consume iodized salt is in the range of 91 per cent to 99.9 per cent. Other such programmes include the National Programme for Prevention and Control of Fluorosis which was implemented in five districts of Assam only, and National Programme for Prevention and Control of Deafness. Together, these programmes contribute to the overall well-being of the individual and the community.

Government interventions also include Mahatma Gandhi National Rural Employment Guarantee Act (MGNREGA) which provided guaranteed hundred days employment of rural households and helps in the creation of community and other assets, including water- and soil-related works towards drought-proofing, leading to better agriculture and nutrition productivity and production. Further, *Pradhan Mantri Gram Sadak Yojana* is yet another intervention to provide better rural connectivity to facilitate in selling farm produce and procuring nutritive items and also for timely access to health facilities.

Other initiatives include vaccination and inoculation and disease-specific interventions such as in malaria and TB.

State governments of the NER have taken a number of initiatives such as Assam's 'Affordable Nutrition & Nourishment Assistance Yojana', Manipur's 'Go to Village Mission', and Meghalaya's healthcare and nutrition programme for poor child and poor female.

In health infrastructure, almost all the NE States are doing better than other regions, with the average population served per government hospital in Manipur and Nagaland more than the national average. In terms of availability of human resources for public healthcare, most states have better than national averages. However, with the region being sparsely populated and hilly, they may need more health personnel to serve the same number of people, especially in such regions. In the recent years, private healthcare has made some progress in the region. As per a 2016 Survey by Government of Manipur, that state has 110 registered private hospitals/clinics. Mizoram has twenty-three private hospitals (Mizoram Economic Survey, 2018–19). There are also private medical colleges in Manipur, Meghalaya, Nagaland, and Sikkim.

In medical education and R&D, the Regional Institute of Medical Sciences, Imphal, Lokpriya Gopinath Bordoloi Regional Institute of Mental Health, Tezpur and Regional Institute of Paramedical and Nursing Sciences, Aizawl are the frontal organizations focus on NER-specific issues.

Health expenditure falls under two categories, one for treatment as an outpatient and the other for hospitalization. The second one is necessitated in all major ailments and that imposes financial burden on the patients and their families. The status of hospitalization expenditure in the NE is presented in the Table 5.1.

While the average expenditure during hospital stay, except for the states Manipur and Tripura in rural areas and Assam and Manipur in urban areas, is less compared to the all-India average, this could largely be because of absence of required specialty hospital facilities in the

Table 5.1: Average Hospitalization Expenditure in NER

State	Rural		Urban	
	Average expenditure during stay at hospital	Average of other expenditure on account of hospitalization	Average expenditure during stay at hospital	Average of other expenditure on account of hospitalization
Arunachal Pradesh	5,678	2,363	8,926	1,789
Assam	6,966	1,554	47,064	5,304
Manipur	20,475	2,011	29,493	1,534
Meghalaya	6,061	2,997	10,215	3,595
Mizoram	2,075	2,023	18,786	3,004
Nagaland	8,744	2,908	13,461	3,756
Sikkim	12,855	2,755	16,731	1,616
Tripura	19,664	2,019	20,617	1,966
All India	14,935	2,021	24,436	2,019

Source: RIS database based on National Health Profile of India, 2019.

Note: Green colour denotes the expenditure being lower than national average, and the red colour denotes the expenditure being higher than national average.

private sector and low paying capacity of the people. It is also instrumental to see that 'other expenditure' on account of hospitalization is more than the national average in the case of the other North Eastern States (CBHI). Empirical studies are not available as to why the expenditure on hospital stay is higher in Manipur. Few possible conjectures are that (i) Manipur has a high share of private healthcare, (ii) a large number of patients opt for cosmetic surgeries, and (iii) the high proportion of foreigners obtaining healthcare in Manipur pushes up the cost. Similar figures for Tripura are also on the high side, maybe because of higher per person burden from ischemic heart disease (49 per cent), stroke (52 per cent), and chronic obstructive pulmonary disease (64 per cent) than national averages (ICMR).

In the NER, public expenditure on health as a percentage of total state expenditure is the highest in India varying between 5.45 per cent in Mizoram to 8.34 per cent in Manipur. Most public expenditure on health comes from the Centre.

An area of concern all across the country is in the matter of health financing in the absence of universal coverage of public healthcare. Of late, health insurance is slowly becoming popular among people, but all states in NER, except Arunachal Pradesh and Tripura, have less than half coverage in any health insurance scheme. The States of Manipur, Nagaland, and Assam are way behind the national average, with Manipur and Nagaland having less than 10 per cent coverage.

In this context, the Ayushman Bharat—Pradhan Mantri Jan Arogya Yojana (PMJAY) is expected to be a major leap forward. Under the PMJAY, states can have locally adapted insurance schemes. Meghalaya has a Megha Health Insurance Scheme launched in 2012, covering all residents irrespective of the poverty line. It has an insurance cover of Rs. 2.80 lakh available for up to five members per family on a floater basis, i.e. the amount can be utilized individually or jointly.

The government has to be the major player in the matter of healthcare in the NER for the foreseeable future, in view of various political and strategic reasons, including the factor that these are sensitive border states and the average income level of the population is much lower than that of the national average which makes the area less attractive to private players. The government needs to do more, for better implementation of its schemes. The PHCs and CHCs are to be the base for improvement of healthcare. They have to be easily accessible to all settlements and, perhaps, the norms even for hilly terrain may have to be liberalized for the NER. An aspect that will have to be given attention is developing the doctor–patient connect. The region has a large number of tribes, and they speak many languages and dialects. Use of local languages for promotion of public health as well as in facilitation of access to healthcare in rural and urban areas is expected to lead to better health outcomes.

One of the demands of the NE is to have more quality tertiary care institutions such as the All India Institute of Medical Sciences. The possibility of establishing such institutions may be examined. Moreover, quality is to be given the highest priority when it comes to medical education and service.

Private sector presence is not very strong in the North East. Large units such as ONGC, Oil India, and Reliance can contribute to the health sector through CSR. The Tea Estates can also play a significant role in the healthcare of their workers—both regular employees and contract or daily wage workers, which will contribute to their own productivity. Private healthcare is gradually picking up in the NER; Manipur is one such example. There is scope for more private hospitals, clinics, and diagnostic centres in the NER. These will attract medical tourism from neighbouring countries such as Myanmar. New ventures can avail of facilities being offered by the governments for startups. Good models will attract foreign investments. They will have to think of innovative ways to provide affordable healthcare. Hub-spoke model used by ERC is an example. Public–private partnerships can also be tried. But reliance on private healthcare for achievement of UHC has to factor the issue of affordability and is to be accompanied by appropriate financial risk protection for the common people.

Wellness Zones in North East India

The NER has the potential to become the major wellness hub of India and can promote Wellness Tourism. The region is endowed with rich cultures practicing different folk medicines, immense biodiversity, and it is also a hotspot for medicinal plant cultivation and collection. With the rise in disposable incomes of urban population in India and other countries, many consumers now seek wellness and recreation as important motives for travelling.

It is for this reason that 'Wellness Tourism' has experienced a surge in recent years. The availability of the three streams of Ayurveda, Sowa Rigpa, and the North Eastern Folk Medicine, coupled with the natural beauty of the area and its salubrious climate, makes the region a unique destination for global wellness tourism. Some recent initiatives by the government have helped to increase the scope of wellness and medical tourism in the NER.

For example, most of the NE States have tourism policies that recognize the immense scope for health and wellness tourism. The Department of Tourism, Government of Assam, also gives Best Medical Tourism Awards to hospitals in the state that attracts medical tourism. But significant challenges in the form of lack of connectivity, poor state of health infrastructure in the remote regions, and inadequate branding and marketing of the region as a wellness destination needs to be taken care of. The promotion of wellness tourism in the region will give the much-needed boost to the economy of the region and could also generate vast employment opportunities for the NE inhabitants.

Source: RIS Policy Brief No. 86 'Healthy City Planning and Traditional Medicines: Learning from International Experiences'.

A nationwide campaign for improving reproductive, maternal, newborn, child, and adolescent health to influence the key interventions for reducing maternal and child morbidity and mortality in the high-risk and vulnerable communities has been undertaken since 2013. UNICEF is the lead development partner of Call to Action Summit and has supported the Government of Assam in launching RMNCH + A strategy in six of its High-Priority Districts of Dhubri, Golaghat, Hailakandi, Karimganj, Kokrajhar, and Nagaon, which constitute 28 per cent of the population of state, 26 per cent of its maternal deaths, 34 per cent of under five deaths, and 45 per cent of neonatal deaths. In Arunachal Pradesh, Sikkim, and Mizoram, RMNCH + A programmes are being implemented by the Government with a vision to provide adequate maternal health services by operationalizing ANC services at all the health facility centre of these states, including free referral transport for pregnant women and new born children.

Way Forward

The position on ground as indicated by a Lancet, etc. study in 2019 indicates (Figure 5.3) that the business as usual approach must change to achieve NNM targets. As an example, the NNM target against the likely achievement gap covered demonstrates that the battle against anaemia among women and children[3] needs to be more intensified in all the states.

---

[3] The study covered women and children up to 6 years.

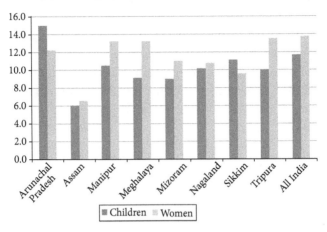

Figure 5.3: Anaemia: Projected Gap in 2022 from NNM Target (%)
Source: RIS database based on *Lancet*, PHFI etc. Study 2019.

A number of initiatives have been taken and schemes intensified to fast-track achievements of SDGs.

In addition to the common interventions at the national level, the following area-specific ones are required in nutrition and health:

i) It is noticed from the NHFS 4 detailed report that among children under five years of age suffering from diarrhoea during the preceding two weeks, 17.8 per cent in India were not given any treatment. Compared to it, in the NER in Meghalaya, only 6.3 per cent children were left out, whereas in Nagaland and Assam, it was higher at 32.9 per cent and 28.6 per cent, respectively. For the Poshan Abhiyan to succeed, no child should be left behind. Assam has put in place a 'District Multi-sectoral Results Based Nutrition Plan', and many NE States are adopting product-specific missions, which all need to be intensified. Notably, in 2019, Mizoram bagged joint 1st rank awards for 2018–19 under Poshan Abhiyan on ICDS–CAS (Common Application Software) implementation, and overall implementation categories, from the Ministry of Women and Child Development, indicating commendable efforts by Mizoram. Practices adopted by Mizoram need to be replicated by all states including other NE States. Some other NE States have also bagged awards for reducing malnutrition.

ii) While implementing the government programmes, be it ICDS or MDM or PDS, etc., the probability of a vulnerable household being left is higher in the vast, hilly, and relatively thinly populated NER tracts than in the rest of country. Therefore, it necessitates localized solutions and efforts on the nutritional and awareness fronts, besides provision of safe drinking water and better sanitation, technology, knowledge sharing, and tertiary health facilities supported by proper primary and secondary health facilities, etc.

iii) Health- and nutrition-centric awareness generation and sensitization of all stakeholders should be undertaken aggressively, which are low-hanging fruits to influence mindsets and to make lifestyles healthier. On one hand, among the vulnerable sections of society, the constraints to overcome are affordability and access of nutritional food items; and on the other hand, among better-off sections, there is a need to prefer healthier food items to keep problems of overweight and obesity at bay. In this endeavour, diversification of the food basket for balanced diets can help a lot, if intake of unhealthy food items is minimized. Role of micronutrients also needs to be emphasized as deficiency of even an innocuous looking and low-priced food item, meeting substantial proportion of RDA (recommended dietary allowance) of a micronutrient, can lead to significant discomfort, invite diseases, and impair abilities.

iv) Focus on the first one thousand days of a child's life should be accorded the top most priority.

v) The local self-governments, etc. need to involve and encourage the Anganwadi workers and SHGs in facilitating the supply of fresh vegetables, whole milk, condiments, etc.

vi) District-level officers need to be sensitized to improve district-level performance, through intensive field visits and meeting the public, beneficiaries, and grassroot-level stakeholders.

At a number of places, civil society organizations (CSOs) can be engaged, such as The Akshaya Patra Foundation (TAPF), which is providing MDM in Guwahati. The financial arrangement is based on supplying MDM free-of-cost to school children by getting subsidy from the state besides getting subsidized foodgrains through the FCI and the

State's Food and Civil Supplies Corporation. This model to feed a large number of children relies upon its centralized and decentralized kitchen units, which have the capacity to have ready meals for 100,000 youngsters in a little more than four hours. Their delivery framework includes uniquely planned vehicles to timely deliver hot-cooked meals to schools. Cleanliness and hygiene are accorded utmost importance in the TAPF kitchens. The Meghalaya Vision envisages mobilizing and engaging civil society and private sector for the development and implementation of policies in the healthcare sector, including for prevention and control of NCDs. Participation of NGOs in other programmes can also be encouraged and enhanced. Management of PHCs by NGOs in Arunachal Pradesh and outsourcing of CHCs to NGOs in Assam are two good examples of involving NGOs.

The NER is rich in good local health practices. They could be assessed from public health angle, and the appropriate ones could be brought into public healthcare. The advantage is that the local people will easily connect with such practices, and they may be cheaper than the formal systems.

Schemes such as ASHA workers could be strengthened. The volunteers be selected from the local communities and given proper training and empowerment. It may, perhaps, be necessary to reduce the norm for number of patients being served by each ASHA worker in these states, considering the topography and problems with access due to scattered population with low density.

Another dimension which is to be built into health policies at the state level is the linking of health systems with educational institutions. Healthy habits and lifestyles need to be inculcated in the young and for this, schools and colleges are the best place.

There is need for grassroots-level awareness and education for preventive healthcare such as healthy life style, sanitation and hygiene, vaccination. This will be much more economical than spending vast amounts on curative healthcare. In healthcare, quality and safety of the services and the medicines and equipment are of primary importance. The Directorate General of Health Services (DGHS), India has already brought out Guidelines on Indian Public Health Standards (IPHS) for PHCs, Community Health Centres, Sub-Centres, District, and other hospitals. The state health administrations should ensure that all the health facilities in their states are established and managed as per the IPHS norms.

The states will have to gear up their efforts towards achievement of good health and well-being for all, within the earmarked time slots for various targets under the NHP, 2017 and the Sustainable Development Goal Targets. They will have to take a number of steps towards this. Some of these are identified in the following:

a) Every state should do a field-level survey to assess the health status in all possible indicators. Where the states have not yet evolved their own state-level indicators, the national-level indicators could be used as a guide.

b) The survey should result in a robust database on healthcare in each state covering both the government and private sectors.

c) Based on the survey, the reports of which should be made public so that third-party observations and suggestions can be received, every state should prepare its own Vision Document, either as part of the SDG vision statement or as a separate health vision statement. This should be made after holding stakeholder consultations with government agencies—both from the State and the Centre, academic institutions, and civil society organizations, including selected national-level institutions. The Vision Statement should have clear goals and targets as well as alternative pathways.

d) The health sector is highly dependent on technology and, therefore, focus on medical innovation and research is also necessary. This is to be done keeping in view the affordability concerns. There is a need to develop cheaper diagnostic devices.

e) A factor that can enable affordable healthcare is widespread use of digital technology and the Internet.

f) Technology and knowledge sharing should be made a fundamental feature of the North East Health Vision. Best practices should be promptly shared with others. Field-level workers and health personnel in the rural sector will have to be trained in the use of medical technologies.

Conclusion

SDG 3 is about ensuring healthy lives and promoting well-being for all at all ages. While it lays down thirteen targets, they do not have the term 'well-being', leading to the presumption that achievement of those targets, which relate to various measurable outcomes of health interventions, is what is required for achieving 'well-being'. In such a well-being index, the North East would present a complex picture with the smaller states remaining high in rankings and Assam lagging. Arunachal Pradesh and even Nagaland also have to make special efforts to improve their index. Two areas that require additional focus to attain well-being are those of mental health and effective use of traditional systems of medicine. This is of equal importance like preventive healthcare. Mental health problems in the North-East have to be tackled with the high threat of substance abuse. Therapies such as yoga would go a long way in nurturing well-being in the North East as in other parts of the world. Institutional bases for development of traditional medicine as a tool for well-being already exist in the North-East in the North Eastern Institute of Folk Medicine, Pasighat, and the newly established North Eastern Institute of Ayurveda and Homoeopathy (NEIAH), Shillong. At the same time, the existence of many and varied folk medicine traditions in the North-East, which have high local acceptability, should also be effectively used for well-being promotion.

Overcoming the challenge of undernourishment and inadequate health coverage must be the priority development agenda not only in the North East but also at the national level. The recent initiatives by the State Governments and the Central Government are expected to yield favourable results. The impact evaluation of these schemes can be assessed through credible studies. The NER has ample natural resources, which if utilized properly, can make it self-sufficient and can also become a hub with its supply of surplus produce of non-foodgrain items such as fruits, vegetables, meat items, etc. to the other parts of the country and outside. Towards this end, efficient utilization, conservation, and management of the precious natural resources have to be ensured by the state governments. Therefore, a strategic action plan based on a holistic view should be put in place and effectively implemented by meticulously redesigning the whole gamut of food, horticulture, vegetable, meat, etc., cold chains, value addition, marketing infrastructure, etc. by internalizing nutritional values and health linkage.

6

Education, Skill Development, and Entrepreneurship

Introduction

The Sustainable Development Goal (SDG) 4 seeks inclusive, equitable, and quality education for all, encompassing technical and vocational training by providing lifelong learning opportunities and to substantially increase the number of youth and adults with relevant skills for employment, decent jobs, and entrepreneurship. Further, SDG 8 calls for full and productive employment and decent work for all, including for young people and persons with disabilities, and equal pay for work of equal value as major component of inclusive and sustainable economic growth. Thus, SDG 4 and SDG 8 are highly interlinked and interdependent for the socio-economic development of the country. The achievements of SDG 4 will also largely affect and be affected by achievements of other SDGs.

The NE States have a mixed level of achievements under SDGs 4 and 8 as captured in the NITI's SDG India Index 2019. On SDG 4 compared to the all India score of 58, Manipur (70) and Mizoram (61) performed better, while Arunachal Pradesh and Sikkim were at the all India level. Other NE States had a score which ranged from 44 to 55. In case of SDG 8, the all India score at 64 was better than that of all India score on SDG 4. On SDG 8, Sikkim (68) and Meghalaya (65) were having better than national scores, while Tripura (63) and Assam (62) were just below it; the remaining NE States have scores varying from 27 to 52.

Education and skilling create the enabling environment for upward socio-economic mobility, which is key to eradicating poverty. Employability of the workforce remains an issue for discourse and action in the international, regional, national, and sub-national development agenda. From a global perspective, as per SDG Report 2019, in 2018,

Rise of the North East, RIS, Oxford University Press. © Research and Information System for Developing Countries 2023.
DOI: 10.1093/oso/9780192849342.003.0006

one-fifth of the world's youth were not engaged in education, employment, or training (NEET). Thus, they were neither gaining professional experience nor acquiring or developing skills through educational or vocational programmes during the formative stages of life. The Report adds that gender differences in this regard are all pervasive; as in 2018, young women were more than twice as likely as young men to be unemployed or outside the labour force and not in school or in a training programme (young women had a NEET rate of 30 per cent compared to 13 per cent for young men).

Generally, the literacy rates of the North Eastern Region (NER) are comparable to the national rates. However, the percentage of persons with education attainment below primary education, including the literacy rates, is an important indicator of educational deprivation. The NER, in this regard, records higher deprivation than the national level for various reasons. Very high dropout rates are observed in most of the NE States compared to the country's average, both for total and girl population, at primary level in the year 2016–17.[1] Not only at the primary and upper-primary levels, the dropout rates at secondary-level workout as very high in the NER (27.7 per cent) as against national figure (22.1 per cent).

Large percentage of schools in the NER have a single teacher, are without a girl's toilet, have inadequate provision and poor quality of mid-day meal (MDM), and low levels of certain other basic amenities—these are some of the possible reasons for high dropout rates. The non-availability of girls' toilets is as high as 12.7 per cent against all India average of 2.4 per cent. The incidence of such schools is high in Assam (15.7 per cent) and Meghalaya (14.4 per cent).

The NER have a large number of universities in relation to their population. Improvement in this over time has also been remarkable. The central government has set up a university in each of the states. And yet, the number of colleges per thousand population in the age group of eighteen to twenty-three years works out to be much below the national figure. The two states that recorded reasonably high figures in 2017–18 are Manipur and Nagaland, but still these are below the national average. Tripura and

[1] Press Information Bureau, Government of India, 28 July 2019, Ministry of Skill Development and Entrepreneurship.

Meghalaya have shown significant improvement in recent years, but that in other states has, at best, been modest.

Gross Attendance Rate (GAR),[2] for higher education in the region, computed by taking enrolment as a percentage of students in 18–23 age groups based on NSS data, was 9.5 per cent in 2004–05, which has gone up to 23.1 per cent in 2014. The corresponding figure for India as a whole has increased from 14.8 per cent to 26.9 per cent—However, despite this improvement in attendance in higher educational institutions in several states, the average figure works out as below the all India level. Unfortunately, the figures for Tripura, Sikkim, and Meghalaya still work out to be alarmingly low.

The gender disparity in GAR in higher education is low in the states of Assam and Meghalaya but here the overall GAR is also very low. However, in the states with high GAR—such as Nagaland, Arunachal Pradesh, and Manipur, the gender disparity is high. This implies that benefits of expansion of higher education are not accruing to women. Interestingly, in the states of Mizoram and Tripura, gender disparity is high in spite of their low GAR. The fact that gender disparity is extremely low in Meghalaya, emerged also from the discussion with officials and researchers. This may be because of the matrilineal tribal society in the state.

The remoteness of rural areas is a major concern as perceived by the officials in all the states which can be inferred also from the high rural urban disparity in the region. High disparity exists even at the national level, but the hilly states in the region, such as Meghalaya and Mizoram, record particularly high values. A positive fact is that GAR among tribals in the region is much higher than the tribals at the national level. Unlike elementary and school education, high gender gap is noticeable in higher education, similar to that at the national level. The share of persons with diploma or graduation and above is lower among women compared to men, as per 2011 Census in the region.

It is observed that people have gone for skill development trainings also after acquiring basic high education. The key issue here is that the courses in most public-funded institutions are offered in conventional streams under general education. Private players are able to read the periodic and

[2] Khuntia, Priyadarsan Amitav, 'Skill Development of Youth in North East India: Way Forward', V.V. Giri National Labour Institute, NLI Research Studies Series No. 124/2017.

Box 6.1: SEQI in North Eastern States

The School Education Quality Index (SEQI) has been developed by NITI Aayog to provide insights and data-based feedback on the success of school education across India. It attempts to provide a platform for promoting evidence-based policymaking and highlights possible course corrections in the education sector catering to the need of improving the quality of education and service delivery. Among all the north eastern states of India, all states except Assam have been grouped together as small states to facilitate a like-for-like comparison while Assam has been included in the group of large states. As per the NITI Aayog report for 2016–17, Assam was one of the top-performing states in the large states category with a performance score of over 60per cent. Among the small states group, Manipur and Tripura were the best performing states with Manipur leading the group with a performance score of 68.8 per cent followed by Tripura with a score close to 65per cent. All the other states had a score between 40 per cent and 60per cent, with an exception of Arunachal Pradesh which had the lowest score of 24.6per cent. While most these states showed an improvement in their rankings from the base year, Mizoram, Sikkim, and Arunachal Pradesh showed a slight dip in their performance rankings from 47.7 per cent to 46.5 per cent, 43.9 per cent to 43 per cent, and 30.4 per cent to 28.4 per cent in 2015–16 to 2016–17, respectively. Within the categories of SEQI, it was observed that most north eastern states, except Sikkim and Assam, fared better in the outcomes category as compared to the governance processes aiding outcomes category, highlighting the areas that need to be strengthened.

Source: School Education Quality Index (SEQI), NITI Aayog (2019).

sporadic demand in certain disciplines well in advance, but there are not many of these in the region. Public institutions have also now started offering professional diploma courses which will go a long way in achieving the goal of quality education and employability.

While schools lacked basic amenities, the budgetary allocation for elementary and secondary education has gone up during the past five years, but a high proportion of it remains unspent—particularly in the state of Assam, where it is as high as 17.5 per cent and 15 per cent of the allocated amount in general education component of higher education during 2016–17 and 2017–18, respectively. In technical education, too, the unspent amount was 47 per cent in the year 2017–18.

From the national and NER growth perspective, youth employability has been a cause of concern for policy makers and several attempts towards this direction are a testimony to it. The Government of India created a separate Ministry, namely, Ministry of Skill Development & Entrepreneurship (MSDE) to exclusively focus on providing the right opportunities to young people and also to encourage youngsters to pursue entrepreneurship as a full time career. National Youth Policy 2014, National Skill Development Mission, National Skill Development Agency (NSDA), and National Policy on Skill Development and Entrepreneurship 2015 are a few initiatives which have a basic approach to enhance skilling opportunities—matching with suitable platforms for the youth. Major flagship programmes such as *Pradhan Mantri Kaushal Vikas Yojana* of Ministry of Skill Development and Entrepreneurship and *Deen Dayal Upadhyaya Grameen Kaushalya Yojana* of Ministry of Rural Development are also being implemented for skill development.

In the backdrop of preceding discussion, the skilling ecosystem in the NE has specific needs to meet the challenges in order to address the aspirations of its youth more is need to equip them in a holistic manner with upcoming demands such as the 4th Industrial Revolution (4IR), and at the same time upgrade skills at all age levels in the traditional sectors to enhance productivity and competitiveness.

Notably, the region has higher literacy than the country, clubbed with better proficiency in English, which unlock many opportunities—matching needs of both international and domestic demands.

The Emerging Scenario

A primary challenge that the NER faces in education is accessibility because of the nature of the topographies of the states which have communities scattered over remote and hilly regions. It would make the requirement of physical infrastructure for both school, and higher and technical education much more intense than in other parts of the country, with the norms for setting them up being different for the hilly states.

The levels of infrastructure for elementary education were noted as higher in the region than that in the country, which possibly were responsible for higher enrolment and attendance rates. This, however, is not the case at secondary and higher secondary level. Understandably, the advantage of the NE, observed in terms of educational indicators at primary level, does not exist in secondary and higher secondary education. Given the high level of poverty and socio-economic deprivation in many of the states, provisioning of MDM scheme can be an important factor in attracting and retaining students at the school level.

The North East Special Infrastructure Development Scheme approved in December 2017 also opens up the possibility of improving infrastructure for secondary and higher secondary school education in remote areas as it has explicitly identified this as one of its priority concerns. The high priority given to this region by the present government is reflected in its budgetary enhancement in recent years. Along with this, a strategy needs to be designed to involve the private sector in strengthening the higher education system, especially in developing professional courses. The low share of diploma courses in most of the states is a matter of special concern from the viewpoint of livelihood of the population in the region. Increasing the coverage of diploma education, catering to the needs and aspirations of the local population merits urgent consideration of the state governments.

People of the NER give high weightage to acquiring education as they aspire to use education and professional skills as their asset to establish their 'entitlement' in the labour market. High value-addition processes and services-based activities can come up in the region, but these require a certain level of skills which is sadly lacking. On the other hand, a large number of illiterates and dropouts without primary education are struggling to find a space in the labour market or struggling to generate a threshold income in primary activities. Given the limited opportunities within the region, many among the educated youth are seeking absorption in the national economy, leading to large-scale out-migration. An appropriate strategy of higher education and skill development can halt migration from the NE region for lower end jobs. Along with this, an exposure to employment and entrepreneurship and professional courses and the opportunities they open up at the school level needs to be a high priority for the NER.

One notable feature of education in the NER is the high dependence on public sector, as in the case of healthcare. The special status given to these states on account of various security and economic grounds leading to very high central share in the government schemes could be a reason for this. The NER faces several development challenges due to lack of channels such as public and private enterprises, industrial activity, and institutional finances which lead to lack of skilling opportunities; besides the specific challenges of digital and physical connectivity and infrastructure deficiency. Externalities such as adverse impact of climate change on the farm and non-farm sector, topographic variations, etc. are added challenges, as the agriculture and allied sector provides livelihood to a sizable population of the region but is highly susceptible to climate variations. The region has a mix of hills and plains, due to which the programme service delivery to target groups in the hill regions is also a major challenge.

Delayed and limited information collection is yet another challenge. Diagnosis of interrelations and interdependence amongst the sectors for working out projected values and recommendations require a large amount of disaggregated information. Official information/data are generally dispersed over a number of departments of the state governments. Moreover, it is not available at the desired disaggregated levels.

The National Policy on Skill Development and Entrepreneurship, 2015, realized the formidable challenge that in the next twenty years while the labour force in the industrialized world was expected to decline by 4 per cent, in India, it would increase by 32 per cent, and also recognized this as a huge opportunity. It pointed out the dual challenge of paucity of highly trained workforce, and at the same time non-employability of large sections of the conventionally educated youth, who possess little or no job skills. This demonstrates a classical mismatch of segmental under supply and over supply, where inadequacy of human capital building trainers persists as a constraint. The problem is compounded by the quality issues to meet industrial and other demands.

The policy also stresses on the need to handle additional challenges arising from inadequate infrastructure, poor investment, and low industrial opportunities, in places such as NER. The policy brings forth the proclivity of large sections of industry, especially in the MSME sectors to treat skilled and unskilled persons at par. This leads to lack of incentives to climb up the skilling ladder and needs redressal through incentives for higher value additions by the more skilled persons. Special attention to job creation for skilled youth persists as a major challenge before the nation, while entrepreneurship based on innovation has immense growth potential. Counselling and guidance remain challenges in the skill space, which if tackled can help reduce the attrition rates during training and employment by helping candidates make informed choices.

The private sector hasn't invested much in most areas owing to continued challenges such as lack of connectivity and resultant higher costs of logistics. Some of the private projects such as medical diagnosis and treatment have fructified but these need to be scaled up. A big bang thrust across the existing and prospective sectors remains to take place, spurring on the infrastructural push already in operation. Once a 'big bang' occurs, all channels of development and multifaceted actions on skilling and upskilling amidst enhanced industrial activities and trainings, internships, would steer forward. The traditional skills that can help generate jobs, with forward-looking techniques and appropriate investments continue to include avenues in dairy, food processing, rubber, rubber-wood furniture, bamboo products, sericulture, pisciculture, apiculture, water conservation, soil analysis, handlooms, handicrafts, health, beauty and wellness, and automotive, construction, and hospitality, sectors.

The ever-changing, forward-looking opportunities as of now encompass, 4IR, IT/ITeS, computer languages, big data analytics, satellite mapping and analysis, medical biotechnology, agricultural biotechnology organic farming, cold chains, civil aviation, resilient and earthquake resistant infrastructure and so on. The skilling needs for NER are not limited to existing or unlocking opportunities within the Region, but to meet the demands in the rest of country, as well as abroad; and some youth who return to these states with better entrepreneurial activities would provide employment in the region.

Overview and Opportunities

According to the 2011 census, literacy rate except for Assam and Arunachal Pradesh was higher than the national average (74.04 per cent) with highest being in Mizoram at 91.33 per cent. This clubbed with better proficiency in English in NER unlocks many opportunities matching needs of both international and domestic demands. However, quality of education needs focused attention. The ASER-2016 read with ASER-2018 (published on 20 January 2020) for assessing standard of primary education and the gaps therein clearly indicate that gaps between official norms and actual practice were evident both when young children enter school and in what they are able to do in terms of foundational skills such as reading and arithmetic. Moreover, it reported that the gap between expectations and ground realities starts very early and needs to be addressed urgently and that once children fall behind, it is very difficult to catch up.

The rates of unemployment for the general population in the region are and have been much higher than the country, both in rural and urban areas over the past one and a half decade. These are about twice the national rate in Manipur and Mizoram and more than three times in Nagaland. Meghalaya and Sikkim, however, record low unemployment rates. The urban rates are generally higher than in the rural areas across the states in the region, as is the case in the country. Studies on employment possibilities in the region suggest low demand for graduate education at government institutions and preference for job driven technical, professional degrees. Understandably, there is relatively higher demand for people with professional qualification than with general education. Attention must, therefore, be paid to the problems on the supply side in order to design skill development programme to ensure employability.

Further, a study[3] by Indian Chamber of Commerce on development and employment generation potential of the north eastern states, between 2011 and 2021, the region will generate only 2.6 million jobs, and almost half of this will be in Assam alone. As opposed to the low demand, there will also be a supply of seventeen million people during 2011–2022, an excess of fourteen million job seekers. So there is need for a twin approach for developing skills for both local employment and for those who seek to migrate.

There are 73 ITIs in NE with seating capacity of 17,000, of which around 13,000 cater to the engineering or technical trades such as electrician, auto-mechanics, etc. However, currently there is a shortage of facility for training of trainers also at these facilities.[4]

In order to achieve the mammoth task of skilling the youth for enhancing employability, MSDE in co-ordination with other administrative ministries and state governments have been making efforts to eliminate disconnect between demand and supply of skilled manpower across the country including NE. The progress of NE States under 'Skill India' programme is highlighted below[5]:

- 2.5 lakh youths have been trained since 2016, of which 1.82 lakh have been certified. To improve the livelihood opportunities of more than 80,000 traditional arts and handicrafts artisans have had their skills certified under the Pradhan Mantri Kaushal Vikas Yojana (PMKVY) in the region.

- MSDE introduced National Skill Training Institute (NSTI) for skilling women of Tripura in non-traditional roles and increasing gender sensitivity in the workplace, under which training is provided in Computer Numerical Control (CNC) mechanics, automation specialists, warehouse packers, mine welders, toolmakers and

---

[3] Indian Chamber of Commerce: India's North-East Diversifying Growth Opportunities (2013).

[4] Press Information Bureau, Government of India, 28 July 2019, Ministry of Skill Development and Entrepreneurship.

[5] Press Information Bureau, Government of India, 28 July 2019, Ministry of Skill Development and Entrepreneurship, Center and State governments review skill development initiatives in the North-Eastern Region to empower youth & create sustainable opportunities of employment.

die-makers, security guards, vermi-composting producers, among others.

- Under a Skill India Special Project to support the Bru Tribe Women, almost 250 women have been trained under PMKVY, who got employed. Jan Shikshan Sansthans under MSDE have been established and re-operated through non-governmental organizations, providing vocational skills.

- In the 2018, in NER 214 applications were received for National Entrepreneurship awards out of which five winners were from North East, including three women, out of a total of 33 winners at the national level.

- MSDE had ensured that there is a single regulator for training ecosystem (for both short-term and long-term training) to streamline all skill trainings to one legal entity. It further established the National Council for Vocational Education and Training (NCVET) which was approved by the Cabinet in October 2018. NCVET would be an overarching skills regulator by merging the existing skill regulatory bodies—NSDA & National Council for Vocational Training.

Interconnects among the flagship programmes are equally vital as Khuntia (2017) argues that Skill India has a vital role in supporting the other flagship initiatives such as Make in India, Smart city, Digital India, Startup India, Standup India, and Swachh Bharat, and youth of NE can boost the skilling and up skilling ambition of the country by 2022.

The NER Vision 2020 aptly identifies that in any people-centric vision of NER, education and the building of skills and knowledge will be the cornerstone. The North Eastern Council (NEC), a government agency for regional development, has also been funding projects for infrastructure development and providing financial support to students in NER, for development of sports and youth activities, development and promotion of education and social sector.

There are institutions that also facilitate skilling in the region, for instance, Indian Institute of Technology, Guwahati, would have extension centres in the NE States to introduce pedagogy of education to large numbers of learners. This would encompass direct instruction, networked learning with supported open learning programmes through outreach

---

Box 6.2: Paryatan Sahayak Prakalp—Tripura

Tripura has very high potential to become a great tourist destination, with many tourist locations and many more that are yet to be explored. In order to enable the tourism sector in Tripura to grow, the best strategy is felt to involve all the stake holders and simultaneously create an ecosystem to increase the number of stake holders. Therefore, with the objective of promotion of entrepreneurship in tourism sector, the access of loans to tourism enterprises setup from 1 July 2019 is provided and upon successful repayments, as an incentive, the interest component is borne by the state government. The Tripura Tourism Interest Subvention Scheme 2019, namely 'Paryatan Sahayak Prakalp', is implemented through Tripura Tourism Development Corporation Ltd. (TTDCL), which through a committee including industry department, lead bank, and other bankers recommends proposals to banks. It provides interest subvention for loans up to Rs. 5 lakh, though a bank may extend a loan beyond this amount as per its norms. It covers individual older than eighteen years up to fifty years with preference to unemployed youth and to those who have completed graduation or diploma in Hotel Management or Travel and Tourism or undergone any skill development in tourism-related skills under the PMKVY or any others schemes.

Source: Official sources.

---

activities, and also create awareness and training for the rural masses about rural technologies.

Notably, Singapore would also be investing in Assam for entrepreneurship development, and there is scope for such bilateral collaborations.

Education and Skill Ecosystem

The Government of India has taken up major skilling initiatives which are being implemented through the States. These emanate from the skilling policy framework which includes National Policy on Skill Development and Entrepreneurship, 2015 as an integral part of the government policy on *Sabka Saath, Sabka Vikaas*, now enlarged as *Sabka Saath, Sabka Vikaas, Sabka Vishwas*, and its commitment to overall human resource development. It aims to take advantage of the demographic profile of country's population in the coming years, through a comprehensive and holistic policy as part of an integral process. Some salient objectives of this policy are:

- to meet the challenge of skilling at scale with speed and standard (quality),
- to provide an umbrella framework to all skilling activities being carried out within the country, and to align them to common standards and link the skilling with demand centres,
- to lay objectives and to identify various institutional frameworks which can act as the vehicle to reach the expected outcomes, and to provide clarity and coherence on how skill development efforts across the country can be aligned within the existing institutional arrangements,
- to link skills development to improved employability and productivity.

In this regard, the *Deen Dayal Uapdhyaya Grameen Kaushalya Yojana* skilling programme intertwines market orientation of demand, skilling orientation, and institutional support, to attain placement linked skilling projects in more than 250 trades for rural youth. Under this, the programme implementing agencies are required to achieve placement of at least 70 per cent of the trainees.

Further, the National Skill Development Mission in synergy with the State Skilling Missions, State Skill Development Missions of NE, NEC, and other facilitating actors such as private sector including prospective investors, training providers, industrial demandeurs, multilateral organizations, CSOs, think-tanks, media, and institutions can play a crucial role to harness potential of youth efficiently for utilizing public, private, and other resources to skill youth to make them employable/employment providers.

Another set of emerging opportunities is in establishing own startups supported by schemes such as Atal Innovation Mission, MUDRA, and other innovative funding options, leading to entrepreneurial initiatives. Towards this endeavour, Startup India is a flagship initiative of the Government of India, intended to catalyse startup culture and build a strong and inclusive ecosystem for innovation and entrepreneurship in India.

Under Atal Innovation Mission, NITI Aayog promotes setting up of Atal Incubation Centres in both public and private sector. Moreover, its Tinkering labs are also set up to foster curiosity, creativity, and imagination in young minds and inculcate skills such as design mindset, computational thinking, adaptive learning, physical computing, etc. right from the schooling years.

Out of the initiatives taken on entrepreneurship in NE six Institutes of Higher Learning participated in the PM-YUVA scheme and 684 students received entrepreneurship training in 2017–18. The Indian Institute of Entrepreneurship, Guwahati, now with MSDE, has helped streamline its role on Entrepreneurship. Further, there would be focus on coverage of local trade-based short-term courses also.

The National Skill Training Institutes for Women are also operating in states; for instance, at Tura in Meghalaya, courses are conducted in the Trades of Craftsmen Instructors Training Scheme (CITS) and Craftsmen Training Scheme (CTS) besides a number of short-term courses in basic beauty, garments, and basic office: Agartala, Tripura also has CITS and CTS.

Steps taken on skilling by some NE States include introduction of vocational education as an additional subject at the secondary level to impart skills to persons in identified vocations/trade along with general education, which in fact would also reduce dropout rates. At the next level, ITIs and polytechnics can attract budding technocrats by offering cutting-edge technical skills making them future ready.

A major pillar of the strength of NSDC is the Sector Skill Councils (SSCs), which aim to bridge the gap between industry's skill demands and skills supplied. NSDC also sets the National Occupational Standards, which is a critical contribution to India's skilling ecosystem. In these effort SSCs, which are national partnership organizations, bring together all the stakeholders, namely industry, labour, and the academia.

Till date, the NSDC Board has approved thirty-eight SSCs, which also have more than six hundred Corporate Representatives in their Governing Councils.

The SSCs operate as an autonomous body and have the flexibility to be registered as a Section 8 Company, or a Society. NSDC is mandated to initiate and incubate SSCs with initial seed funding to facilitate their growth and enable them to achieve self-sustainability in a time bound manner.

On these lines, the Ministry has taken up several measures to bring coherence in skill development through introduction of common norms, placing emphasis on demand-driven training, encouraging Public–Private Partnership (PPP) model; bringing convergence and co-ordination across ministries and departments. Policy measures are being introduced to revamp the Technical Vocational Educational Training track in education, to make both horizontal and vertical mobility possible and bring equivalence in 'general' and 'vocational' certification at all levels through NSQF. The National Skill Development Corporation (NSDC), under MSDE, is a one of its kind PPP in India. NSDC aims to promote skill development by catalysing the creation of large, quality, for-profit vocational institutions. MSDE intends to establish visible and aspirational training centres in every district of the country. These training centres shall be called *Pradhan Mantri Kaushal Kendra (PMKKs)*.

Box 6.3:   State-Level Initiatives on Skill Development

Arunachal Pradesh
- CM Yuva Kaushal Yojana, to provide high-end training to our youths (both within the state and outside).
- Chief Minister's Paryatan Shiksha Yojana-I (CMPSY-I) to sponsor students of the State for taking up B. Sc (H&C) for three-year degree course in prestigious Institutes recognized by Ministry of Tourism, Government of India. Chief Minister's Paryatan Shiksha Yojana-II (CMPSY-II) to sponsor students for Diploma course in Tourism.
- Establishment of White Water Guide Training Centre (Aqua Adventure Centre) in various major river basins (Kameng, Siang, Dibang, Lohit, and Subansiri) to supplement the tourism needs of the state by providing professional hands in handling rafting related activities.
- CM's Hastshilp Yojana to promote premium and niche handicraft productions of exportable items of modern concept of design with introduction of modern technology by providing training to unemployed youths under handloom, handicrafts and weaving sectors.

Assam
- Skills training to the tea tribes for setting up small businesses. Subsequent to the skill trainings, state government provides a one-time grant of Rs. 25,000 for setting up of small businesses.
- State-Level Mega Skill Development Scheme to provide skills training to youth of the State, linked with SVAYEM Yojana so as to ensure employability and encourage entrepreneurship.

Manipur
- The Industrial and Investment Policy of Manipur, 2017 was notified with the objective to provide skill development and entrepreneurial skills and encourage gainful employment.
- Data and Indicator is being strengthened to track of the progress in skilling of youth, employment, and the skilling of vulnerable/ marginalized youth.

Meghalaya

- To bring about such a paradigm shift, the Meghalaya Institute of Entrepreneurship (MIE) has been set up as a Nodal institution in the State for facilitating rapid economic transformation through entrepreneurship education and promotion of micro enterprises involving the youth, women, and other critical target groups in the State.
- In this regard, MIE aims at entrepreneurship creation and promotion, innovation, and application of skills, technologies, and harnessing the rich potential of promising sub sectors with clearly defined focus on apiculture, agriculture, horticulture, floriculture, pisciculture, aromatic and medicinal plantations, animal husbandry, non-farm enterprises, and other locally viable, remunerative income-generating activities.

Mizoram

- Mizoram has made skilling as an integral part of various schemes run by the state such as Integrated Muga Silk Development Project, Intensive Bivoltine Sericulture Development Project, and Integrated Sericulture Development Project. The state government has also put emphasis on the awareness creation for entrepreneurship and also set up a committee named 'Mizoram Entrepreneurship Development Monitoring Committee' to educate the youth of the state on various opportunities beyond the public sector and impart necessary skills.

Nagaland

- Nagaland Startup Policy has evolved the vision to establish Nagaland as a model startup leader, by creating a culture of entrepreneurship that nurtures creative and innovative youth, allowing them to build successful startup companies, become job creators and contribute towards building a healthy and sustainable economy.
- The objective of the policy is to facilitate the growth of startups, with a focus on establishing innovative 'Made in Nagaland'

products and services. The salient features of this new policy are to introduce a Nagaland Innovation Fund, Nagaland Investor Network, create Entrepreneurship, Incubators, and set up Entrepreneurship Development Centres in schools. The policy seeks to promote women entrepreneurship by earmarking 25 per cent of funds for startups led by women entrepreneurs. The eligible startups will also get fiscal incentives.

Sikkim

- Priority of the state government is focused on skill development and entrepreneurship, education, innovative and high-value tourism, and promotion of non-polluting Green Industry. Each Industrial and Service Unit will now make a firm commitment to support professional and technical education, training and skill building of their workers and employees and also fresh recruits.
- To support the products made in Sikkim, the state government now proposes that whatever is produced in Sikkim, in its packaging besides 'Made in India', the producing unit have to add 'A product of Sikkim Himalayas'.

Tripura

- The State Government has established a separate department for dealing the matters related with skill development. The department organizes skill development training programmes and provides certificates.
- Placement support is provided to the successful candidates to private companies based on the acquired skills on different trades.

Source: Official sources.

Conclusion

Educational development must be an integral part of the strategy to streamline the growth process at the grassroot and ensure that the region plays a key role in meeting the goals of the country's Act East Policy and help in breaking the economic and geographical isolation. Importantly, the high population growth and migration in the NE region have transformed the once-land-abundant but ecologically fragile territory into a land scarce region. Its economic carrying capacity is further constrained because of depletion and degradation of certain natural resources and suboptimal utilization of several others and of labour. What is required is technical, higher and professional education suited to the needs and requirements of the NER.

The macro development strategy for the region must focus on skill intensive industrialization and the education system must be linked to the same. The current scheme of Capacity Building and Technical Assistance of the Ministry of Development of North Eastern Region (DoNER) Ministry, designed to support skill development, enhance employability and promote self-employment opportunities is a welcome initiative.

Designing textbooks and other teaching material posing mathematical problems and computer games in the context of the NER would help in improving learning outcomes. An understanding of the local resource base and development potential, leading to inculcation of ecological sensitivity, needs to be imparted at the school level. Specialized colleges and institutions of the highest proficiency should be established in different states so that students of any state can acquire technical, management, and professional degrees from another state within the region. These will provide skill support to numerous existing and prospective industries. Some of the skill sectors/vocational courses for industries which are viable for NE and generate jobs for youth are as under:

From the lens of NE, and aspiration of youth towards a selected sector of tourism, travel and hospitality, it is relevant to have a look at the presence of the partner Training Centres of the sector-specific council named Tourism and Hospitality Skill Council. In fact, NSDC computed skilled manpower requirement for different sectors and within each for different levels is covered. For instance, the hospitality segment requires basic skills in Housekeeping, Skill Category Level-I or Front Office Services, Skill Category Level-II for Management and Entrepreneurship, and Specialized Skill for Tourism Package Development. Training and creating synergies between industry and education through job oriented diploma courses, organized parallel with general education at high schools

Table 6.1: Skill Sectors/Vocational Courses for Industries Which Are Viable

Sector	Courses
Hospitality	Cuisines, food & beverage, pastry & baking
Tourism	Tour operators, hotels, home stay, taxis to places of attraction, etc.
Medical	Nursing, Paramedics, Wellness
Fashion designing	Garments, handloom weaving.
Essential technicians	Electrician, plumbing, repair of ACs, fridge, mobile, etc.
Automobile	Fitter, turner, mechanics, welding.
Retail	Retail merchandising
Aviation	Cabin crew, air hostess, ground crew, etc.
Others	Beauty, etc.
Soft skills	For employability in any sector

Training of trainers in each skill set so that their resources are used to create more human resources.

Source: Ministry of DoNER.

and colleges, would help to bring down the dropout rate and increase their employability, after completion of education.

Skill development can't be left only to the government; all stakeholders should be actively involved in this endeavour. Such a holistic approach necessitates the involvement of industrial and manufacturing units, service providers, institutions, CSOs, and so on. An effective skill gap mapping should be carried out and updated to also encompass upcoming trades and opportunities and be maintained on real time basis and available in the public domain. In a fast-changing demand and anticipated demand scenario, to support it, the course modules need to be updated to keep these realistic, relevant, and remunerative, while instructors need to be trained to meet the varied and technologically updated new demands. Studies, vision documents, and moreover state-specific skill mapping (though some states have undertaken skill mapping) and even within the state, the district- and block-level mapping would be of immense importance in successful handling the skill affair of North East Region.

While strengthening the skill ecosystem, it should be internalized that aspiring youth should venture into those areas of skill training that are in demand in the North East and beyond both domestically as well as abroad, by buttressing the traditional paradigm of conventional skills and breaking the gender stereotype in choosing skill trades. Notably, the National Policy on Skill Development and Entrepreneurship 2015 rightly observes that mainstreaming gender roles by skilling women in non-traditional roles and increasing gender sensitivity in the workplace will have a catalytic effect on productivity and be a smart economic decision. There is a need to fully harness the locked potential and talent of the NER to provide people, especially youth and women, employability and ability to employ others through entrepreneurial initiatives. For instance, emphasis should be on establishing the remaining PMKKs out of the allocated ones not only for the establishment of new training centres but also for assessing and improving the quality of the training imparted, in order to ensure higher proportion of placements.

Given the vibrancy in many sectors in the NE States, there is significant scope to conduct more training courses to meet the current and upcoming demand under CITS and CTS. To harness the demographic dividend, focus on gender equality needs to be sharpened. State statistical systems need strengthening in terms of its capacity to produce reliable and timely information with required disaggregation. Latest ICT and technology innovations can help in this endeavour.

7

Communication, Connectivity, and Infrastructure Development

Introduction

The Sustainable Development Goals (SDGs) envisaged in the Agenda 2030 sets the vision for future of the world economy and the humanity. All the seventeen goals are interrelated and capture all essential dimensions of inclusive and balanced economic, social, and human development. Countries at various levels of development, particularly the developing countries and least developed countries (LDCs) have undertaken suitable and adaptive policy initiatives to achieve SDGs by 2030. SDGs are interrelated and require an integrated approach by the countries across sectors rather than piecemeal and fragmented approaches. Communication, connectivity, and infrastructure play a crucial role in meeting the SDGs. The role of connectivity and infrastructure in all different forms—social, economic, and digital—is not just confined to SDG-9 (a goal that defines a roadmap for resilient and inclusive infrastructure along with industrialization and innovation for all countries, especially for those who lag on these counts) rather it encompasses processes and institutions that facilitate fulfilment of other SDGs. For example, SDG-1 that aims at ending poverty in all its forms requires creation and equitable distribution of income-generating activities and livelihood options in view of potential social and economic vulnerabilities. Lack of physical connectivity in the form of roads, railways, and communication, especially in rural and backward areas, would perpetuate poverty and restrict the communities living in those areas from exploring means to leverage their skills and resources for better standards of life. Likewise, SDG-3, SDG-4, SDG-6, SDG-8, SDG-10, SDG-11, and SDG-13 have direct bearings on infrastructure. Infrastructure is an enabler for creating congenial

Rise of the North East, RIS, Oxford University Press. © Research and Information System for Developing Countries 2023.
DOI: 10.1093/oso/9780192849342.003.0007

conditions for achievement of those goals. SDG-11, in particular, is all about making cities and human settlements livable and vibrant growth centres providing opportunities for lagging regions in a country to catch up with national averages and global standards. Likewise, modern communication facilities and systems facilitated by information technology (IT) would act as an enabler of the systemic changes those developing countries such as India is currently witnessing. In fact, it is not an exaggeration to characterize the slower pace of upward social mobility and economic exclusion in many countries of the world in the past five decades particularly in the rural areas is the outcome of absence of communication. Lack of proper communication in terms of access to modern communication tools at affordable prices impaired proper implementation of government policies, inefficient aggregation of people's needs and ambitions, and lower participation of people due to ignorance. Unlike the past, better deployment of telecommunication and IT infrastructure in the recent years has revolutionized communications in provision of public services through mobile telephony and internet. Access to faster, reliable, and affordable communication is empowering ordinary people by building their self-confidence and real time access to decisions and developments around them.

SDG-8 relies heavily on infrastructure stock in a country at a particular point of time. In fact, the extent and quality of infrastructure available in a region determines the enabling conditions for full and productive employment of land, capital, and labour. Natural resources would remain unutilized or underutilized in absence of proper road and railways connectivity. Lack of affordable commuting between home and workplaces would lead to unemployment of local labour and widen inequality. SDG-4 constitutes a direct component of social infrastructure as education and skilling is central for countries to remain competitive in the emerging trade and industrial landscape. A steady progress in internet penetration would probably enhance skill development through digital mode along with formal education and training. The Fourth Industrial Revolution that depends on new-generation digital technologies would require solid foundation of knowledge economy rooted in education, health, and skill development.

In addition to the catalytic role that infrastructure plays in enabling and facilitating achievement of SDGs, physical connectivity and other forms of infrastructure are important for regional development as well. The symbiotic linkage between infrastructure and balanced regional development has been studied rigorously in the spatial planning and economic geography literature. In most simplistic sense, infrastructure enables linking the hinterland with urban growth centres and facilitates effective dispersal of activities in the economy across different regions within a country than unjust concentration of productive industrial and service activities in urban metropolis.

The North Eastern Region (NER) of India consisting of eight states, recently coined as *Asthalaxmi* by the Prime Minister, presents certain common characteristics as a region for focused regional development strategy. The region is home to precious natural resources including oil and natural gas. Agriculture and small and medium enterprises in sectors such as tea, bamboo, etc. are backbone of the NER economy. Over the years, NER demonstrated spectacular growth potential and resilience in terms of livelihood diversification, trade and investment, and people's mobility. With strong natural resource endowments and strategic locations on the long land borders with Bangladesh, Myanmar, Nepal, and Bhutan, NER presents a unique case for a new model of development beginning with transport corridors, gradually elevating to economic corridors with maturing of production, agglomeration, and trade processes, and finally to growth corridors that link the region with rest of South Asia and Southeast Asia. By enabling better sourcing of local natural resources in the hinterland and smooth supply of finished goods and services to rural and relatively less developed areas, physical connectivity in terms of robust network of roads, railways, ports, and airports can help integrate NER with the regional production networks in South and Southeast Asia and promote cross-border trade with neighbouring countries such as Bangladesh, Myanmar, Nepal, and Bhutan. The Union Government of India at different points of time has given special attention to the unique strengths of the North Eastern States and explored the possibility of leveraging those unique strategic advantages for promoting bilateral trade and investment with neighbouring countries. In the recent years, the focus has shifted from 'Look East Policy' to 'Act East Policy' which implicitly implies greater focus of realization of the policy goals.

The incumbent government at the centre has pursued a comprehensive development strategy for NER within the framework of 'Act East

Policy'. In that spirit, connectivity, communications, and infrastructure development has become the topmost priority for the union and the state governments in NER. Building new roads; rebuilding, repair, maintenance, and upgradation of state and national highways (NHs), proposed spread of railways network linking all the state capitals in NER, laying and activation of digital and IT infrastructure across the region have become the major infrastructure-related interventions in the region. Recently, the Government of Assam has opened a new department called the Act East Policy Affairs Development (AEPA) to provide focused attention on implementation of Act East Policy especially promoting cross-border trade between NER and the neighbouring countries such as Bangladesh, Myanmar, Nepal, and Bhutan using all means of transportation, e.g. land, sea and inland waterways, and air. The Department of AEPA of Assam has recently organized the 'India-Bangladesh Stakeholders' Meet' in Guwahati on 22–23 October 2019 with the overarching theme of 'transformation through transportation'. The deliberations highlighted the potential exists for reduction of trade costs by developing and streamlining alternate modes of cargo transport between Assam, Tripura, Meghalaya, and Bangladesh. Moreover, the thrust on SDGs provides a new basis for renewed focus on infrastructure development in NER. Against this backdrop, this chapter covers the current situation in physical and digital connectivity including digital communication and links its contribution to SDGs in view of the development of regional and sub-regional connectivity and infrastructure initiatives in South and Southeast Asia.

Infrastructure Gaps and SDGs

Poor infrastructure continues to remain a major supply-side bottleneck in the quest for high and inclusive economic growth. Besides institutional and regulatory issues, lack of finance is often viewed as a major reason for the slow pace of infrastructure development in most of the developing and LDCs. As per the McKinsey (2016), the world needs to invest $3.3 trillion annually in economic infrastructure through 2030, and under-investment in critical and new infrastructure would erode future growth potential and productivity. Table 7.1 illustrates the projected

Table 7.1: Estimates of Infrastructure Investment Gaps (2016–30)

Region/Sector	Current Trends	Investment Need	Financing Gap	SDGs (Additional Need)
Sector				
Road	1.0	1.3	0.3	–
Electricity	1.0	1.1	0.1	0.2
Railways	0.4	0.4	0	–
Telecoms	0.3	0.3	0	–
Water	0.2	0.2	0	0.1
Airports	0.1	0.1	0	–
Ports	0.1	0.1	0	–
Region				
Asia	4.0	4.4	0.4	0.3
America	1.7	2.5	0.8	0.1
Europe	2.3	2.6	0.3	–
Africa	4.3	5.9	1.6	3.4
Oceania	3.5	3.8	0.3	–

Source: Oxford Economics and Global Infrastructure Hub (2017).

financing requirements for different sectors and regions for the period 2016–30. It is observed that even the traditional infrastructure sectors including roads and electricity still require substantial funding and financing needs would amplify given the current thrust on attainment of SDGs. Asia and Africa, the two populous and fast-growing regions of the world, need infrastructure investment of 0.3 per cent and 3.4 per cent of gross domestic product (GDP), respectively. Given the magnitude of infrastructure financing gaps globally as well as in fast-growing economies in emerging Asia, the existing sources of financing by the multilateral and regional Development Finance Institutions including the World Bank, Asian Development Bank, Inter-American Development Bank, African Development Bank, and others would fall short of; hence, there arises a need for new and supplementary sources of funding. Further, the achievement of SDGs would require additional flows of investments to infrastructure sectors covering physical connectivity, digital connectivity, and communication networks.

Infrastructure development constitutes physical infrastructure and soft infrastructure across urban and rural sectors. Along with traditional infrastructure sectors such as transportation, water and sanitation, power, importance of promoting inclusive, resilient, and sustainable infrastructure is increasingly felt across developing countries. Further, there is strong acknowledgement of the need for diversification of funding sources in the form of blending, introduction of new and innovative instruments of financing, mode of participation with greater participation of the private sector, regulatory and institutional reforms, and other relevant aspects.

Traditionally, infrastructure development in the developing countries focused on expansion of the physical network of roads, railways, airports, sea ports, telecommunications, and so on. Despite high GDP growth and infrastructure development in aggregative terms, many regions in most of the developing countries, including India, have remained relatively backward as compared to the growth centres. In consequence, these aspirational regions/areas faced stagnation while economic activities got concentrated in the growth centres. As production fragmentation and spread of global and regional value chains have revolutionized the scope for promoting exports, investments, and job creation, it is critical to link the aspirational regions to mainstream economy. Infrastructure development would enable the local industries especially the small and medium enterprises to access markets in other parts of the country. These specially targeted area development projects carry high risks and often face bureaucratic delays. It may require sustained flow of institutional finance, as commercial finance is less likely to flow to such projects on the grounds of high perceived risks.

The economic, environmental, and social dividends of a well-laid connectivity and communication and infrastructure network are enormous. Quality and resilient infrastructure covering all areas of infrastructure such as roads, railways, ports, health, education, energy, etc. together as a portfolio of projects would contribute to three essential pillars of SDGs such as economic, environmental, and social. Addressing poor governance, financing gaps, and silo approaches along with reforms could enhance the contribution of infrastructure to development (EIU, 2019).

As discussed in the previous section, connectivity could be a game changer in the NER development process. By laying out well-planned network of roads, railways, and airports, the fragmented small size of the local economies in different states in NER can be integrated which would not only yield the much-needed scale economies but also enable greater linkages with other regions of the country. This section briefly highlights the current status of connectivity in NER and the future roadmap.

Roadways

The total road length in the NER was 498,545 km in 2016–17 with a net addition of 127,815 km in the past six years. All the eight states of NER have experienced steady addition to their road network during 2010–17. Assam being the biggest state in NER accounted for the dominant segment of the region's roadways. After Assam, Tripura, and Nagaland shared the largest road networks of the region. Manipur, having borders with Myanmar, the gateway for India to Southeast Asia, had total road length of 24,776 km (Table 7.2).

The total length of NHs in NER is 13,082 km as of 2016–17 marking a 4,600-km addition in the past six years. Unlike the total road length (inclusive of all types of roads), the regional network of NHs is relatively

Table 7.2: State-wise Length of Road, 2003–04 to 2016–17 (km)

States	2010–11	2011–12	2012–13	2013–14	2014–15	2015–16	2016–17
Arunachal Pradesh	21,122	21,555	14,980	28,095	24,469	25,362	30,692
Assam	239,394	241,789	284,232	288,135	313,621	326,512	329,520
Manipur	18,604	19,133	19,252	20,837	21,661	24,247	24,776
Meghalaya	11,702	11,984	12,103	12,317	13,260	13,372	21,727
Mizoram	8,727	9,810	11,293	10,939	9,803	9,831	8,108
Nagaland	33,423	34,146	35,189	38,281	36,600	37,176	36,114
Sikkim	4,420	4,630	5,616	6,570	6,525	7,450	8,243
Tripura	33,338	33,772	29,248	31,021	41,857	37,384	39,365
NER	370,730	376,819	411,913	436,195	467,796	481,334	498,545

Source: RIS database based on North Eastern Development Finance Corporation Ltd. (NEDFi) Databank.

evenly distributed. Assam and Arunachal Pradesh have NHs of 3,821 km and 2,513 km, respectively, in 2016–17. The rest four states including Manipur, Meghalaya, Mizoram, and Nagaland have NH length between 1,200 km and 1,800 km. Besides NHs, the network of state highways in NER has improved considerably over the years. However, the annual addition to state highways in the region is reasonably low for states such as Sikkim, Tripura, Manipur, and Meghalaya. Overall, the total length of state highways has gone down from 7,656 km in 2010–11 to 5,939 km in 2016–17. It may be due to upgradation of state highways to NHs.

Although the progress in development of roads in the region appears to be satisfactory in aggregate terms, the adequacy, quality, design of roads for human mobility and movement of cargo is to be carefully assessed. It can be examined from the ease of transport from improvement in connectivity within the NER as well as linkages with rest of the country. In that sense, the density of NHs probably serves as a good indicator of adequacy of roadways. Compared to the national average of 35.1 km per sq km of NHs, the North Eastern States have performed well. As of June 2017, all the seven states in NER except Arunachal Pradesh have very high density of NHs. Three states such as Nagaland, Tripura, and Manipur have maintained road density of 93.3 km, 81.4 km, and 78.2 km, respectively, which is significantly higher than the national average (Table 7.3). Looking at the population numbers, the estimate of road density needs to be carefully examined. Assam is the most populous state in the region, whereas human habitation in other states is scattered, and most parts of the geographical areas in the region are hilly terrains. From that perspective, the comparison of road density in NER with national average is not that straight and simple, as with other states in the plain areas.

Another way of assessing the efficiency of roads is in terms of vehicle traffic. In terms of motor vehicle traffic per thousand population, all the states in NER have experienced modest rise in vehicular traffic in the recent years. The vehicular traffic in the region is highest for Mizoram (144) followed by Nagaland (141), Manipur (119), and Arunachal Pradesh (116). With seventy-eight vehicles per thousand population, Assam has the lowest motor vehicle density. However, the scenario is entirely different when total number of registered vehicles is considered. During 2009–15, the total number of registered vehicles in NER increased from 2,007 to 3,894 marking 94 per cent growth in a period of six years.

Table 7.3: Distribution of Density of National Highways (NHs) Length (As on 30 June 2017)

States	Total NH length in Km	Area in 1,000 sq km	Population in lakh (2011 census)	% age of NH	Length of NH in km/1,000 sq km	Length of NH in km/lakh population
Arunachal Pradesh	2,537.4	83.74	13.83	2.20	30.3	183.5
Assam	3,844.7	78.44	311.69	3.33	49.0	12.3
Manipur	1,745.7	22.33	27.22	1.51	78.2	64.1
Meghalaya	1,204.4	22.43	29.64	1.04	53.7	40.6
Mizoram	1,422.5	21.08	10.91	1.23	67.5	130.4
Nagaland	1,546.7	16.58	19.81	1.34	93.3	78.1
Sikkim	463.0	7.10	6.08	0.40	65.2	76.2
Tripura	853.8	10.49	36.71	0.74	81.4	23.3

Source: RIS database based on NEDFi Databank.

Railways

Although road network in NER has expanded remarkably over the years, the modernization, upgradation, and expansion of railways infrastructure is critical to the future socio-economic development of NER. Besides providing an alternative means of passenger and cargo movements, railways serves as the most feasible mode of transportation for certain trade routes in the region. In view of the progress made in cross-border connectivity with Bangladesh, Nepal, Bhutan, and Myanmar, the importance of railways is being felt widely in the region as well as in other parts of India. Seven states of NER have railways connectivity and Sikkim is being connected with Indian railways network through the 44 km Sivok-Rangpo line (Ministry of Railways, 2018). Despite hilly terrain and varying weather patterns, the Northeast Frontier Railway has achieved substantial progress in execution of existing and new projects.

The total length of railways in NER is 2,662 km as of 2016–17. While vast hilly terrain of region has held back rapid expansion of the railway network and entails high investment costs, railways is a viable alternative to address the issue of slow traffic/cargo movement by road and ensuring safe and secure mobility. While road network would, by and large, be expanded negotiating the terrain, rail network can be futuristic in terms of additional infrastructure such as longer bridges and tunnels. This, however, needs attention to environmental and ecological fragilities in these regions (See Box 7.1). The regional distribution of rail network is heavily skewed in favour of Assam. With 2,443 km of rail length, Assam constitutes 91.8 per cent of north-eastern railways network, whereas Manipur, Mizoram, Arunachal Pradesh, and Nagaland are yet to make significant footprint in the country's railway map (Table 7.4).

In recent years, particularly in the past five years from 2014 to 2019, there has been notable progress in execution of railway projects in the region. Seven major railway projects covering total length of 122.91 km and total cost of Rs. 21,412.8 crore have been completed during 2014–19. It included construction of four new lines and three lines for gauge conversion. While most of the railway lines have passed through Assam, several important routes across NER covering Manipur, Mizoram, Meghalaya, Arunachal Pradesh, and Tripura have been successfully completed in

Box 7.1: Can Increased Road Connectivity Contribute to Reduced Extent of Shifting Cultivation in the North Eastern Region?

The Working Group III formed by NITI Aayog submitted its report titled 'Shifting Cultivation: Towards a Transformational Approach' in 2018. It noted that 'despite the desire of the community and efforts by the government to usher in change, shifting cultivation remains an enigma and persists in large parts of the region even today'. The North Eastern States account for a lion's share in the land used under shifting cultivation in the country. It is found that the schemes designed to re-store jhum lands through alternate land use failed significantly as they did not incorporate adequate measures to provide or enhance liveli-hood options and food security of the shifting cultivators. The Report also noted that shifting cultivation had over the years shrunken to re-mote areas 'where the fruits of development like roads, schools, mar-kets and hospitals are yet to reach'.

Notwithstanding the debate on the negative environmental impact of shifting cultivation or otherwise, it is imperative that the technique does not necessarily ensure food, nutritional and livelihood security on a longer term and leaves the communities into what is often re-ferred to as 'low-level equilibrium trap'. It is difficult to break this trap by supply driven factors such as regulatory measures or state-induced direct curative interventions alone. Relevant drivers that create forces big enough to unleash the aspirations of communities to move out of this subsistence based economic structure are needed to be in place.

A meta-analysis of land cover transformation in respect of shifting cultivation in a global perspective reveals that it decreases in regions with access to local, regional, and international markets that en-courage cattle production and cash crops. Unequal and insecure ac-cess to market opportunities and investment, on the other hand, create incentives for pursuing shifting cultivation. It was observed that such practice declined considerably in China, Cambodia, and Thailand, whereas increased in Madagascar and the Democratic Republic of Congo. However, the study also underscored the fact that transition from shifting to intensive permanent agriculture had the potential to enhance permanent deforestation, loss of biodiversity, and associated ecological and environmental concerns. Negative effects on the social and human capital of local communities to varying degrees were also recorded (Vliet et al., 2012).

India's Act East Policy that emphasizes on increased road connectivity between the North Eastern States and the South-East Asian countries can play an important role in creating deepening access of the communities to the local, regional, and international markets would induce the farmers to opt for a diversified cropping pattern resulting in increased income generation and thereby reduce their dependence on shifting agriculture. The 'low-level equilibrium trap' can thus be broken. Needless to add, the required transformation would take a considerable period to be realized, provided simultaneous efforts are initiated that mitigate the potential and associated risks of decline in ecological and environmental services, market failure, and even climate change.

Source: Author's compilation.

Table 7.4: Railway Routes in NER (km)

State	2010–11	2013–14	2016–17
Arunachal Pradesh	1	1	12
Assam	2,433	2,459	2,443
Manipur	1	1	1
Mizoram	2	2	2
Nagaland	13	13	11
Tripura	151	151	193
NER	2,601	2,627	2,662

Source: RIS database based on NEDFi Databank

this period (Table 7.5). Besides those projects, several projects are at various stages of implementation in the region. As per the Ministry of Development of North Eastern Region (DONER), as of 31 August 2019, the ongoing rail projects in NER cover 1,076 km of length with total cost of Rs. 40,698.1 crore. Out of twelve major projects, one project is on the verge of completion, whereas ten other projects are likely to be completed

Table 7.5: Major Railway Projects (Costing Rs. 100 Crore and Above) Completed during 2014–19

Sl. No	Project Description	Type of Project	Length (km)	States Covered	Estimated Cost (Rs. Crore)	Year of Completion
1.	Kumarghat–Agartala	New BG Lines	107.45	Tripura	1,733.2	2016
2.	Bogeebil Rail-cum-Road Bridge (with link lines on North and South Banks)	New Lines	73.00	Assam	5,920.0	2018
3.	Harmuti to Naharlagun	New BG Lines	20.00	Assam	613.0	2014
4.	Dudhnoi–Mendipathar	New BG Lines	19.20	Assam, Meghalaya	321.0	2014
5.	Katakhal–Bhairabi	Gauge Conversion	83.55	Assam, Mizoram	509.0	2016
6.	Rangiya–Murkongselek (Including finger line of Balipara–Bhalukpung)	Gauge Conversion	505.00	Assam, Arunachal Pradesh	4,585.0	2015
7.	Lumding–Badarpur–Silchar, Arunachal–Jiribam & Badarpur-Kumarghat GC & MM for GC of Baraigram–Dulabchera, Karimganj–Maishashan & Karimganj bypass line	Gauge Conversion	420.90	Assam, Manipur, Tripura	7,731.6	2017

Source: RIS database based on Ministry of Development of North Eastern Region (DONER) website.

in 2021 and 2022 (Table 7.6). These projects include the railway routes which are aimed at connecting the state capitals in NER.

The railway projects connecting all the state capitals in the NER are at different stages of implementation. A total of forty-three projects are underway in NER which include completion of fourteen projects, three projects awaiting clearance from the Cabinet Committee on Economic Affairs (CCEA) and four projects at initial stage of planning. Some of the important projects connecting state capitals include Kumarghat–Agartala (Tripura), Jiribam–Imphal (Manipur), Harmuti–Naharlagun (Assam), Bairabi–Sairang (Mizoram), Dimapur–Zubza or Dhansiri–Sukhobi-Zubza (Nagaland), and Sivok–Rangpo (Sikkim). The recent developments in road connectivity and trade infrastructure including Integrated Check Post, Land Customs Stations in Moreh and the Jiribam–Imphal broad gauge line which is expected to be completed in March 2022 would be strategically important for India–Myanmar trade via Moreh–Tamu border in Manipur. Likewise, the New Mayanguri–Jogighopa line assumes importance as Jogighopa is being developed as a multimodal logistics hub which would be the gateway for the NER to Southeast Asia.

The completion of Bogibeel Bridge over Brahmaputra is a major milestone in north-east connectivity. The 4.94-km long road-cum-rail bridge would connect the North with the South banks of Brahmaputra and reduce the travel time between Tinsukia in Assam and Naharlagun of Arunachal Pradesh by more than ten hours. Besides construction of new lines and gauge conversion, modernization of stations has been undertaken across the region. With conversion of 943 km of meter gauge lines to broad gauge, all the rail lines in NER are operating on broad gauge now. State capitals of Arunachal Pradesh and Tripura and Barak Valley of Assam are now connected well through broad gauge (Yadav, 2018). Two railway routes under the jurisdiction of Northeast Frontier Railway such as Rangapara North Lakhimpur–Murkongselek and Siliguri–Jogighopa including broad gauge conversion of Siliguri–Haldibari serve as strategic lines for the country from the defence point of view.

Railways network has strengthened India's international connectivity with Bangladesh, Nepal, and Bhutan. Rail connectivity with Bangladesh exists through three lines: (1) Sealdah–Dhaka through Gede, (2) Old Malda–Rohanpur through Singhabad, and (3) Radhikapur–Birol. In addition, a new line from Agartala to Akhaura of 15.06 km length is under

Table 7.6: Major Ongoing Railway Projects (Costing Rs. 100 Crore and Above)

Sl. No	Project Description	Type of Project	Length (km)	States Covered	Estimated Cost (Rs. Crore)	Overall Physical Progress (%)	Date of Completion
1.	New Maynaguri–Jogighopa	New BG Line	288.88	Assam	3,300.0	92.00	March 2021
2.	Agartala–Sabroom	New BG Line	112.00	Tripura	3,407.0	99.15	June 2019
3.	Jiribam–Imphal	New BG Line	110.62	Manipur	13,809.0	67.54	March 2022
4.	Dhansiri–Sukhobi-Zubza	New Line	82.50	Assam, Nagaland	3,000.0	16.86	March 2022
5.	Bhairabi–Sairang	New BG Line	51.38	Mizoram	4,968.0	59.24	2021–22
6.	Sivok–Rangpo	New BG Line	44.96	Sikkim	4,085.0	1.00	June 2021
7.	Teteliya–Byrnihat	New BG Line	21.50	Assam	1,532.0	59.35	2021–22
8.	Agartala–Akhaura (Bangladesh)	New BG Line	15.06	Tripura	967.5	11.44	2020–21
9.	Murkongselek–Pasighat	New BG Line	26.15	Assam, Arunachal Pradesh,	661.0	7.00	Not Fixed
10.	Lumding–Hojai Patch	Doubling	44.92	Assam	650.6	78.42	August 2019
11.	Digaru–Hojai Patch	Doubling	102.00	Assam	2,136.0	32.04	2020–21
12.	New Bongaingaon–Kamakhya via Goalpara	Doubling	176.00	Assam	2,182.0	23.68	2020–22

Source: RIS database based on Ministry of Development of North Eastern Region (DONER) website.

progress and estimated to be completed in 2021. Likewise, the restoration work of Haldibari to Chitali line is under progress now. Along with improvement in bilateral engagements between India and Bangladesh especially in the form of progress in BBIN Motor Vehicle Agreement and Coastal Shipping Agreement, trade between the two countries is expected to flourish through this rail route. This route could emerge as an economically viable route for cargo movements for trade.

Currently, India does not have any rail links with Bhutan. However, Indian Railways have undertaken surveys of the possible routes between the two countries. The five possible routes are Kokrajhar (Assam) to Gelephu (Bhutan) (57.7 km), Pathsala (Assam) to Nanglam (Bhutan) (51.15 km), Rangia (Assam) to Samdrup Jongkhar (Bhutan) (48.04 km), Banarhat (West Bengal) to Samtse (Bhutan) (23.15 km), and Hasimara (West Bengal) to Phuentsholing (Bhutan) (17.52 km). The Northeast Frontier Railway has submitted feasibility studies on these routes to the Ministry of External Affairs in 2017. These studies were undertaken in the spirit of improving connectivity with South and Southeast Asian neighbours as part of 'Act East Policy'.

Rail connectivity between India and Nepal has attracted significant attention in the bilateral diplomatic engagements over the years. Currently, three projects including Raxaul (Bihar)–Birgunj (Nepal) line, Jayanagar (Bihar) to Janakpur/Kurtha (Nepal), and Jogbani (Bihar) to Biratnagar (Nepal) are being considered for improving railway links between India and Nepal (Embassy of India, Kathmandu). The construction work in the Jogbani–Biratnagar line has made significant progress. This line covers 5.45 km on the India side and 13.15 km on the Nepal side. Land acquisition has been completed on the India side, and IRCON International Limited has been entrusted with the construction of the line. Once the land acquisition is completed on the Nepal side, the line would be ready for commissioning (Yadav, 2018). As far as trade cargo is concerned, both the governments in India and Nepal have agreed to some bilateral frameworks in the past. The creation of ICD at Birgunj and Raxaul–Birgunj rail link facilitates direct movement of goods in transit to Nepal. In addition, India has extended Nepal direct transit access to Bangladesh for bilateral and third country traffic through the Radhikapur–Birol Interchange on India–Bangladesh border. Both the countries has also signed a Rail Service Agreement in May 2004 for extending cargo train service to the Inland Container Depot in Birgunj which was modified in 2008 covering oil/liquid traffic in tank wagons and bilateral break-bulk cargo in flat wagons (Embassy of India, Kathmandu).

Inland Waterways

Inland waterways are cheapest modes of cargo transport in India. Realizing this potential, the Union Government has allocated more re-sources and implemented schemes for developing waterways in the country including the North Eastern States. Total navigable length of main rivers in NER is 3,839 km. Inland waterway is a promising alter-native for transport of people and cargo in NER given good coverage of rivers including Brahmaputra; which has the longest river length of 724 km. Although the powered vessels employed for cargo has increased considerably over time, the quantity of cargo carried by the waterways presents dismal picture. Compared to 865.1 thousand tonne in 2009, the quantity of cargo transported through waterways has declined to 178.7 thousand tonne in 2015 for the waterways in Assam. Likewise, total number of passengers carried by the water vessels has also gone down during 2012–13 in Assam. Surprisingly, the number of powered ves-sels introduced for cargo and passengers have fallen in subsequent years (Table 7.7).

Table 7.7: Passengers and Cargo Carried by Inland Water Vessels

State	Year	Powered Vessels Employed (Nos.)		Cargo Carried (Thousand Tonne)
		Cargo	Passengers	
Assam	2012	66	66	37.7
	2013	56	56	71.8
	2014	56	56	338.5
	2015	56	56	178.7
Mizoram	2015	48	48	1,000.0

Source: RIS database based on NEDFi.

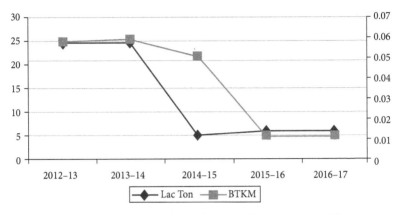

Figure 7.1: Cargo Movements through National Waterways-2 (The Brahmaputra)
Source: RIS database based on data from IWAI.

A similar pattern in cargo movements through National Waterway (NW)-2, i.e. the Brahmaputra was observed in the past few years. Although cargo traffic was almost same for 2012–13 and 2013–14, it has declined sharply in 2014–15 and stabilized at that level for 2015–16 and 2016–17 both in lac tonne and billion tonne-kilometre terms. It is alarming to notice the sharp fall in cargo traffic from 25 lac tonne in 2013–14 to 5 lac tonne in 2016–17 (Figure 7.1). Since the current policy of waterways development considers Brahmaputra as a major waterway in NER and for trade with other parts of India and Bangladesh, the better utilization of NW-2 and revival of cargo traffic appears to be feasible in the coming years.

In general, most of the waterways in India are operationally inefficient and commercially unviable due to low and variable draft. The inland waterways in NER suffer from similar problems. Since the current policy focus of India is on promoting inland waterways for movement of cargo for international trade, the feasibility of major cargo routes needs to be studied. Table 7.8 presents the nature of cargo or the commodities that can be transported through the waterways identified by the governments. For instance, two routes, e.g. Tezpur–Kolkata and Dibrugarh–Kolkata, are suitable for tea, whereas other routes could be effective for movement of minerals such as coal, bitumen, iron and steel, gypsum, and so on. These waterways would not only decongest cargo traffic on roads and

Table 7.8: Waterways: Major Identified Cargo

Identified Route	Nature of Cargo
Kolkata–Pandu	Coal, bitumen, iron and steel
Pandu–Kolkata	Gypsum, tea, coal
Jogighopa–Kolkata	Coal (Meghalaya)
Tezpur–Kolkata	Tea
Dibrugarh–Kolkata	Tea
Silghat–Budge Budge	POL
Namrup	Urea
Bongaigaon Refinery	RP Coke

Source: RIS database based on NEDFi.

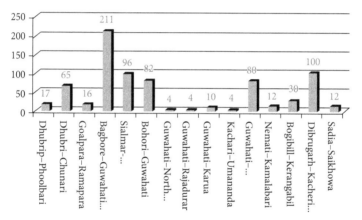

Figure 7.2: Ferry Service through Waterways in NER (in km)
Source: RIS database based on data from NEDFi.

railways but also provide viable and cheaper modes of cargo transport in the region.

There are fifteen ferry services in the NER covering 743 km of distance. The longest ferry service is Bagbore–Guwahati–Sialmari route with 211 km followed by other significant routes such as Dibrugarh–Kacheri–Oriumghat (100 km), Sialmari–Vijoynagarh–Guwahati (96 km), Bohori–Guwahati (82 km), and Guwahati–Kanchanmari (80 km) (Figure 7.2). These ferry services mostly involve passenger movements among different areas in the NER.

Air Connectivity

Aviation sector in India in general has experienced high growth in recent years. Sharp rise in air traffic has been registered both for domestic and international routes with regional variations in the country. The domestic air traffic has increased significantly during the past four years. The growth rate witnessed for domestic passengers during the past four years were 21.5 per cent, 21.5 per cent, 18.3 per cent, and 13.1 per cent, respectively, during 2015–16, 2016–17, 2017–18, and 2018–19. Three-year Compounded Annual Growth Rate (CAGR) for domestic passengers handled at all Indian airports taken together is 17.6 per cent (Ministry of Civil Aviation). In light of the enormous potential of the sector to contribute to economic growth, regional development and employment generation in India, the first Integrated Civil Aviation Policy was adopted in 2016. Subsequent to this, two important initiatives have been launched, viz., NABH (NextGen Airports for Bharat) Nirman initiative and the *'Regional Connectivity Scheme (RCS) UDAN–Ude Desh Ka Aam Naagrik'*.

Alongside passenger traffic air-cargo movement has also been on the rise to support trade aided through improved logistics. Both hard and soft infrastructure has undergone significant transformation in the recent past with major Indian airports setting global standards. However, air connectivity in the North Eastern part of India is of high priority for variety of reasons that often extends beyond demand and supply considerations. First, given the unique geographical location, topographical specificities, and political compulsions, the region still faces serious shortfall of hard infrastructure for connectivity through land, sea, and water routes. While air connectivity has been relied upon for quicker connectivity with rest of India its reach remains restricted due to inadequate airport facilities and commercial viability at many destinations in the sub-region. Topography and terrain definitely poses challenge for fast expansion of airport infrastructure across the region.

Secondly, NER of India is a bridge with ASEAN and is at the heart of sub-regional initiatives such as Bay of Bengal Initiative for Multi-Sectoral Technical and Economic Cooperation (BIMSTEC), Bangladesh, Bhutan, India and Nepal (BBIN), and Bangladesh-China-India-Myanmar (BCIM). Therefore, NER can become more self-reliant and prosperous if trade and investment receives a boost with adequate and reliable connectivity with India's extended neighbourhood. Direct air connectivity between NER and some of these countries has the potential to bring people closer and also facilitate trade to certain extent through air cargo. The latter is considered important for seamless market access since some of the primary products principally produced in NER require faster and efficient movement to mainland India as well as foreign export destinations, especially in ASEAN.

The seven states in NER, except for Sikkim which so far did not have any civil aviation services, noticed considerable improvement in passenger and cargo traffic between 2015 and 2018. However, alongside Sikkim, both Arunachal Pradesh and Nagaland remain most poorly connected through air services. As captured in Table 7.9, passenger traffic has registered most significant rise in Nagaland followed by noticeable improvements in Mizoram, Manipur, and Tripura with great divergences in absolute number of passengers depending on populations and other development conditions. Assam needs to be treated differently as it is the largest of the eight states and is ahead of others as the only regional air hub. Following Assam, the two states that have somewhat close volumes of passenger and cargo traffic are Tripura and Manipur, with Tripura having significantly higher aircraft movements. However, the fall in cargo volumes for both the states during this period possibly has implications for trade and market access. On this front, the remaining states have to catch up significantly. One potential trigger for improvement in air connectivity is tourism that can enhance prospects of the civil aviation sector significantly. Encouragingly, under Swadesh Darshan Scheme of Ministry of Tourism, projects worth Rs. 1,400.03 crore have been sanctioned for the NER and Rs. 896.12 crore has been released for the same.[1]

The Union Government has taken major steps to improve infrastructure in airports including in the NER. This is part of the ongoing efforts under the NABH Nirman initiative. The new green field airport that has come up in the region under this scheme is that in Pakyong, Sikkim

[1] Government of India, Ministry of Development of North Eastern Region Rajya Sabha Unstarred Question No. 3677 answered on 25 July 2019, Subject: North Eastern Region Vision 2020.

Table 7.9: Snapshot of the Aviation Sector in North Eastern Region

S. No.	STATE	Aircraft Movements (in Thousand)		CAGR (%) (2015–18)	Total Passengers (in Lakh)		CAGR (%) (2015–18)	Total Cargo (in '000 MT)		CAGR (%) (2015–18)
		2015	2018		2015	2018		2015	2018	
1	Arunachal Pradesh	0.1	0.0	–100.0	0.0	0.0	–100.0	0.0	0.0	–
2	Assam	35.0	49.9	12.6	27.9	54.7	25.1	11.2	23.6	28.1
3	Manipur	4.8	6.7	11.9	6.1	9.9	17.3	4.5	4.3	–1.2
4	Meghalaya	0.4	0.5	3.3	0.1	0.1	7.8	0.0	0.0	–
5	Mizoram	2.9	3.5	6.9	1.6	3.0	22.0	0.3	0.7	41.0
6	Nagaland	0.6	1.5	35.5	0.5	1.9	52.2	0.2	0.6	48.3
7	Tripura	7.6	10.1	9.8	8.8	13.8	16.2	5.7	5.3	–2.2
8	Sikkim	–	–	–	–	–	–	–	–	–

Source: RIS database based on Ministry of Civil Aviation–Report on 48 Months of Transforming Aviation in India 2014–18.

which is being hailed as an engineering marvel in a mountainous terrain. Under NABH, Nirman new terminal buildings are being constructed in Guwahati and Agartala. The airport-wise aircraft movement as per the latest figures for NER including existing and new cities to be connected under UDAN is presented in Table 7.10. Proposals for new airports in Arunachal Pradesh, Nagaland, and Meghalaya are currently under serious consideration (Table A in Appendix).

To cater to the needs of regional connectivity and balanced regional development, RCS-UDAN scheme was launched on 21 October 2016 to fulfil the aspirations of people outside major air hubs. This scheme is of particular relevance for the North Eastern States that are eligible for additional support along with the Union Territories (see Box 7.2). It is suggested that introduction of new routes under UDAN (including in helicopters) shall boost intra-regional connectivity in NER, where state capitals remain poorly connected except for some hub and spoke connectivity between Guwahati and other cities in the region (Tables B and C in the Appendix). Such expansion should also be innovatively designed to cater to additional needs such as availability of air ambulances, needs of evacuation in times of natural disasters, etc., keeping in mind the existing connectivity challenges. While there is strong indication for several new domestic routes getting connected with other cities in India, the additions of new international routes particularly supporting India's Act East engagement has to be prioritized. In this regard, the North Eastern Council has already identified possible routes for which Viability Gap Funding (VGF) in line with UDAN could be helpful (Table D in the Appendix). The need for connecting neighbouring countries by direct routes would brighten the prospects of promoting exports from the NER in high-value fruits, flowers, spices, herbal plants, items of sericulture and handicrafts, etc.

Digital Connectivity and Communication

One of the most important pillars of connectivity under the present-day realities is that of digital connectivity. India is by far one of the best examples from the developing world to have taken great leaps in that direction. The Government of India launched 'Digital India' programme in

Table 7.10: North Eastern Region Airports and Air Connectivity in Summer 2019 (30 June 19 to 6 July 19) with Additional Details*

State	Airport	No. of Movements (Arr.+Dep.)/Week	Airlines Operating	Cities Connected
Arunachal Pradesh	Passighat	8	Alliance Air	Guwahati, Lilabari, Jorhat
	Tezu	–	–	Jorhat, Kolkata, Guwahati
Assam	Guwahati	1,029 (Domestic)	Indigo, Alliance Air, Air India, Go Air, Spicejet, Air Asia India, Air Vistara	Ahmedabad, Aizawl, Amritsar, Bhubaneswar, Bengaluru, Mumbai, Kolkata, Cochin, Delhi, Dibrugarh, Hyderabad, Imphal, Agartala, Bagdogra, Lilabari, Silchar, Passighat, Jaipur, Chennai, Patna, Tezpur, Varanasi, Pakyong, Cooch Behar, Rupsi, Tezu
		38 (International)	Druk Air, Spicejet; NOK AIR	Dhaka, Paro, Singapore, Bangkok
	Dibrugarh	112	Indigo, Air India, Spicejet, Air Vistara	Kolkata, Delhi, Guwahati, Bagdogra
	Silchar	70	Air India, Spicejet	Kolkata, Guwahati, Delhi
	Jorhat	14	Indigo	Kolkata, Delhi
	Lilabari	22	Alliance Air, Spicejet	Guwahati, Passighat, Kolkata
	Tezpur	6	Alliance Air	Guwahati, Kolkata
Manipur	Imphal	210	Indigo, Air India, Air Asia India	Aizawl, Bengaluru, Kolkata, Delhi, Guwahati, Hyderabad, Agartala, Chennai
Meghalaya	Barapani	14	Alliance Air	Kolkata, Agartala, Aizawl, Dimapur, Imphal, Tezpur
Mizoram	Aizawl	22	Air India	Kolkata, Imphal, Delhi
Nagaland	Dimapur	26	Indigo, Air India	Kolkata, Shillong
Sikkim	Pakyong	–	–	Delhi, Guwahati, Kolkata
Tripura	Agartala	192	Indigo, Air India	Bangalore, Chennai Kolkata, Guwahati, Imphal

Source: Ministry of Civil Aviation, Government of India.

Note: * New routes/airlines introduced in 2018 and 2019 under UDAN 1&2 are marked in bold–compiled from responses to various Rajya Sabha questions.

Box 7.2: Regional Connectivity Scheme-UDAN

UDAN is an innovative scheme to develop the regional aviation market. It is a market-based mechanism in which airlines bid for seat subsidies. This first-of-its-kind scheme globally will create affordable yet economically viable and profitable flights on regional routes so that flying becomes affordable to the common man even in small towns.

The twin objectives of the scheme are: promoting balanced regional growth and making flying affordable for masses. The scheme, which would be in operation for a period of ten years, envisages providing connectivity to un-served and undeserved airports of the country through revival of existing air strips and airports. The scheme is being executed by the Airport Authority of India (AAI), the implementing agency.

Under this Scheme, State Governments are also required to provide following concessions:

1. RCS will be made operational only in those States which reduce VAT on Aviation Turbine Fuel (ATF) at these airports to 1 per cent or less for a period of ten years.

2. State Government will provide land free of cost and free from all encumbrances and also provide multimodal hinterland connectivity (road, rail, metro, waterways, etc.) as required.

3. State government will provide police and fire services free of cost. Power, water, and other utilities will be provided at substantially concessional rates.

4. VGF will be shared between MoCA and the State Government in the ratio of 80:20. For the North Eastern States, the ratio will be 90:10. The payment of the full amount of VGF will be made to the airline operator from the Regional Connectivity Fund (RCF)[a] and the State Governments will be subsequently asked for reimbursement.

Source: PIB 21 October-2016, Annual Reports of the Ministry of Civil Aviation 2016–17 and 2017–18.

[a] The Central Government has issued the order to a levy on scheduled flights operated within India to fund Regional Air Connectivity Fund, in the following manner: (i) Rs. 7,500 with stage length up to 1,000 km, (ii) Rs. 8,000 with stage length more than 1,000 km to 1,500 km, and (iii) Rs. 8,500 with stage length above 1,500 km.

2015 creating unprecedented momentum in establishing nation-wide digital infrastructure. This has been tremendously helpful in promoting inclusive development; bridging digital divides and empowerment through AADHAAR-enabled Direct-Benefit-Transfer programmes; delivery of social security schemes; and in reaching out to all age groups particularly youth, women, and the elderly. However, the hard infrastructure component in Digital India, apart from the massive software based platforms, is critical to the success of all associated initiatives. The hard infrastructure requirements include both wireline (covering optical fibre network and broadband), as well as wireless and satellite telephony. The much-appreciated success of the private sector in providing voice services has been critically dependent on the initiatives by the Government in laying the hard infrastructure for Digital India in the first place. Reliable and high-speed internet connectivity is also critical for supporting entrepreneurship ecosystem emerging in different parts of the country including in the NER, particularly for design, development, and user interface of e-commerce platforms and multimedia services. Some of the states in NER are rightly poised to leverage technology-driven entrepreneurship and digital platforms to support retail, trade, and tourism sectors critical to the region and hence promote livelihood opportunities.

The key initiative of the Government under the Digital India programme is that of BharatNet project which is being implemented in a phased manner to provide broadband connectivity to all the Gram Panchayats (GPs) throughout the country (approx. 250,000) of which 11,252 GPs are in the North East Region. As per the strategy, last mile connectivity, through Wi-Fi or any other suitable broadband technology to access broadband/internet services, will also be provided at all the 2.5 lakh GPs in the country. It is reported that 345,779 km Optical Fibre Cable (OFC) has been laid (as on 4 July 2019) by which 131,392 GPs have been connected. Out of these, 120,562 GPs have been made service ready. Additionally, 854 GPs have been connected on satellite media.[2] Due to unique geographical and climatic challenges including long monsoon,

---

[2] A lump sum of Rs. 20,431 crore (Rs. 10,286 crore for Phase-I and Rs. 10,145 crore for Phase-II) has been allocated and disbursed from Universal Service Obligation Fund to Bharat Broadband Network Limited under BharatNet project. It is mentioned that the funds are allocated for the project as a whole and not State/Union Territory-wise.

the states in the North East would be connected through satellite media aided by GSAT-11.[3] State-wise progress of BharatNet in the NER is presented in Table 7.11.

However, ensuring delivery of government subsidies through dedicated platforms in remote and rural areas; and connecting sparsely distributed populations in North Eastern States critically depends on efficient functioning of Common Services Centres (CSC) that are planned for all 2.5 lakh GPs under Digital India. Utilization of such platforms for development interventions would be important for ensuring the larger aspirations of the SDGs. This effort also includes strengthening the CSC network through standardization of service availability and capacity building of all stakeholders involved. There is urgent need to bridge that gap between registered and functional CSCs in the North Eastern States apart from completing connectivity through OFCs for the identified GPs in all states. For the remaining GPs, it is believed that other technological options need to be harnessed in an expedited manner since in all likelihoods such habitations and habitants would be most remotely located. It may be noted that Tripura is the country's third international internet gateway after Mumbai and Chennai (through Cox's Bazar-Bangladesh.). Full serviceability of this gateway would be critical for promoting economy and development in the entire NER by bringing down service costs. Robust cooperation and understanding with Bangladesh would ensure reliability of this gateway.

Finally, monitoring of the progress of SDGs would be crucial as per the targets laid under specific goals. In this connection, all indicators linked to tele-density would be important parameter for national benchmarking and global reporting (particularly SDG-9 and specifically target 9.c). As per available information, state-wise tele-density measures for the North East is poor due to systemic factors such as standard reporting of aggregate numbers by certain service providers. Nevertheless, in terms of NER aggregate vis-à-vis all India average for mobile and wireline connectivity between 2010–11 and 2015–16, NER registered significantly higher growth. But at the same time, tele-density remains much below the all India levels, even as there is improvement

---

[3] Compiled from MeITY's/Minister's responses to parliament questions.

Table 7.11: State-wise Progress of BharatNet in NER

State	Number of Districts	Number of Districts with BharatNet Exposure	Total No. of GPs	No. of Identified GPs for Broadband/ Optical Fibre	No. of Services Ready GPs	No. of GPS where Implementation Is Pending	Common Service Centres (CSC) Registered#	Common Service Centres (CSC) (Functional)#
Arunachal Pradesh	16	2	1,795	675	84	591	289	76
Assam	27	22	2,648	1,627	1,622	5	8,083	3,213
Manipur	9	5	2,749	531	325	2,424	1,219	995
Meghalaya	7	2	5,965	–	87	722	610	217
Mizoram	8	2	763	763	41	722	240	145
Nagaland	11	5	994	874	123	751	249	157
Sikkim	4	2	176	176	62	114	76	32
Tripura	4	1	1,178	1,178	381	797	969	460

Source: RIS database based on RBI (as on June 2019), #MeiTY.

Table 7.12: Telephony and Teledensity in the North Eastern Region

		2010–11	2015–16	% Change
Wireless	NER	18,855,288	29,635,734	57.17
	All India	811,595,317	1,034,108,663	27.42
Total (Wireless + Wireline)	NER	19,382,366	29,920,603	54.37
	All India	846,325,166	1,059,333,231	25.17
Tele-density (%)	NER	44.26	64.43	
	All India	70.89	83.4	
Broadband Connection (in Mn)	NER	0.2	4.43	
	All India	11.89	149.75	
Internet Connection (in Mn)	NER	1.1	10.82	
	All India	19.67	342.66	

Source: RIS database based on TRAI.

in penetration in terms of broadband as well as internet. While the rate at which broadband connectivity has improved in NER is better than national average, the number of times internet connectivity has grown during the same period is much lower than the national average. The faster growth of broadband networks is an encouraging sign, as mere tele-density or internet penetration may not help in ensuring adequate download speed for information as well as development support services. Table 7.12 captures the details on telephony and internet penetration with focus on NER.

Improved Connectivity and Infrastructure Leading to Development Corridors

The NER of India is a crucial component of several national and regional transport corridors linking South Asia and Southeast Asia. These transport corridors are catalysts for rapid infrastructure development and greater access to communication in NER. The identified projects under these connectivity corridors contribute to improvement of roads, railways, and waterways in the region and connect the vital trade routes existing between India, South Asia, and Southeast Asia. Among the national initiatives, Bharatmala Pariyojana is a major nation-wide transport corridor in India.

Some of the notable sub-regional connectivity initiatives include Trilateral Highways (THs) and its possible extension to Cambodia, Laos and Vietnam; Kaladan Multimodal Connectivity Project; and South Asia Sub-regional Economic Cooperation (SASEC). Five corridors under SASEC involving India are (1) Delhi–Mumbai Industrial Corridor, (2) Bengaluru–Mumbai Economic Corridor, (3) Chennai–Bengaluru Industrial Corridor, (4) East Coast Economic Corridor, and (5) Amritsar–Kolkata Industrial Corridor. The North-East Economic Corridor covering total length of 3,246 km includes various alignments such as Bongaigaon–Guwahati–Nagaon–Tezpur–Dibrugarh–Margherita, Dudhnoi–William Nagar, Gohpur–Itanagar, Nagaon–Dimapur, Numaligarh–Dimapur–Kohima–Imphal, Kohima–Jessami–Ukhrul–Imphal, Jorabat–Jowai–Silchar–Karimganj–Agartala, Manu–Simlung–Aizawl–Imphal, Silchar–Aizawl, and Silchar–Jiribam–Imphal.

It is imperative to understand the strategic connectivity points in the NER from the angle of cross-border trade and movement of people. Six states of the NER have borders with neighbouring countries. With two roads in Assam and three roads in Mizoram, there are nine international connectivity points in NER. These nine roads connect the land border points which have potential to become major trading routes for India's bilateral trade with Bangladesh, Nepal, Bhutan, and Myanmar. For instance, Imphal–Moreh road facilitates border trade between India and Myanmar at Moreh–Tamu border between the two countries. The route details of international connectivity and border roads and their respective lengths are mentioned in Table 7.13. The border roads need to be developed for enhancing connectivity between different states in NER and neighbouring countries.

There are several choke points in NER, which lead to unwanted delay and congestion in surface transport. An integrated transport corridor approach is suitable for releasing traffic on those routes and enables faster movement of cargo. Specific types of interventions by the transport authorities have been conceived to decongest those choke points. For Guwahati along the East-West corridor, a flyover is being considered, whereas bypass appears to be effective solutions for another five choke points on the North East Economic Corridor including Imphal, Silchar, Shillong, Dibrugarh, and Dimapur.

Table 7.13: International Connectivity and Border Roads of North
Eastern States

State	International Connectivity Roads	Length (km)	Border Roads	Length (km)
Assam	Darranga-Guwahati	49	Kochigain–Raimana– Jaigaon–Lamkapura—Birpara	123
	Sutarkandi–Karimganj	14		
Manipur	Imphal–Moreh	106	Sangshak–Nampisha	90
Meghalaya	Dawki–Shillong	95	Baghmara-Rongra-Mahadeo–Ranikor	206
Mizoram	Zorinpui–Lunglei	172	–	–
	Kawarpuchiah–Seling	294		
	Zowkhathar–Kawlkulh	92		
Nagaland	Avakhung–Jessami	149	–	–
Tripura	Sabroom–Agartala	–	Teliamar–Amarpur-Sabroom	216
			Khowai–Agartala	55
Sikkim	–	–	Mangan–Kodyong–Chungtang–Lachung–Yumthang–Yume-Samdang–Border	90
			Chumtang–Lachen Monastry–Log Bridge–Pashi–Naku-Nakpolatok–Nakula	75

Source: National Portal of India, 'Bharatmala Pariyojana-A Stepping Stone Towards New India'. (https://www.india.gov.in/spotlight/bharatmala-pariyojana-stepping-stone-towards-new-india.

Bharatmala Pariyojana

Bharatmala Pariyojana is a grand connectivity initiative introduced by the Government of India in 2017 that aims to connect North-South-East-West Corridor covering the Golden Quadrangle, port connectivity, and road upgradation with 2/4/6 laning over a five-year period in four different phases. By 31 March 2019, the total road length completed under the Bharatmala Pariyojana was 33,808 km which accounts for 73 per cent of the target road length under the scheme. Under this scheme, 12,000 km of highways are to be developed in NER; mostly by the National

Highways Infrastructure Development Corporations (NHIDCL) and the rest by NHAI and state Public Works Departments (PWDs). Detailed Project Reports have been completed for a number of projects to be implemented by NHIDCL (MORTH, 2019). Besides highways development, the Special Accelerated Road Development Programme for the North Eastern Region (SARDP-NE) aims to provide connectivity to eighty-eight district headquarters in the NER. NHIDCL has completed 2,101 km of roads till March 2019. In addition, the Arunachal Pradesh Package of SARDP-NE covers 2,319 km of roads which are to be completed by March 2023–24. Along with other union and state government scheme for road development, the Bharatmala Pariyojana is contributing significantly to transformative changes taking place in the connectivity landscape of the NER.

South Asia Sub-Regional Economic Cooperation

The SASEC was conceived in 2001 for promoting sub-regional cooperation in connectivity development and economic cooperation. SASEC was envisaged to realize regional economic integration in the framework of South Asia Growth Triangle. Several connectivity corridors have already been implemented in India and in other member states. SASEC has wider developmental implications for the NER as several projects are linked to the trade routes between India, Bangladesh, Nepal, Bhutan, and Myanmar (See Box 7.3). A number of connectivity projects have been implemented in NER and some are in the pipeline. In 2011, SASEC identified three focus sectors—transport, trade facilitation, and energy. The SASEC Operational Plan has formulated the road map for the upcoming projects. For the NER of India, twenty projects are identified as potential SASEC projects (Table E in the Appendix).

Trilateral Highways

THs is a multicountry connectivity project connecting India, Myanmar, and Thailand. TH serves as the bridge between South Asia and Southeast Asia and has potential to enhance seamless connectivity between the two

---

Box 7.3:   Creation of North East Industrial Corridor

Government of India is planning to set up North East Industrial Corridor that will create numerous job opportunities for the people of the region. This was stated by the Defense Minister during his address at the 11th Maitree Diwas Celebrations in Tawang, Arunachal Pradesh on 14 November 2019. He elaborated that Arunachal Corridor will act as a land bridge between India and South East Asia that will provide employment opportunities and give fillip to trade and tourism. This indicates special emphasis of the Government on the development of the North East region under the Act East Policy. He said, 'Road to "New India" runs through "New North-East India"'. Reaffirming Government's commitment to improve connectivity in border areas, he said, approval to construct a tunnel at Sela Pass to Tawang, operationalization of Pasighat Airport, nod to set up Hollongi Airport near Itanagar and work to establish three strategic Railway lines in the region are some of the decisions in that direction. The projects are expected to provide all-weather connectivity to the local population, facilitate the movement of the Armed Forces, and give a boost to tourism. The Defense Minister lauded the Five-Year Road Plan of Chief Minister of Arunachal Pradesh under which all the existing inter-state and inter-district roads will be upgraded to State highway specifications by 2024.

Source: PIB.

sub-regions. In view of high costs of cargo movements by sea and long delay in shipments, TH offers a viable alternative means of connectivity and access points to India's NER. TH covers the road corridor connecting Moreh (India)–Kalewa (Myanmar)–Mandalay (Myanmar)–Mae Sot (Thailand). The Thailand side of the highway is already developed and India–Myanmar road routes need repair. With India's offer of rebuilding seventy-one bridges in the Myanmar side as part of TH, the road construction work in Myanmar has received significant policy priority by the Government of Myanmar. Keeping in mind the emerging economic opportunities along this trade route, the feasibility study on extension of TH to Cambodia, Lao, and Vietnam is being conducted. Since TH connects India at Moreh and does not have any coverage on the Indian side, the benefits of TH in terms of higher bilateral trade between India and Myanmar can be harnessed properly through development of feeder routes and NHs in Manipur, Mizoram, and Nagaland. The four-laning and rehabilitation work of 109 km Imphal–Moreh highway is being developed on a fast track basis. In that perspective, TH is a promising connectivity project for the region.

Kaladan Multimodal Transit Transport Project

The Kaladan Multimodal Transit Transport Project (KMTTP) is another milestone in India-ASEAN connectivity. The 'Act East Policy' would further boost connectivity in NER once KMTTP becomes fully operational in terms of cargo movements. KMTTP is another effort to reduce the burden of high costs of carrying goods across South Asia and Southeast Asia regions. With unique package of roads and waterways, KMPTT is a futuristic connectivity corridor for promoting trade, investment, and integration of NER with regional production networks in Asia. KMPTT was conceptualized in the year 2010 with an aim to connect Indian ports with Sittwe port in Myanmar. Most of the India-bound cargo from Myanmar can be carried over on the Kaladan river up to Paletwa (the waterway component), and from Paletwa goods can move by road up to Mizoram (the road component) (RIS, 2014). Once the waterway is complete, KMPTT would serve as an efficient route for movement of regional cargo meant for international trade. The ensuing transition in Myanmar's economic policymaking and political institutions makes KMPTT an important venture to further economic, commercial, and strategic linkages between India and Myanmar. The North Eastern States of India would get alternate access via water route and promote trade, investment, and people-to-people interactions. This project would significantly reduce traffic on Siliguri corridor and pave the way for proper use of waterways for expanding trade in the region.

Conclusion

Connectivity, communication, and infrastructure development are inter-related and constitute an important supply-side enabler of development in the North Eastern States of India. While progress in programmes and projects on each of three pillars are notable, the combined synergistic outcome can have transformative impact on the development trajectory in NER. The need for robust connectivity networks and related economic and social infrastructure for achievement of SDGs is a derived demand. Although connectivity-specific SDGs and targets are not many compared to other sectors, the importance of connectivity as an underlying force behind meeting certain SDGs cannot be undermined. The goals that would have direct bearing with infrastructure are SDG-3, SDG-4, SDG-6, SDG-8, SDG-10, SDG-11, and SDG-13. As the State Governments in NER are gradually orienting their policies and institutions in line with SDG requirements, connectivity and infrastructure along with improved digital communication assumes special policy focus. Unlike other parts of India, the hilly terrains of NER demand careful planning of connectivity routes and their distribution across various modes. The current policies of the Government of India towards development of roads and railways in NER, by and large, reflect this approach. There has been significant progress in development of physical connectivity in the form of roads, railways, and airports in different parts of NER in the recent years. The additions to national and state highways and massive modernization and broad gauge conversion works by the Northeast Frontier Railway in NER indicate the pace of development in regional connectivity. Further, notable progress has been observed in case of digital connectivity infrastructure. Access to digital connectivity and communication has increased considerably in the region.

Along with the ongoing projects being implemented by the National Highways Authority of India, State Road Transport departments and Border Roads Organization, the Government of India has adopted a development-oriented approach towards connectivity and infrastructure in the NER. Economic corridor approach has inspired the design and implementation of major connectivity projects in NER in the recent decade. The Bharatmala Pariyojana is an ambitious and integrated connectivity initiative for improving road connectivity in NER. The progress under the scheme is notable and promising, given the specific challenges faced by the implementing agencies. In addition, the cross-border connectivity projects such as the THs and Kaladan Multimodal Transport Transit Project which are at different stages of development promise significant developmental gains for the people in the region. Once operational, these projects would open NER for higher trade and investment flows from Southeast Asia and ASEAN. The possible spurt in trade and economic activity would facilitate better internal market integration within NER and with other parts of the country.

Appendix

Table A: Plan for New Airports in NER

State	Status of New Airports
Arunachal Pradesh	Ministry of Civil Aviation has granted 'Site Clearance' and 'In-principle' approval on 18 January 2019 for setting up a New Greenfield Airport at Holongi, ltanagar, for which Airports Authority of India (AAI) has already initiated preparation of bidding documents.
Nagaland	The State Government of Nagaland has proposed to set up a Greenfield airport at Ciethu, Kohima. As per the feasibility study conducted by the multidisciplinary team comprising officials from Directorate General of Civil Aviation, Ministry of Environment, Forest and Climate Change and AAI in August 2018; though the project is technically feasible, the financial implication of site development is exorbitant making the project financially unviable.
Meghalaya	Tura airport, in the State of Meghalaya, is a non-operational airport. AAI has projected a requirement of 50.50 acres of land to the State Government of Meghalaya for the development of the airport for operation of ATR-72 type of aircraft.

Source: Government of India, Ministry of Development of North Eastern Region, Rajya Sabha Unstarred Question No-3677, Answered on 25 July 2019, North Eastern Region Vision 2020.

Table B: Intra-Regional Air Connectivity in NER—New Operational Routes

Shilling–Silchar–Shillong–Imphal–Shillong–Dimapur–Shillong–Aizawl–Shilong–Agartala–Shillong	Shillong—Imphal Shillong—Dimapur Shillong—Aizawl Shillong—Agartala Shillong—Silchar	Operator: Deccan Air

Source: As on FEB 2018 Lok Sabha Starred Question 90 UDAN.

Table C: Helicopter Routes awarded under UDAN 1and 2

Daparizo (AP)	Yinghiong (AP), Dibrugarh (Assam)
Itanagar (AP)	Lilabari (Assam)
Itanagar(AP)	Tezpur (Assam)
Passighat (AP)	Tuting (AP)
Tezu (AP)	Walong (AP), Dibrugarh (Assam)
Tuting (AP)	Dibrugarh (Assam)
Walong (AP)	Dibrugarh (Assam)
Yinghiong (AP)	Dibrugarh (Assam)
Ziro (AP)	Dibrugarh (Assam)
Dibrugarh (Assam)	Lilabari (Assam), Jorhat (Assam)
Guwahati (Assam)	Nagaon (Assam)
Tezpur (Assam)	Nagaon (Assam), Itanagar (AP), Jorhat (Assam),
Imphal (Manipur)	Moreh (Manipur), Tamenglong (Manipur), Thanlon (Manipur)
Jiribam (Manipur)	Tamenglong (Manipur)
Parbung (Manipur)	Thanlon (Manipur)

Source: Response to Rajya Sabha Unstarred Question No. 308.

Table D: Proposed International Routes in NER

Agartala—Dhaka
Agartala—Dimapur—Yangon
Guwahati—Imphal—Yangon
Guwahati—Mandalay—Kumming
Guwahati—Shillong—Dhaka
Guwahati—Yangon—Bangkok
Imphal—Mandalay—Bangkok
Kolkata—Dimapur—Bangkok
Kolkata—Guwahati—Kumming
Silchar—Imphal—Mandalay

Source: RIS database based on Draft North Eastern Council Regional Plan (2017–18 to 2019–20).

Table E: Potential SASEC Projects in NER

Project	Estimated Cost ($ Million)	Indicative Source of Funding
Road		
Completion of four-laning of Bijni–Guwahati	200	Government
Upgrading of Imphal–Moreh NH 39	180	ADB
Completion of Road upgrades between Lumding and Imphal	400	Government
Upgrading of Wangjing to Khudenthabi section in Manipur	95	ADB
Upgrading of the NH44 Silchar–Agartala–Sabroom (NH-53 and NH-44) with spur (Karimganj to Sutrakhandi) of NH-151 to Bangladesh Border	610	Government; ADB
Silchar to Guwahati via Harangjao–Turuk in Assam	452	Government, ADB
Maram–Peren–Dimapur road in Manipur and Nagaland	360	Government, ADB
Hafflong to Tamelong via Lia Sang and Tavesam in Assam and Manipur	300	Government, ADB
Split four-lane between Kohima and Kedima, Kromg and Imphal section of NH 39 in Manipur	280	Government, ADB
Ukhrul–Jessami, NH 202 in Manipur	230	Government, ADB
Jiribam to Tiparmukh in Manipur	210	Government, ADB
Four-laning of Imphal–Mairang NH 150 in Manipur	100	Government, ADB
Development of link roads between Srirampur to Dhubri and Phulbari to Tura with new bridge across river Brahmaputra on NH 127B	530	ADB, JICA
Tura to Dalu connecting to Kaladan multimodal transport corridor	320	JICA
Shilong to Dawki including rehabilitation of Dawki bridge at India–Bangladesh border	31	JICA
Aizawl to Tuipang connecting to Kaladan multimodal transport corridor	594	JICA
Development of Gangtok highway (Bagrakot to Menia)	770	Government, ADB
Khowai–Agartala link road	85	Government
Construction of new bridge on Feni river in South Tripura connecting Bangladesh	TBD	Government

Table E: Continued

Project	Estimated Cost ($ Million)	Indicative Source of Funding
Railways		
Jiribam–Imphal in Manipur (New Line)	500	NF
Double tracking of new Bongaigaon–Kamakhya in Assam	320	NF
Akhaura–Agartala rail link	100	NF
123 km Dimapur–Kohima (New Line)	500	NF
Ports		
New container port at Diamond Harbour	250	Concession
Development of Haldia Port	280	PPP
Development of Sagar Island Port	1,300	NF

Source: Compiled from Appendix 1 in SASEC Operational Plan 2016–25.
Note: No funding identified.

8

Financing of SDGs

Introduction

The previous chapters in this volume dwelt at length the achievements and challenges linked to the Sustainable Development Goals (SDGs) in the context of the North Eastern Region (NER). The chapters highlighted the efforts initiated in localizing the efforts to concretize sustainable development at the operational level, followed by a macro profile of the region. The important components that would facilitate a smooth passage to the achievement of SDGs within the targeted timeline—health status, education, and skill development, coupled with the issue of gender justice—have been discussed elaborately in the previous sections. Connectivity and regional development are considered *sine qua non* to ensure sustainable development that leaves no one behind. The section on connectivity and regional development probes the efforts and challenges in this regard. The present chapter wraps up the document through generating an insight about the availability of financial resources to the states in NER in implementing the actions to achieve the desired operational targets.

Existing Sources of Finance

Finance and technology are identified as key means of implementation for the SDGs globally. It may be noted that, sustainable development of a region is connected not only to availability to resources alone. Such resources are characterized by their capacity to generate additional resources, without being exhausted in the process. The resources required to this effect consist of natural, human, and man-made ones. To ensure their availability in a seamless manner, driven by a monetary economy, availability of financial resources that facilitates acquiring the other

Rise of the North East, Oxford University Press. © Research and Information System for Developing Countries 2023.
DOI: 10.1093/oso/9780192849342.003.0008

resources through exchange mechanisms is a necessary condition. The importance and relevance of finances for sustainable development, therefore, cannot be overemphasized. SDG 17 calls for the necessity to mobilize resources from all possible sources in a coordinated manner and utilize them through effective institutions of partnership. The partnership profiles engage both internal and external players. The previous section enumerated the efforts made in engaging internal partners in localizing the implementation of efforts towards achieving the SDGs. This section will focus on the extent of flow of financial resources—internal and external—for facilitating the implementation efforts. In the process, it will highlight the importance of not only the flow of financial resources in facilitating sustainable development but also that of ensuring a judicious expenditure of the resources available.

We have identified five main sources of financial resources that would play important roles in the achievement of Agenda 2030 in the North–East at the state level. They are:

- State government
- Central government
- External sources
- Private investment
- Credit from the banking sector

Internal Finance Generated by Respective State Governments

The role of the respective state governments in facilitating development is of primary importance. Such a role is dependent on the capacity of the state governments in generating their own resources—own tax revenue and own non-tax revenue. The following analysis captures generation of own revenue of the North Eastern states as share of its revenue expenditure. To make the understanding comparable, we have estimated the state-specific values as the difference between the value for the state and that pertaining to all the states of the country clubbed together. Thus, a positive value indicates that the state in question fares better than the national average of all the states taken together, while a negative value indicates the reverse. The relevant estimates were arrived at using data from Reserve Bank of India (2019).

Own Revenue

The analysis from the compiled data indicates that all the North Eastern states are relatively handicapped in generating their own financial resources in comparison to the average capability of all the states taken together. Assam and Sikkim appear to be a little better off than the other states with the average gap from 2014–15 to 2019–20 being around -20 per cent and -25 per cent for the two states, respectively. In 2019–20, according to the budget estimates, the proposed gap for Assam was lower than its average at around -19 per cent, while for Sikkim, it was greater at around -29 per cent. Arunachal Pradesh, Manipur, Mizoram, Nagaland, and Tripura require to put in further efforts to catch up with their peers and break the glass ceiling at the earliest as the average gap over 2014–15 to 2019–20 for these states is at around -39 per cent, -43 per cent, -41 per cent, -43 per cent, and -34 per cent, respectively.

The capacity of a state to raise its own resources for development purposes is often measured by own tax to Gross State Domestic Product (GSDP) ratio. Non-tax revenues raised by the state also contribute to financing development processes. The compiled data allow for the comparison of the Own Tax-GSDP ratio of all the states combined together with those pertaining to the North Eastern states. It reveals that while the combined average of the states was between 6 per cent and 7 per cent between 2011–12 and 2015–16, for Arunachal Pradesh, Manipur, Mizoram, and Nagaland, it hovered between 2 per cent and 3 per cent till 2016–17. While the ratio for Meghalaya shows a secularly increasing trend, that for the rest of the states began recording an increasing trend during 2017. Arunachal Pradesh, in fact, realized an Own Tax Revenue-GSDP ratio higher than that of the country as a whole during 2017–18. A fundamental effort towards achieving SDGs would have to increase the capacity of the NE states in consistently and sustainably raising their Own Tax GSDP ratio. Own Tax Revenue of a state comprises three components: (i) taxes on income, (ii) taxes on property and capital transactions and taxes on commodities and services, and (iii) taxes on commodities

Table 8.1: Major Sources of Own Non-Tax Revenue
for North Eastern States

State	Sources
Arunachal Pradesh	Power
Assam	Petroleum, Dividends and Profits, Interest Receipts, Forestry and Wildlife
Manipur	State Lotteries
Meghalaya	Industries
Mizoram	Power
Nagaland	Education, Sports, Art and Culture, Power
Sikkim	State Lotteries, Power
Tripura	Power

Source: State Finances: A Study of Budgets of 2019–20, Reserve Bank of India.

and services. Needless to add, the states have to make efforts at tapping the potential sources towards raising their own tax revenue.

Upon the analysis of the compiled data, it is revealed that there is an almost reverse feature vis-à-vis the share of Own Non-Tax Revenue as a share of GSDP. Compared to a low share that characterizes the average of all states, the North Eastern states show a higher propensity in terms of generating Own Non-Tax Revenue compared to that generated by all the states together. However, Manipur and Tripura have bucked the trend. Another worrying feature is the drastic decline in the same for Sikkim during the period under review. It will be interesting to identify some of the major sources of Own Non-Tax Revenue for the North Eastern states. Table 8.1 gives some insights. The interesting point to be noted here is the fact that most of the sources are linked to either use of natural resources—power and petroleum or recreation—lotteries and sports and culture.

Development Expenditure

Development Expenditure is defined as the component of expenditure (social and economic services) on revenue and capital account and loans and advances extended by the state for development purposes, whereas aggregate disbursement is the summation of aggregate expenditure and debt repayments. Aggregate expenditure is the summation of revenue expenditure, capital outlay, and loans and advances. From the compiled data, we get an idea of the development expenditure carried out by the North Eastern states as percentage of their aggregate disbursement. It is clear that some of the NE states fare better than the national average— Meghalaya with a high level of consistency and Arunachal Pradesh, Assam, and Mizoram, sporadically. According to 2019–20 budget estimates, Meghalaya is projected to spend 6 per cent more than the national average, while over the past six years, its average spending has been 3.4 per cent above the national average. The states of Nagaland and Manipur require urgent attention towards this fiscal component as they have been consistently lagging behind. Between 2014 and 2019, the gap of Nagaland and Manipur was around -10 per cent and -6 per cent. For the fiscal year 2019–20, according to the budget estimates, the proposed gap for Nagaland stood at -8.8 per cent while for Manipur it was -4.1 per cent.

Non-Development Expenditure

From the compiled data, it was possible to analyse the state of non-development expenditure (general services) in the NE states. In the gap analysis, a positive value indicates that a state is spending more on non-developmental activities as a share of its total disbursement on a comparative scale vis-à-vis the average of all states. Non-development expenditure may well be coined as the cost of governance, and the data suggest that the cost of governance is relatively high in the north eastern states in comparison with their peers in the country. All states are heavily into non-development expenditure, barring some few exceptional years.

The five-year trend from 2014–15 till 2018–19 suggests that the cost of governance only in Arunachal Pradesh has been found to be lower in comparison to the whole of the country. According to the 2019–20 (BE), the cost of governance is set to see a steep increase with the gap rising to 8.8 per cent. Manipur, Nagaland, and Tripura have consistently borne a higher cost of governance as the average gap from 2014 to 2019 stands at 5.7 per cent, 12.5 per cent, and 4.1 per cent for these states, respectively. Mizoram has seen a couple of years when its gap became lower than the national scenario, but the 2019–20 (BE) suggests that the gap may increase to 14 per cent; the highest for any NER state over 2014–19.

Achievement of SDGs clearly calls for a reversal in the general trend in the NE states, i.e. there is need for increase in the share of development expenditure. Nagaland, Manipur, and Tripura call for special attention in this context.

Interest Payment as Share of Revenue Receipts and Revenue Expenditure

Interest payments constitute a considerable drag on the resources available to the states to pursue development. The compiled data allow for the exposition of gaps in interest payment by the states as a share of their revenue receipt and revenue expenditure. From 2014–15 to 2019–20, if seen from a comparative perspective, the gap appears to be negative, indicating that the NER states bear a lesser interest burden than all the states as a whole bear. Arunachal Pradesh, Assam, Manipur, and Meghalaya not only have lower interest payments as a share of their revenue receipts and revenue expenditure, but they also spend lower than Nagaland, Sikkim, and Tripura. The average gap of interest payment as a share of revenue receipts stand at around: -8 per cent for Arunachal Pradesh; -6 per cent for Assam, Manipur, and Meghalaya, while -7 per cent for Mizoram. The average gap of interest payment as a share of revenue expenditure stands at around: -7 per cent for Arunachal Pradesh; -6 per cent for Assam, Manipur, and Mizoram, while -5 per cent for Meghalaya. This positive feature in terms of significantly lower level of burden of interest payments may be leveraged effectively in the coming days.

Committed Expenditure as Share of Revenue Expenditure

Committed expenditure is the fixed expenditure on interest payments, salaries and wages, and pensions and subsidies. Between 2014–15 and 2019–20, in the states of Manipur, Nagaland, and Tripura, the committed expenditure as a part of the revenue expenditure exceeds the Indian level. On an average, the spending for the aforementioned states is 6 per cent,

11 per cent, and 8 per cent, respectively. According to the budget estimates of 2019–20, Manipur and Tripura are projected to spend around 6 per cent and 8 per cent, respectively, more than the national level on its committed expenditure as part of its revenue expenditure.

Special attention may be desirable for the state of Nagaland as it has unwaveringly had the most spending on committed expenditure from 2014–15 to 2019–20, with gap for the 2019–20 (BE) was estimated to be 10.5 per cent over the national scenario. Entirely reverse trend is seen in this regard for Arunachal Pradesh. Over the period under review, it is the only NER state for which the committed expenditure is lower than the average of the rest of the states in the country. Arunachal Pradesh, on an average, has spent 4 per cent lower than the national average, while according to the budget estimates for 2019–20, the gap is proposed to stand at around 3 per cent lower than the national scenario.

Finance from the Central Government

The North Eastern states receive considerable financial support from the Central Government, having been accorded special status. The flow of funds from the Central government to these states happens in three forms:

- State's share in central taxes;
- Grants from the centre, and;
- Gross loans from the centre.

These three components are together termed as gross transfers from Centre. Data used for analysis in this section have been sourced from Reserve Bank of India (2019).

Gross Transfers as Share of Aggregate Disbursements

The analyses of these three components from the compiled data provide the details over the issue. It clearly shows that the NE states enjoy a superior position with respect to the situation that prevails in the states on the average. Among the NE states, the flow of gross transfers as share of aggregate disbursements for Arunachal Pradesh, Manipur, Mizoram, and Nagaland stands at 47.8 per cent, 43 per cent, 45.6 per cent, and 45.6 per cent, respectively, which is found to be relatively higher than the national scenario. The gross transfers for these states for the year 2019–20 (BE) are projected to be 44.4 per cent for Arunachal and Mizoram, 35.9 per cent for Manipur, and 43.2 per cent for Nagaland. Out of the eight NER states, the gap of Assam has had been consistently the lowest from 2014–15 to 2019–20. According to the budget estimates of 2019–20, the gap of Assam is estimated to be 19.4 per cent more than the national average.

Rehabilitation of Bru-Reang Refugees

A historic agreement was signed by Government of India, Governments of Tripura, and Mizoram and Bru-Reang representatives on 20 January 2020, to end the twenty-three-year-old Bru-Reang refugee crisis. The agreement is in line with the Government vision for the progress of the NE and the empowerment of the people of the region.

With this permanent solution to the longstanding issue of rehabilitating thousands of Bru-Reang people, they can now look towards a bright future. Under the new agreement, around 34,000 Bru refugees will be settled in Tripura and would be given aid from the Centre to help with their rehabilitation and all round development, through a package of around Rs. 600 crore. These people would get all the rights that normal residents of the States get and able to enjoy the benefits of social welfare schemes of Centre and State governments.

Source: PIB.

Social Sector Expenditure as Share of Aggregate Expenditure

The compiled data considered the nature and extent of expenditure on social sector and specifically those into education and health (Reserve Bank of India, 2019). It is to be taken in consideration that the aggregate expenditure considered for the analysis includes the central transfers as well. Upon analysis, it was clear that social sector expenditure appears to be given a leg up in Assam, Meghalaya, and Tripura. Over the past six years, from 2014–15 to 2019–20, Assam and Tripura have had a better performance vis-à-vis the rest of the country. Tripura has, on an average, spent 7.1 per cent more than the average of the rest of the states in the country, while Assam has spent, on an average, 4.3 per cent more. Barring a blip in 2015–16, Meghalaya has also fared better than the rest of the country spending 3.8 per cent more than the national average.

Upon further disaggregating the social expenditure, it emerges that but for a few outliers, the states of NER have been consistently spending more than the national average towards spending on medical, public health, and family welfare. Meghalaya, Mizoram, Nagaland, and Tripura emerge as the standout performers of the sector as they have steadily eclipsed the national performance from 2014–19. On an average, Meghalaya has spent 2.4 per cent more than the rest of the country with its highest spending being in 2015–16; it should be noted that not only it was the highest among the NER states but also being 2.9 per cent greater than all other states of the country.

The performance of NER states in the education sector is not uniform. Own expenditure for Assam and Meghalaya has consistently been more than what prevails in the states of the country on an average. Assam has over the past six years up to 2019–20 spent on an average 7 per cent more than all the states, while the spending of Meghalaya has been only marginally greater than the state-wise national scenario. Barring 2014–15 for Sikkim and 2014–16 for Tripura, the two states have relatively spent more on education. Arunachal Pradesh, Manipur, and Nagaland require urgent attention in the fiscal considerations of the education sector as their own spending has been consistently lower than the national scenario. With an average gap of -3.6 per cent, the state of Arunachal has spent least on education from its own resources from 2014–15 to 2019–20.

In addition to the transfer of central funds to the states, 10 per cent of the Annual Plan Budget of 52 Ministries of the Union Government is earmarked every year for spending in NER since 1998–99. Table 8.2 gives some insights into the allocation of funds to the NER states by non-exempted union ministries.

To summarize, we find that the capacity of the states in NER is considerably low in terms of raising domestic tax revenue compared to their

Table 8.2: Allocation of Funds to NER States by
Non-exempted Union Ministries

Year	Allocation (Rs. Crore)	Expenditure (Rs. Crore)	Expenditure (as % of Allocation)
2007–08	12,968.38	11,048.07	85.19
2008–09	14,846.91	12,446.74	83.83
2009–10	16,229.46	14,689.98	90.51
2010–11	21,772.22	19,779.06	90.85
2011–12	21,721.55	16,872.3	77.68
2012–13	NA	NA	NA
2013–14	25,947.16	23,170.63	89.30
2014–15	27,359.17	24,483.42	89.49
2015–16	29,669.22	31,294.75	105.48
2016–17	32,180.08	29,367.9	91.26
2017–18	40,971.69	39,753.41	97.03
2018–19	47,087.95	45,518.14	96.67

Source: Compiled from annual outlays for NER States by Ministry of Development of North Eastern Region.

peers in the rest of the country, while they have succeeded in raising a significantly large part of their revenue receipts through collection of non-tax revenue mostly through central grants. Own non-tax revenue accrues from sources linked to harnessing of natural resources among others. State lotteries, industrial activities, and even entertainment taxes in respect of Nagaland are significant state-specific sources of non-tax revenue. It is intriguing to regard that the share of development expenditure in total expenditure vis-à-vis that of non-development expenditure is considerably low in the NER region, even though the interest burden is relatively lower in these states compared to that in their counterparts in the rest of the country. Higher ratio of committed expenditure to aggregate expenditure is also a matter of concern. All the NER states being considered 'special category' ones, enjoy a relatively higher share of gross transfer of resources from the centre. However, the relative expenditure on education appears lower than that incurred by the rest of the states. With the 'cost of governance' relatively higher, some efforts at introducing expenditure reforms are considered useful to rationalize the expenditure pattern of the governmental resources in NER region. Further, it is of utmost importance to locate potential new sources of tax revenue in these states or enhance the tax base effectively.

Externally Aided Interventions

Besides transferring resources to the states, the Centre also arranges externally aided projects to the states. Bilateral and multilateral development projects (in the form of loans) in the region have focused on energy, infrastructure, urban development, environment as well as poverty and livelihoods. Table 8.3 and 8.4 capture the quantum of flows, phases of project implementation, and the partner institutions along with the sectors. Two externally aided projects specially designed for the NER states may be mentioned here:

North Eastern States Roads Investment Programme (NESRIP) assisted
    by Asian Development Bank (ADB) (Table 8.5 and 8.6)
North East Rural Livelihood Project assisted by World Bank

Details about these schemes are furnished in Box 8.1.

Private Investment

The quest for sustainable development may remain unachievable in the absence of allocation of financial resources from the private entities. Such investments are required to create new productive capacities and add value to the available resources in an optimal manner. They are relevant to generate opportunities for more exchange of goods and services across regions, help innovate and harness new technologies, add to the employment potentials, and thereby improve the quality of life of individuals. Private investments may be categorized under two heads: domestic investments and foreign direct investments (FDIs).

Table 8.3: Externally Aided Projects in North East India (USD Million)

Description	Agreement Date	Terminal Disbursement Date	Loan Amount (USD million)
GOJP [Japan]			
IDP-182—Tripura Forest Environmental Improvement & Poverty Alleviation Project	30-03-07	11-07-17	65.60
IDP-201—Guwahati Water Supply Project	31-03-09	28-07-19	287.64
IDP-201A—Guwahati Water Supply Project	31-03-09	28-07-19	27.12
IDP-211—Sikkim Biodiversity Conservation & Forest Management Project	31-03-10	15-06-22	57.72
IDP-211A—Sikkim Biodiversity Conservation & Forest Management Project	31-03-10	15-06-22	3.61
IDP-242—Guwahati Sewerage Project	27-02-15	14-07-25	116.85
IDP-242A—Guwahati Sewerage Project	27-02-15	14-07-25	12.19
ADB [Asian Development Bank]			
2592-IND—Assam Power Sector Enhancement Invest. program--Project 1	15-02-10	30-06-17	49.60
2677-IND—Assam Power Sector Enhancement Investment Prog. Projeclt-2	17-01-11	30-06-17	66.90
2684-IND—Assam Integrated Flood and Riverbank Erosion Risk Management Invest. Prog.	10-05-11	31-07-16	48.50
2770-IND—North Eastern State Roads Invest. Program-Project 1	09-07-12	31-12-16	74.80
2800-IND—Assam Power Sector Enhancement Investment Program (MFF)—Project-3	27-02-12	28-02-18	33.30
2806-IND—Assam Urban Infrastructure Investment Prog. Project-1	09-03-12	30-06-18	61.00
2834-IND—North Eastern Region Capital Cities Dev. Investment Prog project-2	19-11-12	30-06-18	60.00

Table 8.3: Continued

Description	Agreement Date	Terminal Disbursement Date	Loan Amount (USD million)
3033-IND—Supporting Human Capital Development in Meghalaya	23-01-14	31-03-19	100.00
3073-IND—North Eastern State Roads Investment Program—Project 2	17-02-14	31-03-20	125.20
3118-IND—SASEC Road Connectivity Investment Program (Tranche-1)	26-03-15	30-06-22	300.00
3140-IND—Assam Power Sector Investment Program (Project-1)	20-02-15	30-06-19	50.00
3200-IND—Assam Power Sector Enhancement Investment Program-Project 4	20-02-15	31-12-18	50.20
3327-IND—Assam Power Sector Investment Program Project-2	07-11-16	31-12-19	48.00
3337-IND—North Eastern Region Capital Cities Development Investment Prog Tranche 3	28-01-16	22-06-19	80.00
9168-IND—JFPR Assistance—Livelihood improvement for river erosion victims in Assam	10-01-13	31-05-16	2.50
GODE [Germany]			
1642595E—Climate Change Adaption in North Eastern Region	31-05-12	30-12-19	0.78
3990289E—Participatory Natural Resource Management in Tripura	21-05-08	31-03-17	8.16
IBRD [I B R D]			
8136-IN—Assam State Roads Project	05-11-12	31-03-18	320
IDA [I D A]			
Q942-IN—Preparation of Proposed Nagaland Health Project Preparation Advance	17-10-14	31-12-16	1
5035-IN—North East Rural Livelihood Project	20-01-12	15-03-19	80.8
IFAD [I F A D]			
794-IN—North Eastern Region Comm. Resource Management proj. for upland areas II	12-07-10	31-03-17	12.6

Source: Ministry of Finance, GOI.

Note: Japan and Germany's loan data are converted in USD.

Table 8.4: Present Status of the Projects as on 30 September 2019

State	Project	Sanction Date	Approved Cost	Present Status	Total Funds Released	Date of Completion
Assam	Barpeta to Kalitakuchi (AS-37)	10-12-12	224.01	Ongoing	133.81	31-12-19
Meghalaya	Garobada to Dalu (NH 51) (MLN-01)	26-03-14	267.60	Ongoing	189.26	31-12-19
Sikkim	Meli (from km 17.10) to Nayabazar (SK-01), Nayabazar to Namchi (SK-02	28-03-13	191.03	Ongoing	63.47	31-12-19
Assam	Tamulpur to Paneri (AS-02), Paneri to Udalguri (AS-03), Major bridges, 5 nos. {4 nos. on Tamulpur to Paneri (AS-02) and 1 no. on Paneri to Udalguri (AS-03)}	10-02-15	421.86	Ongoing	226.00	31-03-20
Manipur	Tupul (NH 53) to Bishnupur, Thoubal to Kasom Khullen (MN-06)	1-10-14	475.68	Ongoing	228.19	31-03-20
Mizoram	Serchhip to Buarpui (MZ-02)	3-12-14	301.97	Ongoing	108.09	31-03-20
Tripura	Udaipur(NH44) to Melaghar (TR-02)	06-04-15	139.84	Ongoing	44.28	31-03-20

Source: Dashboard of Ministry of Development of North Eastern Region (available at https://mdoner.gov.in/dashboard/schemetables/common_all_project_list_scheme.php?scheme=nesrip)

Box 8.1: Externally Aided Interventions

North Eastern States Roads Investment Programme (NESRIP) Assisted by Asian Development Bank (ADB)

The scheme, North Eastern State Roads Investment Programme (NESRIP), with financial support from ADB, was approved on 19 May 2011 at estimated cost of Rs. 1,353.83 crore ($298.2 million @ $1 = Rs. 45.4). It planned construction/upgradation of total 433.425-km long roads in six North Eastern States of Assam, Manipur, Meghalaya, Mizoram, Sikkim, and Tripura.

Five roads (length – 197.30 km) were taken up in Tranche—I and six roads (length – 236.125 km) were considered for financial support in Tranche-II. The mode of sharing of resources among the different stakeholders was fixed as follows (Table 8.5).

North East Rural Livelihood Project Assisted by World Bank

The objective of the North East Rural Livelihood Project (NERLP) with financial support from the World Bank is 'To improve rural livelihoods especially that of women, unemployed youth and the most disadvantaged, in four North Eastern States'. The project consists of four major components:

- Social empowerment
- Economic empowerment
- Partnership development & management
- Project management

The objectives of the intervention were identified as follows:

- Creation of sustainable community institutions around women Self-Help Groups (SHGs), youth groups of men and women (YG), and Community Development Groups (CDG).
- Building capacity of community institutions for self-governance, bottom up planning, democratic functioning with transparency and accountability.

- Increasing economic and livelihood opportunities by developing partnership of community institutions for natural resource management, microfinance, market linkages, and sectoral economic services.

The project that was designed to cover nearly 300,000 households.

Even though designed for a project cycle of five years, it appears that the intervention is still going strong. As per the latest newsletter of NERLP published in July 2019, the project so far facilitated formation of 28,154 Women's Self-Help Groups (SHG), 1,212 SHG Federations, 501 Producers' Groups, and 22 Producers' Organizations. A total of 10,462 boys and girls have been trained in various job skills, and 5,494 of them are employed. Some of the successful schemes under this project relate to clothing shop, production of fermented bamboo shoots, setting up general store, polyhouse farming, and homestay services.

Source: NERLP Newsletter

Table 8.5: Mode of Sharing of Resources between NESRIP and ADB

Agency	Amount (Rs. Crore)	Amount (US$ millions)	Share (%) Tranche-I	Share (%) Tranche-I
M/o DoNER (GoI)	378.4	83.3	24.9	14.2
State Govts.	67.4	14.9	6.8	6.1
ADB Loan	908.01	200.0	68.3	79.7
Total	1,353.8	298.2	100	100

Source: Ministry of Development of North Eastern Region [available at: https://mdoner.gov.in/activities/nesrip-project-details]

Unfortunately, the flow of private domestic investments in the NER is significantly low. The data from Reserve Bank of India (2019) suggest that most of the private investments made in NER are concentrated in only a few states, namely Assam, Meghalaya, and Sikkim. It should be mentioned that Assam has seen the heaviest private investments in the region from 1990–91 to 2016–17.

Table 8.6: Districts Covered under NESRIP

State	District	Blocks
Mizoram	Aizawl	Phullen, Aibawk, Darlawn, Thingsulthliah, Tlangnuam
	Lunglei	Lungsen, Bunghmun, Lunglei, Hnahthial
Nagaland	Peren	Tenning, Peren, Jalukie
	Tuensang	Longkhim, Chare, Noksen, Sangsangyu, Shamator, Chessore, Noklak, Thonoknyu
Sikkim	South	Namchi, Jorethang, Namthang, Ravongla, Yangang, Temi-Tarku, Sumbuk, Sikkip
	West	Gyalshing, Soreng, Yuksom, Dentam, Kaluk, Daramdin
	15 poorest Panchayat wards of East district	Ben, Thasa, Upper Lingtam, Dhanbari, Lower Samlik, Mamring (Amba Mamring Gumpa), Premlakha, Singaneybas, Lower Tarpin, Dokchin, East Machong, Namrang (Tumin Karma Choling Gumpa), Simik (Simik Daduling Gumpa), Kutitar, Namin
Tripura	West	Khatalia, Melaghar, Boxanagar, Bishalgarh, Jampuijala, Dukli, Hezamara, Mohanpur, Jirania, Mandwai, Mungiakami, Teliamura, Kalyanpur, Khowai, Tulashikhar, Padmabill
	North	Kumarghat, Gaurnagar, Kadamtala, Panisagar, Dhamchhara, Pecharthal, Dasda, Jampuihill

Source: Website of Ministry of DONER, Government of India.

Based on the Fact Sheet on FDI from April 2000 to March 2019, during this period, the flow of FDI in NER states (barring Sikkim) was found to be meagre Rs. 591 crore or 116 million USD. The amount corresponds to 0.03 per cent of the total inflow of FDI to India (Rs. 2,378,353 crore or a little over 420 billion USD) during this period. Figures for Sikkim could not be culled out separately as it falls under the jurisdiction of the Kolkata Regional Office of the Reserve Bank of India, and the data available are clubbed with those for West Bengal and Andaman and Nicobar Islands (Rs. 31,119 crore or 6.43 billion USD)

Flow of Commercial Bank Credit Facilitating Financial Inclusion

Financial inclusion through increased accessibility to bank credit is a necessary condition for sustainable development. NER performs poorly on this count. The compiled data compared the credit deposit ratios (CDRs) at the level of place of utilization for the NE states expressed as the gap with the national average (Reserve Bank of India, 2019). Barring 1990, 1992, and 1993, the gaps are consistently found to be negative and, therefore, well below the national average. The gaps for the years 2013, 2014, and 2015 were over -40 per cent lower than the national value. However, in the recent years of 2016 and 2017, the gaps of CDR have dropped with the value for 2017 being around -35 per cent lower than the national scenario.

A low level of CDR can be indicative of many possible malaises. It indicates lack of bankable projects that are found worthy to be financed. It also underscores the creation of personal/corporate savings at a rate higher than the rate at which credit facilities are disbursed to the residents of this region. Given that the growth and development of a region immensely depend on the availability of credit, it is imperative that conscious efforts are taken to increase the same. The features of NER that depress the CDR are to be identified forthright and necessary steps are to be initiated to ensure that it experiences a healthy increase in the coming years. Dedicated state-specific project development units (PDUs) managed professionally may help creation of baskets of bankable projects that would attract interest of the commercial lending agencies.

Suggestive Roadmap for Action

Given the state of efforts made in the NE states in actualizing the SDGs at a localized level and the availability of development finance therein, it will be pertinent to identify some possible actionable points that may facilitate and enhance resource generation capacities for the whole region.

Given the high propensity of non-development and committed expenditure in most of the NE states, a rationalization of the expenditure pattern in favour of more allocation of resources towards development of the region cannot be overemphasized. Such an effort calls for conscious reforms in the expenditure profiles of the states with considerable reductions in non-developmental and committed expenditures as a share of their total disbursements. The low CDR in the North Eastern states calls for an institutional effort at facilitating the identification of bankable and feasible projects for the region. Establishment of dedicated 'Project Development Units' (PDUs) manned by local experts having exposure to the local situations may be effective in enhancing the CDR in these states. Such PDUs would engage in designing suitable bankable projects that ideally use local skills and local resources in larger proportion and help produce goods and services that are competitive enough to contribute to external trade and be sold locally.

NER enjoys a unique status of having the largest share of India's international boundary. Till the other day, it was considered as a source of disadvantage to this region. The emphasis on 'Act East Policy' has the potential to convert the disadvantage into a source of new resources for this region. The India-Japan Act East Forum launched in 2017 is a good step for mobilization of financial resources and joint projects (See Box 8.2). The existing infrastructure of border trade is necessary to be strengthened to this effect. There are nineteen land customs stations located in the international border of the NER facilitating some semblance of trade with Bangladesh, Bhutan, and China. However, the share of trade through the land custom stations compared through the overall trade between India and these countries is very insignificant. An effective mechanism to utilize these opportunities for border trade can go a long way in contributing to the sustainable development of this region. A case in point is the example from Myanmar. Myanmar's trade with foreign countries though border gates with China, Thailand, Bangladesh, and India reached $4.83 billion during the fiscal year 2018–19. Between 1 October 2017 and 30 September 2019, Myanmar's trade volume through border increased by 1,007 million USD whereas that by sea declined by 1922.5 USD (Border Trade Data: Ministry of Commerce, Republic of the Union of Myanmar).

Box 8.2: Launch of India-Japan Act East Forum

In pursuance of the Memorandum of Cooperation to establish the
India-Japan Act East Forum signed on 14 September 2017 during
the visit of Prime Minister Abe to India, Ministry of External Affairs
and Embassy of Japan held the first joint meeting of the Forum on 5
December 2017. The meeting was co-chaired by Foreign Secretary
Dr S. Jaishankar and the Japanese Ambassador to India Mr Kenji
Hiramatsu. The Act East Forum aims to provide a platform for India–
Japan collaboration under the rubric of India's 'Act East Policy' and
Japan's 'Free and Open Indo-Pacific Strategy'. Besides the Ministry
of External Affairs and the Embassy of Japan, participants included
representatives from Ministry of Development of North Eastern
Region (DONER), Department of Economic Affairs in the Ministry
of Finance, Ministry of Road Transport and Highways, Ministry of
Home Affairs and the States of North-East region from the Indian
side, and Japan International Cooperation Agency, Japan External
Trade Organization, Japan Foundation and Japan National Tourism
Organization from the Japanese side.

The second meeting of India - Japan Act East Forum' (IJAEF) was
held on 8 October under the co-chairmanship of Ambassador Kenji
Hiramatsu and Foreign Secretary Vijay Keshav Gokhale. The Forum
aims to further expand the cooperation between Japan and India in
North East and to strengthen the relationship between Japan and
North East, as well as that between Japan and India. In this regard, the
Forum discusses cooperation in various fields and promotes Japan's
cooperation in the region. The Forum comprises Embassy of Japan
and other government-affiliated Japanese organizations based in New
Delhi from Japan's side; the Ministry of External Affairs (MEA) and
other relevant government offices as well as State governments of the
NER from India's side. The immediate key outcomes cover road and
bridge connectivity projects; forest management projects in States of
Tripura and Meghalaya; a new initiative to utilize bamboo which is
abundant in the region; to people-to-people exchanges.

The second IJAEF reaffirmed the commitment of all the stakeholders towards the realization of the region's connectivity to expedite

the implementation of the ongoing projects. Meghalaya North East Connectivity Phase 1: Tura-Dalu (NH-51) Phase 2: Shillong-Dawki (NH-40) Mizoram North East Coonectivity Phase 1 and 2: Aizawl-Tuipang (NH-54). The second JIAEF meeting decided to pursue the realization of Gelephu-Dalu Corridor in collaboration with the ADB. This corridor is expected to enhance connectivity in North East as well as with neighbouring countries. Japan is prepared to proceed with Dhubri/Phulbari bridge project, which will be the longest river bridge in India if realized, as Phase 3 of North East Road Network Connectivity Improvement Project. The two sides affirmed their intentions to consider further projects based on actual demand. The importance of Main District Roads (MDRs) in the NER in improving the livelihood of people in North East as economic lifelines was highlighted.

Source: Press Releases of Ministry of External Affairs and Embassy of Japan in India.

In spite of the ethnic variations across NER, there are several interesting economic features that bind this region together. Firstly, all the sates in NER have more than 60 per cent of their geographical area under forests which can provide environmental services to the country and beyond. Most of them are also rich in hydro power generation potential. The region is home to a number of exotic products such as spices and horticultural crops. The mountainous landscape of this region adds to potential touristic attractions. Traditional skills in handloom and handicrafts abound in these states. These similarities may well be tapped to integrate NER into a common economic structure that would contribute to creation of unique value chains spread across them. Given similarities in respect of some of them across the international border and the longstanding cultural linkages with the neighbouring communities would be an added advantage of such integration.

References

'90 per cent of Kaziranga inundated, animals flee park in droves' (16 July 2020). *The Times of India*.

ADB. 2016. *SASEC Operational Plan 2016-2025*. Manila: Asian Development Bank.

'All India Consumer Price Index numbers for agricultural and rural labourers' (May 2020). Labor Bureau.

Anand, P. K., Kumar, K. and Khanna, S. 2019. 'Sustainable Agriculture and Nutritional Security: Emerging Policy Options with Production Choices'. *Discussion Paper # 240*, Research and Information System for Developing Countries, Government of India, New Delhi.

Ansari, M. I. Z. 2019. 'Exploring the North Eastern region for Future Business Opportunities in the Era of Ease of Doing Business'. *International Journal of Research in Business Studies*, 4 (1), 23–34.

'Arunachal: Bamang Felix calls coordination meeting with CBOs on Covid-19' (1 June 2020). *Arunachal24.in*

'As floods wash over Assam, state government left facing a cascade of disasters' (2020). *The Wire*.

'Aviation flies towards Rs 25,000 crore revenue loss, which would spur structural changes' (2020). CRISIL.

Ayushman, Bharat. 2019. *Best Practices and Innovations: One Year of Implementation Across States, India 2018-19*. New Delhi.

Baishya, M. and Goswami, G. 2017. 'Public Debt of Assam: An Analysis'. *Assam Economic Review*, 10, 231–43.

Barua, A and Das, S. K. 2008. 'Prospectuses on Growth and Development in the Northeast: The Look East Policy and Beyond', *Journal of Applied Economic Research*, 2 (4), 327–50.

Barua, S. 2017. 'Whose River Is It, Anyway?: The Political Economy of Hydropower in the Eastern Himalayas', in *Water Conflicts in Northeast India*. India: Routledge.

Borah, A. and Barman, S. 2019. Flood Havoc and Its Strategic Management for Enhancing Farmers Income in Barak Valley Zone of Assam.

Bose, P. R. 2019. 'Connectivity Is No Panacea for an Unprepared Northeast India'. *Strategic Analysis*, 43 (4), 335–41.

Brunner, H. P. 2010. 'North East India: Trade and Investment and Comparative Advantage', in H. P. Brunner (ed.) *North East India: Local economic development and global markets*. Chapter 3. India: SAGE Publications.

Budget Documents of NE States.

CBHI. 2018. *National Health Profile 2018*. New Delhi: Central Bureau of Health Intelligence.

Centre for Development Goals, Assam Administrative Staff College. 2019. *Journey Towards Sustainable Development Goals in Assam*. Guwahati.

Centre for Development Goals, Assam Administrative Staff College. 2019. *Journey Towards Sustainable Development Goals in Assam*. Guwahati.

Chang, H. J. 2007. 'Institutional Change and Economic Development: An Introduction'. 1–14.

Chang, H. J. 2011. 'Institutions and Economic Development: Theory, Policy And History'. *Journal of Institutional Economics*, 7 (4), 473–98.

Chao, E. 2005. 'A Study in Social Change: The Domestic Violence Prevention Movement in Taiwan'. *Critical Asian Studies*, 37 (1), 29–50. DOI: 10.1080/1467271052000305250

Chattopadhyay, Saumen. 2009. 'The Market in Higher Education: Concern for Equity and Quality'. *Economic & Political Weekly*, 44 (29), 53–61.

Chaturvedi, Sachin; Kharas, Homi; Rehman, Mustafizur and Scholz, Imme. 2019. T20 Japan Policy Brief on 'Sustainable Financing for Development'. March.

Chaturvedi, Sachin; Rehman, Mustafizur and Srinivas, Ravi. 2019. T20 Japan Policy Brief on 'Leveraging Science, Technology and Innovation for Implementing the 2030 Agenda'. March.

Chaturvedi, Sachin. 2018. 'Global Partnership Needed to Achieve Sustainable Development Goals'. *The Asian Age*, 9 July.

Chaturvedi, Sachin. 2018. Localise SDGs to Meet Targets. *Financial Express*, 15 June 2018.

Chaturvedi, Sachin. 2019. 'Agricultural Trade in South Asia: Issues, Challenges and the Way Forward', in Nagesh Kumar and Joseph George (eds.) *Regional Cooperation for Sustainable Food Security in South Asia*. Taylor & Francis.

Chaturvedi, Sachin. 2019. 'Introduction: Challenges Confronting a Rising South Asia—Industry and Employment' and 'Conclusion: Manufacturing and Employment in South Asia', in Sachin Chaturvedi and Sabyasachi Saha (eds.) *Manufacturing and Jobs in South Asia: Strategy for Sustainable Economic Growth*. Springer.

Chaturvedi, Sachin. 2019. 'Introduction: Sustainable Development Goals and India', in Sachin Chaturvedi, T. C. James, Sabyasachi Saha and Prativa Shaw (eds.) *2030 Agenda and India: Moving from Quantity to Quality* (pp. 1–13). Springer, Singapore.

Chaturvedi, S., James, T. C., Saha, S. and Shaw, P. 2019. 'India's Pursuit of SDGs: Unfolding Paradigm Shifts and Convergence', in S. Chaturvedi, T. James, S. Saha and P. Shaw (eds.) *2030 Agenda and India: Moving from Quantity to Quality. South Asia Economic and Policy Studies*. Springer, Singapore.

Chongloi, P. 2011. 'Business Opportunities with Special Reference to Northeast India and Realigning Strategies towards the Look East Policy'. *Journal of North East India Studies*, 1 (1), 81–99.

Choudhury, J. 2018. Sustainable Development Goals in Nagaland. Unpublished manuscript.

Chutia, S. 2015. 'Prospects of Border Trade for North East Region of India with South Asian Countries'. *International Journal of Research in Economics and Social Sciences*, 5 (10).

CII. 'CII COVID-19 Interventions—State Government Notifications' (https://www.ciicovid19update.in/state-govt-notifications.html)

CII. 2020. State Government Notifications. *CII Publication*.

Cline, L. E. 2006. 'The Insurgency Environment in Northeast India'. *Small Wars & Insurgencies*, 17 (2), 126–47.

'Consumer Price Index numbers on base 2012=100 for rural, urban and combined for the month of December 2019' (13 January 2020). Ministry of Statistics & Programme Implementation, PIB New Delhi.

'Coronavirus: Arunachal Pradesh temporarily bans entry of foreigners' (9 March 2020). *Science The Wire.*

'Coronavirus: Northeastern states sound alert' (7 March 2020). *The Economic Times.*

'COVID-19 & tourism in Northeast post 2020' (2020). *The Sentinel.*

'COVID-19 deepens existential crisis for Assam tea sector; stiff competition, rising costs and diminishing prices threaten 180-year-old industry' (2020). *The FirstPost.*

'Covid-19 impact: Q1 to be a washout for IT sector, say analysts' (6 July 2020). *The Economic Times.*

'Covid-19 lockdown: Buses, tempos, trucks to remain off roads in Assam till March 24' (23 March 2020). *The Economic Times.*

'COVID-19 lockdown: Impact on agriculture' (20 May 2020). International Development Economics Associates.

'Covid-19 lockdown: Petroleum sector throttled' (May 2020), *The Telegraph Online.*

'COVID-19: Assam tea planters stare at Rs 1,218 crore loss' (15 April 2020). *The Economic Times.*

Das, R. and Das, A. K. 2011. Industrial Cluster: An Approach for Rural Development in North East India. *International Journal of Trade, Economics and Finance*, 2 (2), 161.

Das, K. 2005. 'Industrial Clustering in India: Local Dynamics and the Global Debate'. *Indian Industrial Clusters*, 1–19.

Das, R. and Das, A. K. 2011. 'Industrial Cluster: An Approach for Rural Development in North East India'. *International Journal of Trade, Economics and Finance*, 2 (2), 161.

Das. K. 2017. 'Conflicts Leave a Trail of Poverty and Malnutrition: Evidences from Assam', in U. K. De, et al. (eds.) *Inequality, Poverty and Development in India.* Singapore: Springer Nature.

Datta, S. 2008. 'What Ails the Northeast: An Enquiry into the Economic Factors'. *Strategic Analysis*, 25 (1), 73–87.

De, L. C. 2018. 'Organic Production of Horticultural Crops in North East Region of India'. *International Journal of Horticulture*, 8.

Deka, B. C., Thirugnanavel, A., Patel, R. K., Nath, A. and Deshmukh, N. 2012. 'Horticultural Diversity in Northeast India and its Improvement for Value Addition'. *Indian Journal of Genetics and Plant Breeding*, 72 (2), 157.

Dhar, B., and Ghosh, S. K. 2015. Genetic assessment of ornamental fish species from North East India. Gene, 555(2), 382–392.

'"Disciplined" northeast emerges as model of Covid-19 management: Jitendra Singh' (9 May 2020). *The Times of India.*

Dutta, P. and Dutta, M. K. 2014. 'Fiscal and Debt Sustainability in a Federal Structure: The Case of Assam in North East India'. *Romanian Journal of Fiscal Policy (RJFP)*, 5 (1), 1–19.

Economic Survey of NE States.

EIU. 2019. 'The Critical Role of Infrastructure for the Embassy of India, Kathmandu. https://www.indembkathmandu.gov.in/ Sustainable Development Goals'. *The Economist Intelligence Unit.*

Esfahani, H. S. and Ramírez, M. T. 2003. 'Institutions, Infrastructure, and Economic Growth'. *Journal of Development Economics*, 70 (2), 443–77.

'Fight against COVID-19: Government of Tripura distributes vitamin c-rich fruits for free to boost immunity' (15 July 2020). *NDTV India.*

Forest Survey of India. 2019. *Carbon Stock in India's Forests. In India State of Forest Report* (16th ed., pp.136–53). Forest Survey of India.

Ghani, A., Donnelly, C., Cox, D., Griffin, J., Fraser, C., Lam, T., et al. 2005. 'Methods for Estimating the Case Fatality Ratio for a Novel, Emerging Infectious Disease'. *American Journal of Epidemiology*, 162 (5), 479–86.

GOI. Agricultural Statistics at a Glance' for different years. Directorate of Economics and Statistics, Department of Agriculture, Cooperation & Farmers Welfare, Government of India.

Goraya, G. S., and Ved, D. K. 2017. Medicinal plants in India: an assessment of their demand and supply. Dehradun: Ministry of AYUSH.

Goswami, C. and Saikia, K. K. 2012. 'FDI and its Relation with Exports in India, Status and Prospect in North East Region'. *Procedia-Social and Behavioral Sciences*, 37, 123–32.

Government of Assam. 2020. 'Launching of Dhanwantari Scheme: Delivery of Essential & Lifesaving Medicines at Doorstep'. Office of the Mission Director, National health Mission, Assam, Letter No. NHM-18017/7/2020-PROC-NHM/ ECF-139421/1566, 24 April.

Government of India and United Nations, Sustainable Development Framework, 2018–2022.

Government of India, Central Bureau of Health Intelligence. 2018. *National Health Profile 2018.* New Delhi.

Government of India, Ministry of Health and Family Welfare. 2015. *Annual Report 2014-2015.* New Delhi.

Government of India, Ministry of Health and Family Welfare. 2017. *National Health Policy 2017.* New Delhi.

Government of India, Ministry of Health and Family Welfare. 2018. *Annual Report 2017-2018.* New Delhi.

Government of Manipur. 2017. 'Report on Private Hospitals/Clinics in Manipur 2016'. Government of Manipur. 2020. 'Manipur Gazette'. 2 June.

Government of Meghalaya. 'Meghalaya: Vision 2030'.

Government of Meghalaya. 2019. Meghalaya Vision 2030: Towards Building State Capability, Enhancing Freedom and Accel.

Government of Mizoram. 2018. 'Progress of SDGs Implementation in Mizoram'.

Government of Mizoram. 2018. Progress of SDG Implementation in Mizoram.

Government of Nagaland. 2018. Review of Sustainable Development Goals 2030 Nagaland Background - Sustainable Development Goals 2030. Retrieved from http://niti.gov.in/writereaddata/files/Nagaland_0.pdf

Government of Sikkim. 2020. 'A special meeting was held at Samman Bhawan today to discuss and deliberate on the current education situation and future road map of digital education in the State'. News & Announcement, 28 July.

Government of Tripura. 2018. Sustainable Development Goals: Vision-2030, 7 Year Strategy, 3 Year Action Plan & Indicators- NITI Aayog's Review meeting on SDGs. Retrieved from http://niti.gov.in/writereaddata/files/tripura.pdf

'GST Revenue collection for March, 2020 Rs. 97,597 crore of gross GST revenue collected' (March 2020). *PIB New Delhi.*

Humphrey, J. and Schmitz, H. 2000. *Governance and Upgrading: Linking Industrial Cluster and Global Value Chain Research (Vol. 120).* Brighton: Institute of Development Studies.

ICAR. 2020. 'Prospects of Northeast Agriculture in post COVID 19 scenario'. ICAR-Agricultural Technology Application Research Institute, Umiam.

ICFA. 2017. *Untapped Potential of North East Region-National Round Table Conference.* Indian Council of Food and Agriculture, 15 March.

ICMR, PHFI and ICMR, et al. 2017. *India: Health of the Nation's States – The India State-level Disease Burden Initiative.* Indian Council of Medical Research; Public Health Foundation of India; Institute for Health Metrics and Evaluation, New Delhi.

IFPRI. (2020). 'Addressing COVID-19 impacts on agriculture, food security, and livelihoods in India'. International Food Policy Research Institute.

IMF. 2020. World Economic Outlook. Washington: International Monetary Fund (IMF).

IWAI. 2017. *Annual Report 2016-17. Inland Waterways Authority of India.* Ministry of Shipping, Government of India.

Jain, K. A. 2018. Meeting with States & UTs on SDGs: Implementation of SDGs. Retrieved from https://niti.gov.in/writereaddata/files/NITI-Aayog-SDG-Presentation-to-States.pdf

Jalan, J. and Glinskaya, E. 1999. Improving Primary School Education in India: An Impact Assessment of DPEP-Phase I, unpublished paper. Retrieved from http://siteresources.worldbank.org/INTISPMA/Resources/Training-Events-and-Materials/india_primaryschool.pdf

Jayaraman, Rajshri. Simroth, Dora and Vericourt, Francis De. 2010. The Impact of School Lunches on Primary School Enrollment: Evidence from India's Midday Meal Scheme. Retrieved from https://www.isid.ac.in/~pu/conference/dec_10_conf/Papers/RajiJayaraman.pdf

Jena, N. R. 2017. 'The Micro, Small and Medium Enterprises (MSME) Manufacturing Sector in India: Role of MSME Clusters and the Idea of MSME Manufacturing Cluster Density'. *IOSR Journal of Economics and Finance (JOSR-JEF),* 8 (5), 49–59.

Kalita, P. (15 April 2020). 'Assam gets 50,000 kits, imported independently from Guangzhou'. *The Times of India.*

Khan, K. 2017. The impact of privatization among social and income groups. *Artha Vijnana,* 59 (1), 34–54.

Kolhe, P. 2017. 'Tax Incentive Policy for Development of Himalayan and North-eastern States in India'. *Indian Journal of Public Administration,* 63 (1), 136–56.

Konwar, P. 2015. Socio-Economic Conditions, Inequality and Deprivation in North East India.

KPMG. 2020. 'Impact of the COVID-19 on the Mining Sector in India'. May.

KPMG and FICCI. 2015. Emerging North-East India - Economically and Socially Inclusive Development Strategies. November.

Kumar K. and Anand P. K. 2018. 'Evolving Conceptual Framework and Monitoring Mechanism for SDGs in India'. *Discussion Paper # 234*, Research and Information System for Developing Countries, Government of India, New Delhi.

Kumar K. and Anand P. K. 2019. 'Pathways for Country's Official Statistical System to Surmount Over Policy Midget'. *Discussion Paper #238*, Research and Information System for Developing Countries, Government of India, New Delhi.

Kundu, S., Chandra, K., Tyagi, K., Pakrashi, A., & Kumar, V. 2019. DNA barcoding of freshwater fishes from Brahmaputra River in Eastern Himalaya biodiversity hotspot. Mitochondrial DNA Part B, 4(2), 2411–2419.

Khuntia, P. A. 2017. Skill Development of Youth in North East India: Way Forward. *NLI Research Studies Series No. 124/2017*.

Lallianthanga, R. K., Sailo, R. L. and Colney, L. 2013. Identification of Potential Wet Rice Cultivation Areas in Mizoram, India: A Remote Sensing and GIS Approach. *International Journal of Geology, Earth & Environmental Sciences*, 3, 49–56.

Lewis, W. A. 1980. The slowing down of the engine of growth. *The American Economic Review*, 70(4), 555–564.

'Lockdown makes a heavy impact on brick business; production season disrupted' (25 April 2020). *Guwahati Plus*.

Loitongbam, B. S. 2015. Regional Economic Agglomeration and Openness: The Economic Development of the North Eastern Region (NER).

Manuela, B., Richarda, K., Sarah, T.-S., Hirsch, H. H., Widmer, A. F. and Neher, R. A. 2020. '2019-Novel Coronavirus (2019-nCoV): Estimating the case fatality rate—A word of caution'. *Swiss Medical Weekly*.

'Manipur Govt signs MoU with Pvt hospitals to fight COVID pandemic' (4 August 2020). *The Hills Times*.

Martin, E. (24 June 2020). 'IMF projects deeper global recession on growing virus threat'. *Bloomberg*.

Mathur. 2020. 'Fight Against COVID-19: Government of Tripura Distributes Vitamin C-Rich Fruits for Free To Boost Immunity'. 15 July.

McKinsey. 2016. *Bridging Global Infrastructure Gaps*, McKinsey Global Institute, June.

'Meghalaya has spent over Rs 100 crore in fight against Covid-19: Conrad Sangma' (21 May 2020). *The Telegraph Online*.

'Midday News' (6 August 2020). *All India Radio*.

Ministry of Agriculture & Farmers Welfare. Annual Reports. Department of Animal Husbandry, Dairying & Fisheries, Ministry of Agriculture & Farmers Welfare, Government of India.

Ministry of Agriculture & Farmers Welfare. Annual Reports. Department of Agriculture, Cooperation & Farmers Welfare, Ministry of Agriculture & Farmers Welfare, Government of India.

Ministry of Civil Aviation. 2018. Report on 48 Months of Transforming Aviation in India 2014-2018, Government of India.

Ministry of Commerce and Industry. 2020. 'India's Foreign Trade'. *PIB New Delhi*.

Ministry of Development of North Eastern Region. Annual Reports. Ministry of Development of North Eastern Region, Government of India.

Ministry of DONER. 2019. Rajya Sabha Unstarred Question No-3677, Answered on-25.07.2019, North Eastern Region Vision 2020, Government of India.

Ministry of DONER. Retrieved from www.mdoner.gov.in

Ministry of Food Processing Industries. Annual Reports. Ministry of Food Processing Industries, Government of India.

Ministry of Food Processing Industries. Prime Minister's Kishan Sampada Yojana. Ministry of Food Processing Industries, Government of India.

Ministry of Railways. 2018. Lok Sabha Unstarred Question No. 2391. Government of India.

Ministry of Statistics and Programme Implementation (MoSPI)'s Various Publications Available in Public Domain.

Ministry of Women and Child Development (MWCD)'s Various Publications Available in Public Domain.

Mishra, R.A. (24 June 2020). 'IMF reverses its optimism for India, sees 4.5 per cent GDP contraction in FY21'. *The Livemint.*

'MoFPI continues to engage with concerned departments to resolve issues of food processing industry' (5 April 2020). *The Economic Times.*

Mohanty, S. K. 2014. 'India-China Bilateral Trade Relationship'. Reserve Bank of India, January. Retrieved from http://www. ris. org. in/images/RIS_images/pdf/India% 20china% 20report. pdf

Mohanty, S. K. 2019. India and China in the Arab World. Conference on 'India, China and the Arab World: Exploring New Dynamics'. India Arab Cultural Centre, Jamia Milia Islamia, 25–26 March, New Delhi.

Mohanty, S. K. and Arockiasamy, R. 2009. Prospects for Making India's Manufacturing Sector Export Oriented, Ministry of Commerce and Research and Information System for Developing Countries, Government of India. New Delhi.

Mohanty, S. K., Gaur, P., Fernandez, S. and Sikri, U. 2019. 'India's Economic Engagement with LAC'. Strategy for Trade and Investment. March, Ministry of Commerce and Industry, and Research and Information System for Developing Countries, Government of India, New Delhi.

Mohapatra, B. K., Vinod, K., and Mandal, B. K. 2007. Inland indigenous ornamental fish germplasm of northeastern India: status and future strategies. Biodiversity and its significance (Tandon, P., Abrol, YP, and Kumaria, S., Eds), 134–149.

MoHFW. 2017. National Health Policy 2017. Ministry of Health and Family Welfare (MoHFW), Government of India.

MoHFW. 2018. Annual Report 2017-2018. Government of India. New Delhi.

MOHFW. National Family Health Survey (NFHS). Ministry of Health and Family Welfare (MOHFW), Government of India.

MORTH. 2019. Annual Report 2018-19. Ministry of Road Transport and Highways, Government of India.

MoSJ&E. 2019. Magnitude of Substance Use in India. Ministry of Social Justice and Empowerment, Government of India.

Munnell, A. H. 1992. Policy Watch: Infrastructure Investment and Economic Growth. *Journal of Economic Perspectives*, 6 (4), 189–98.

MWCD. Annual Reports. Ministry of Women & Child Development, Government of India.

NACO. 2017. 'India HIV Estimations 2017 Technical Report'. National Aids control Organisation, New Delhi.

Nag, Biswajit and Willem van der Geest. 2020. 'Economic Impact Analysis of Covid-19 Implication on India's GDP, Employment and Inequality', Working Papers, EC-20-41, Indian Institute of Foreign Trade.

Nair, M., Ravindranath, N. H., Sharma, N., Kattumuri, R. and Munshi, M. 2013. 'Poverty Index as a Tool for Adaptation Intervention to Climate Change in Northeast India'. *Climate and Development*, 5 (1), 14–32.

Nair, Malini, Ravindranath, N. H., Sharma, Nitasha, Kattumuri, Ruth and Munshi, Madhushree. 2013. Poverty Index as a Tool for Adaptation Intervention to Climate Change in Northeast India. *Climate and Development*, 5 (1), 14–32. ISSN 1756-5529

Nandy, S. N. 2014. 'Road Infrastructure in Economically Underdeveloped Northeast India: A District Level Study'. *Journal of Infrastructure Development*, 6 (2), 131–44.

Nayak, Purusottam and Mahanta, Bidisha, Women Empowerment in India (December 24, 2008). *Bulletin of Political Economy*, Vol. 5, No. 2, pp. 155–183, 2012, Available at SSRN: https://ssrn.com/abstract=1320071 or http://dx.doi.org/10.2139/ssrn.1320071

NEC. Basic Statistics of North Eastern Region 2015. North Eastern Council, Government of India.

NEC. Regional Plan (2017-18 to 2019-20). North Eastern Council, Government of India.

NITI Aayog 2018. SDG India Index. Retrieved from https://niti.gov.in/sdg-india-index

NITI Aayog. 2019a. Localising SDGs Early Lessons from India. Retrieved from https://niti.gov.in/writereaddata/files/LSDGs_July_8_Web.pdf

NITI Aayog. 2019b. SDG India Index 2.0. Retrieved from https://niti.gov.in/sites/default/files/2019-12/SDG-India-Index-2.0_27-Dec.pdf

NITI Aayog. Minutes of the NITI NE Forum.

NITI Aayog. 2017. Three Year Action Plan (Chapter 9). NITI Aayog, Government of India.

NITI Aayog. 2018. Strategy For New India @75. NITI Aayog, Government of India.

NITI Aayog. 2018. Aspirational Districts - Unlocking Potentials, 2018. NITI Aayog, Government of India.

NITI Aayog. 2018. Meeting with States & UTs on SDGs: Implementation of SDGs. NITI Aayog, Government of India.

NITI Aayog. 2018. SDG India Index, Baseline Report 2018. NITI Aayog, Government of India.

NITI Aayog. 2018a. Presentation on Review of Sustainable Development Goals 2030 Nagaland Background - Sustainable Development Goals 2030, Government of India.

NITI Aayog. 2018b. Sustainable Development Goals: Vision-2030, 7 Year Strategy, 3 Year Action Plan & Indicators- NITI Aayog 's Review meeting on SDGs, Government of India.

NITI Aayog. 2019. Localising SDGs Early Lessons from India. NITI Aayog, Government of India. Retrieved from www.niti.gov.in

NITI Aayog. 2019. SDG India Index and Dashboard 2019-20. NITI Aayog, Government of India.

NITI Aayog. 2020. SDG India Index & Dashboard 2019-2020. December.

North Eastern Council, Regional Plan 2017-18 to 2019-20.

North Eastern Development Finance Corporation Ltd (NEDFi), Data Bank.

North Eastern Development Finance Institution (NEDFi). Retrieved from www. nedfi.com

Pandey, D. 2012. Carbon Stock of World Heritage Sites. Retrieved from https://whc. unesco.org/uploads/activities/documents/activity-43-12.pdf

'Personal protective equipment in India: An INR 7,000 Cr industry in the making' (25 May 2020). *Invest India.*

PIB. 2018. Traditional and Sustainable Farming in North Eastern Region. Ministry for Development of North-East Region, Press Information Bureau, Government of India, 18 July.

'Pradhan Mantri Garib Kalyan Anna Yojana to provide free rations during coronavirus lockdown extended, what does it mean for people on the ground?' (14 July 2020). *NDTV India.*

Rahman, M. M. 2014. 'Trade Potential and Economic Cooperation between Bangladesh and Northeast India'. *Economic Corridors in South Asia*, 179, Asian Development Bank.

Rais, M., Acharya, S. and Vanloon, G. W. 2014. 'Food Processing Industry: Opportunities in North East Region of India'. *The Nehu Journal*, 12 (1).

Rasul, G., Karki, M. and Sah, R. P. 2008. 'The Role of Non-timber Forest Products in Poverty Reduction in India: Prospects and Problems'. *Development in Practice*, 18 (6), 779–88.

RBI. 2019. *State Finances: Study of Budgets of 2019-20*. Reserve Bank of India https:// doi.org/10.1017/CBO9781107415324.004

RBI. 2020. Consumer Confidence Survey, 4 June.

RBI. 2020. Governor's Statement, 22 May.

Reddy, A. Amarender. 2018. Report on Impact Evaluation Study of Mission Organic Value Chain Development for North Eastern Region (MOVCDNER). National Institute of Agricultural Extension Management, Ministry of Agriculture.

Regional Variation in Literacy in North-East India. Retrieved from https://shodhga nga.inflibnet.ac.in/ bitstream/10603/61233/9/ 09_chapter%203.pdf

RIS. 2014. *Transforming Connectivity Corridors between India and Myanmar into Development Corridors.* Research and Information System for Developing Countries, New Delhi.

RIS. 2016. *India and Sustainable Development Goals: The Way Forward.* Research and Information System for Developing Countries, New Delhi and United Nations.

RIS. 2018. *SDG 2 Roadmap Framework.* Research and Information System for Developing Countries, New Delhi and World Food Programme.

Rivkin, S., Hanushek, E. and Kain, J. 2005. 'Teachers, Schools and Academic Achievement'. *Econometrica*, 73 (2).

Rodrik, D. 2004. 'Institutions and Economic Performance-getting Institutions Right'. *CESIfo DICE Report*, 2 (2), 10–15.

Rodrik, D. 2005. 'Growth Strategies'. *Handbook of Economic Growth*, 1, 967–1014.

Romer, P. M. 1994. 'The Origins of Endogenous Growth'. *Journal of Economic Perspectives*, 8 (1), 3–22.

Roy, A., Singh, N. U., Dkhar, D. S., Mohanty, A. K., Singh, S. B. and Tripathi, A. K. 2015. Food Security in North-East Region of India—A State-wise Analysis. *Agricultural Economics Research Review*, 28 (347-2016-17191), 259–66.

Rymbai, D. and Sheikh, F. M. 2018. The Insight of Agricultural Adaptation to Climate Change: A Case of Rice Growers in Eastern Himalaya, India. *International Journal of Biometeorology*, 62 (10), 1833–45.

Sahoo, U. K., Singh, S. L., Gogoi, A., Kenye, A. and Sahoo, S. S. 2019. 'Active and Passive Soil Organic Carbon Pools as Affected by Different Land Use Types in Mizoram, Northeast India'. *PLoS One*, 14 (7), e0219969. https://doi.org/10.1371/journal.pone.0219969

Sarma, A. 2008. 'Economic Development of the Northeastern States in the Context of Globalisation'. *Strategic Analysis*, 25 (2), 295–312.

Sharma, Eklabya, Chettri, Nakul, Tshe-ring, K., Shrestha, Arun, Jing, F., Mool, Pradeep and Eriksson, Mats. 2009. Climate Change Impacts and Vulnerability in the Eastern Himalayas.

Sharma, U. and Sharma, V. 2018. Greenhouse Gases Emissions from Agriculture Sector in Northeastern Region of India. *Acta Scientific Microbiology*, 1 (12), 36–43.

'Section 144 clamped in Mizoram to contain Covid-19' (22 March 2020). *NorthEast Now.*

Singh, D.A. (8 May 2020). 'Towards an 18th SDG: Managing pandemics'. *TimesNowNews.Com.*

Singh, S. N. 2018. 'Regional Priority and Sustainable Development in North-Eastern States of India: A Policy Prospective'. *Socio Economic Challenges*, 2 (2), 41–48.

Sinha, G. N. 2018. Status of SDGs Implementation in Arunachal Pradesh SDGs Implementation Framework.

Sinha, G. N. 2018. Status of SDGs Implementation in Arunachal Pradesh SDGs Implementation Framework. Retrieved from http://niti.gov.in/writereaddata/files/Arunachal Pradesh_0.pdf

Sridhar, Devi. 2019. 'Supporting a Healthy Population' in SDGs: Transforming our World, UNA-UK Publication.

Sustainable Development Goals in Nagaland. 2018.

Telephone Regulatory Authority of India (TRAI). Retrieved from main.trai.gov.in

Thacker, S., Adshead, D., Morgan, G., Crosskey, S., Bajpai, A., Ceppi, P., Hall, J. W. and O'Regan, N. 2018. *Infrastructure: Underpinning Sustainable Development.* Copenhagen, Denmark: UNOPS.

Thorat, Sukhadeo and Khan, Khalid. 2017. 'Private Sector and Equity in Higher Education: Challenges of Growing Unequal Access', in N. V. Varghese, Nidhi S. Sabhrawal and C. M. Malish (eds.) *India Higher Education Report 2016: Equity* (pp. 92–128). New Delhi: SAGE Publications.

Tilak, J. B. G. 2005. 'Higher Education in Trishanku: Hanging between State and Market'. *Economic & Political Weekly*, 40 (37), 4029–37.

Tlusty, M. F., Rhyne, A. L., Kaufman, L., Hutchins, M., Reid, G. M., Andrews, C., ... and Dowd, S. 2013. Opportunities for public aquariums to increase the sustainability of the aquatic animal trade. *Zoo biology*, 32(1), 1–12.

Tooley, James and Paula Dixon. 2007a. 'De facto' Privatisation of Education and the Poor: Implications of a Study from Sub Saharan Africa and India'. *Compare*, 36 (4), 443–62.

Tooley, James, Pauline Dixon and Gomathi, S. V. 2007b. 'Private Schools and the Millennium Development Goal of Universal Primary Education: A Census and Comparative Survey in Hyderabad, India'. *Oxford Review of Education*, 33 (5), 539–60

UNCTAD. 2018. 'Bridging Gaps or Widening Divides: Infrastructure Development and Structural Transformation', in *Trade and Development Report 2018*. *United Nations Conference on Trade and Development*.

Union Budget Documents of different years.

United Nations High Level Political Forum. 2017. On the Implementation of Sustainable Development Goals Voluntary National Review Report India. New York.

Viner, J. 1960. *Theory of Customs Union*.

Vision 2030 Documents of NE States.

Vliet, Nathalie van, et al. 2012. 'Trends, Drivers and Impacts of Changes in Swidden Cultivation in Tropical Forest-Agriculture Frontiers: A Global Assessment'. *Global Environmental Change*, 22 (2), 418–29.

'With highest ever single day recoveries of nearly 30,000, the total number of recoveries crosses 7.82 lakhs' (23 July 2020). Ministry of Information and Broadcasting, PIB New Delhi.

Worldometer. https://www.worldometers.info/coronavirus/coronavirus-cases/#total-cases

Yadav, A. K. 2018. 'Rail Connectivity Enhancement in North Eastern States'. Presentation made at the AIIB Lead Up Event on 'Physical Infrastructure and Regional Development' held in Guwahati on 14–15 April 2018.

Ingram Content Group UK Ltd.
Milton Keynes UK
UKHW020150200323
418724UK00001B/2